VIBRANT
PUBLISHERS

TEST PREP SERIES

MATH PRACTICE TESTS FOR THE
ACT®

First Edition

- ◆ 8 Full Length Math Tests
- ◆ 480 Practice Questions
- ◆ Level of Difficulty marked for each question
- ◆ Detailed explanations for all questions

Math Practice Tests
for the ACT®

Paperback ISBN-10: 1-949395-86-3
Paperback ISBN-13: 978-1-949395-86-0

E-book ISBN-10: 1-949395-87-1
E-book ISBN-13: 978-1-949395-87-7

Library of Congress Control Number: 2020936601

This publication is designed to provide accurate and authoritative information in regard to the subject matter covered. The Author has made every effort in the preparation of this book to ensure the accuracy of the information. However, information in this book is sold without warranty either expressed or implied. The Author or the Publisher will not be liable for any damages caused or alleged to be caused either directly or indirectly by this book.

Vibrant Publishers books are available at special quantity discount for sales promotions, or for use in corporate training programs. For more information please write to bulkorders@vibrantpublishers.com

Please email feedback / corrections (technical, grammatical or spelling) to spellerrors@vibrantpublishers.com

To access the complete catalogue of Vibrant Publishers, visit www.vibrantpublishers.com

ACT is the registered trademark of ACT Inc, which neither sponsors nor endorses this product.

Table of Contents

Dear Student,

Thank you for purchasing **Math Practice Tests for the ACT**. We are committed to publishing books that are content-rich, concise and approachable enabling more students to read and make the fullest use of them. We hope this book provides the most enriching learning experience as you prepare for your ACT exam.

Should you have any questions or suggestions, feel free to email us at reachus@vibrantpublishers.com

Thanks again for your purchase. Good luck for your ACT!

– Vibrant Publishers Team

ACT Math
Practice Test 1

Mark Your Answers For Test 1 Here

Date: _____

Marking Directions: Mark only one oval for each question. Fill in response completely. Erase errors cleanly without smudging.

Correct mark: ○ ◉ ○ ○ ○

1 Ⓐ Ⓑ Ⓒ Ⓓ Ⓔ	11 Ⓐ Ⓑ Ⓒ Ⓓ Ⓔ	21 Ⓐ Ⓑ Ⓒ Ⓓ Ⓔ	31 Ⓐ Ⓑ Ⓒ Ⓓ Ⓔ	41 Ⓐ Ⓑ Ⓒ Ⓓ Ⓔ	51 Ⓐ Ⓑ Ⓒ Ⓓ Ⓔ
2 Ⓕ Ⓖ Ⓗ Ⓙ Ⓚ	12 Ⓕ Ⓖ Ⓗ Ⓙ Ⓚ	22 Ⓕ Ⓖ Ⓗ Ⓙ Ⓚ	32 Ⓕ Ⓖ Ⓗ Ⓙ Ⓚ	42 Ⓕ Ⓖ Ⓗ Ⓙ Ⓚ	52 Ⓕ Ⓖ Ⓗ Ⓙ Ⓚ
3 Ⓐ Ⓑ Ⓒ Ⓓ Ⓔ	13 Ⓐ Ⓑ Ⓒ Ⓓ Ⓔ	23 Ⓐ Ⓑ Ⓒ Ⓓ Ⓔ	33 Ⓐ Ⓑ Ⓒ Ⓓ Ⓔ	43 Ⓐ Ⓑ Ⓒ Ⓓ Ⓔ	53 Ⓐ Ⓑ Ⓒ Ⓓ Ⓔ
4 Ⓕ Ⓖ Ⓗ Ⓙ Ⓚ	14 Ⓕ Ⓖ Ⓗ Ⓙ Ⓚ	24 Ⓕ Ⓖ Ⓗ Ⓙ Ⓚ	34 Ⓕ Ⓖ Ⓗ Ⓙ Ⓚ	44 Ⓕ Ⓖ Ⓗ Ⓙ Ⓚ	54 Ⓕ Ⓖ Ⓗ Ⓙ Ⓚ
5 Ⓐ Ⓑ Ⓒ Ⓓ Ⓔ	15 Ⓐ Ⓑ Ⓒ Ⓓ Ⓔ	25 Ⓐ Ⓑ Ⓒ Ⓓ Ⓔ	35 Ⓐ Ⓑ Ⓒ Ⓓ Ⓔ	45 Ⓐ Ⓑ Ⓒ Ⓓ Ⓔ	55 Ⓐ Ⓑ Ⓒ Ⓓ Ⓔ
6 Ⓕ Ⓖ Ⓗ Ⓙ Ⓚ	16 Ⓕ Ⓖ Ⓗ Ⓙ Ⓚ	26 Ⓕ Ⓖ Ⓗ Ⓙ Ⓚ	36 Ⓕ Ⓖ Ⓗ Ⓙ Ⓚ	46 Ⓕ Ⓖ Ⓗ Ⓙ Ⓚ	56 Ⓕ Ⓖ Ⓗ Ⓙ Ⓚ
7 Ⓐ Ⓑ Ⓒ Ⓓ Ⓔ	17 Ⓐ Ⓑ Ⓒ Ⓓ Ⓔ	27 Ⓐ Ⓑ Ⓒ Ⓓ Ⓔ	37 Ⓐ Ⓑ Ⓒ Ⓓ Ⓔ	47 Ⓐ Ⓑ Ⓒ Ⓓ Ⓔ	57 Ⓐ Ⓑ Ⓒ Ⓓ Ⓔ
8 Ⓕ Ⓖ Ⓗ Ⓙ Ⓚ	18 Ⓕ Ⓖ Ⓗ Ⓙ Ⓚ	28 Ⓕ Ⓖ Ⓗ Ⓙ Ⓚ	38 Ⓕ Ⓖ Ⓗ Ⓙ Ⓚ	48 Ⓕ Ⓖ Ⓗ Ⓙ Ⓚ	58 Ⓕ Ⓖ Ⓗ Ⓙ Ⓚ
9 Ⓐ Ⓑ Ⓒ Ⓓ Ⓔ	19 Ⓐ Ⓑ Ⓒ Ⓓ Ⓔ	29 Ⓐ Ⓑ Ⓒ Ⓓ Ⓔ	39 Ⓐ Ⓑ Ⓒ Ⓓ Ⓔ	49 Ⓐ Ⓑ Ⓒ Ⓓ Ⓔ	59 Ⓐ Ⓑ Ⓒ Ⓓ Ⓔ
10 Ⓕ Ⓖ Ⓗ Ⓙ Ⓚ	20 Ⓕ Ⓖ Ⓗ Ⓙ Ⓚ	30 Ⓕ Ⓖ Ⓗ Ⓙ Ⓚ	40 Ⓕ Ⓖ Ⓗ Ⓙ Ⓚ	50 Ⓕ Ⓖ Ⓗ Ⓙ Ⓚ	60 Ⓕ Ⓖ Ⓗ Ⓙ Ⓚ

This page is intentionally left blank

MATHEMATICS TEST

60 Minutes—60 Questions

DIRECTIONS: Solve each problem, choose the correct answer, and then fill in the corresponding oval on your answer document.

Do not linger over problems that take too much time. Solve as many as you can; then return to the others in the time you have left for this test.

You are permitted to use a calculator on this test. You may use your calculator for any problems you choose, but some of the problems may best be done without using a calculator.

Note: Unless otherwise stated, all of the following should be assumed.

1. Illustrative figures are NOT necessarily drawn to scale.
2. Geometric figures lie in a plane.
3. The word *line* indicates a straight line.
4. The word *average* indicates arithmetic mean.

---

1. Julian wants to have an 85-grade average in his Chemistry course. There are 5 assignments that are graded for the course, each having an equal weight. If Julian scores grades of 79, 84, 92, and a 79 on his first four assignments, what must his median score be if he is to end up with an 85-grade average?

   A. 85
   B. 91
   C. 88
   D. 84
   E. 79

2. Which of the following statements is true for x if $2^{x^2-2x} = 2^3$?

   F. $x = 3$ only
   G. $x = -1$ only
   H. $x = -1$ or 3
   J. $x = -3$ only
   K. $x = -3$ or 1

3. You need to enclose a rectangular area of land. You have 1000 feet of fence to use for your enclosure. What is the largest area, in square feet, of the enclosure?

   A. 250
   B. 500
   C. 62,500
   D. 125,000
   E. 25,000

DO YOUR FIGURING HERE.

GO ON TO THE NEXT PAGE.

4. A right circular cone has a height of 10 inches as shown below. A 45-degree angle is formed by the radius and the slant height of the cone. What is the volume of the cone in cubic inches?

F. $\dfrac{100}{3}\pi$

G. $\dfrac{1000}{3}\pi$

H. $\dfrac{2000}{3}\pi$

J. 1000π

K. 2000π

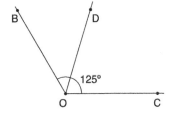

5. The time for a certain chemical reaction to take place at different temperatures is represented by the equation $t = 7\sqrt{d-10}$ where t is time, in seconds, and d is the temperature, in degrees Celsius. If it takes 53 seconds for a chemical reaction to take place, what is the approximate temperature?

A. 67
B. 46
C. 18
D. 411
E. 2107

6. What is the value of $\dfrac{a+1}{\frac{1}{b}}$ if $a = \dfrac{2}{5}$ and $b = 3$?

F. $\dfrac{7}{15}$

G. $\dfrac{9}{5}$

H. $\dfrac{21}{5}$

J. 10

K. 2

7. In the figure below, $m\angle BOC = 125°$, and $m\angle DOC = d + 13°$. Which of the following represents the expression for the measure of angle BOD?

A. $112° + d$

B. $112° - d$

C. $138° + d$

D. $d - 112°$

E. $138° - d$

8

8. The ABC automobile repair shop has given you a quote of $535.50 to repair the damaged bumper on your car. There is a flat fee of $125 plus $75 for each hour the car is worked on. How many hours will it take for the repair shop to repair your car?

   F. 8.2
   G. 8.8
   H. 5.5
   J. 10
   K. 12

9. The 1st term for an arithmetic sequence is 15, and the 4th term is 24. What is the 45th term in the sequence?

   A. 411
   B. 420
   C. 144
   D. 147
   E. 150

10. You know the probability of your flight being delayed for any length of time due to a mechanical issue is 12%. What is the probability that there will **not** be a delay on a round trip (a flight to your destination and a flight back)?

    F. 1%
    G. 12%
    H. 24%
    J. 77%
    K. 50%

11. Let $f(x) = 3x + 5$, and $g(x) = x^2 - 3$. What is the value of $f(g(-4))$?

    A. 46
    B. 44
    C. −52
    D. −91
    E. 286

DO YOUR FIGURING HERE.

9

GO ON TO THE NEXT PAGE.

DO YOUR FIGURING HERE.

12. Rectangle ABCD shown below has diagonals $\overline{AC}$ and $\overline{BD}$. The measure of angle CBD is 30 degrees. If $BD = 12$ meters in length, what is the area, in square meters, of the rectangle?

   F. $36\sqrt{3}$
   G. $36\sqrt{2}$
   H. $36\sqrt{6}$
   J. 72
   K. 144

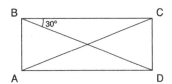

13. You design a model car for your physics project that is propelled by a rubber band. The car moves along a line and the distance it travels, in feet, from a fixed point is recorded in the table below.

t	1	2	3	4	5
d	5	9	13	17	21

   If t is time in seconds, which equation best represents the distance, d, the car has travelled from the fixed point?

   A. $t = d + 4$
   B. $t = 4d + 1$
   C. $d = 5t + 1$
   D. $d = t + 4$
   E. $d = 4t + 1$

14. In the figure given below, the circle with center O is inscribed in square $ABCD$. If $AB = 8$, what is the area of the region that is outside of the circle and inside of the square.

   F. $64\pi - 64$
   G. $64 + 16\pi$
   H. $64 - 16\pi$
   J. $32 - 8\pi$
   K. $64 + 8\pi$

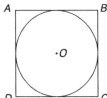

15. Which of the following is equivalent to $y = x^2 + 8x - 5$?

   A. $y = (x - 4)^2 - 21$
   B. $y = (x + 4)^2 - 21$
   C. $y = (x + 4)^2 + 11$
   D. $y = (x + 8)^2 - 21$
   E. $y = (x - 8)^2 + 11$

GO ON TO THE NEXT PAGE.

16. The pie chart given below shows the results from a survey of the percentage of different ways people get to work each day. If 45 people that were surveyed walked to work, how many people from the survey drove a car to work?

DO YOUR FIGURING HERE.

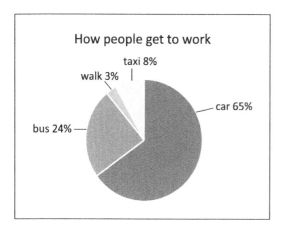

F. 1000
G. 975
H. 1500
J. 175
K. 69

17. What is the slope of the line $4x + 5y = -10$ that is graphed in the standard (x, y) coordinate plane?

A. -4
B. $\dfrac{2}{5}$
C. $-\dfrac{5}{2}$
D. $-\dfrac{4}{5}$
E. $\dfrac{5}{4}$

18. Which of the following is equivalent to the expression $\dfrac{4}{\sqrt{-2}}$ where $i = -1$?

F. 2
G. -2
H. $2\sqrt{2}i$
J. $-2\sqrt{2}i$
K. $-4\sqrt{2}i$

11

GO ON TO THE NEXT PAGE.

19. On a number line, point C lies two-thirds of the distance from point A to B. If point A is at 5 and point B is at 23 on the number line, then point C lies at which number on the number line?

    A. 9
    B. 14
    C. 12
    D. 21
    E. 17

DO YOUR FIGURING HERE.

20. For the circle $x^2 + y^2 = 48$ in the standard (x, y) coordinate plane, where does the point $(6, -5)$ lie?

    F. Inside of the graph of the circle
    G. Outside the graph of the circle
    H. On the graph of the circle
    J. At the center of the circle
    K. On the radius of the circle

21. Given below is a table of values for a polynomial function $y = f(x)$.

x	-5	-2	1	3	6
$f(x)$	-4	0.5	-1	-3	-6

    Which of the following values for x could be a zero for the polynomial function?

    A. -3 and -1
    B. -3 and 2
    C. 0 and 2
    D. 0 and 4
    E. -1 and 4

22. What is $\dfrac{3}{5}$ of 32% of 115?

    F. 37.4
    G. 14.72
    H. 22.08
    J. 134.2
    K. 88.2

23. Let $u = \langle 1,3 \rangle$ and $v = \langle 5,8 \rangle$. If $u - 2v + w = \langle -13,25 \rangle$, which of the following must be w?

    A. $\langle -13,25 \rangle$
    B. $\langle 38,-4 \rangle$
    C. $\langle -4,38 \rangle$
    D. $\langle -9,30 \rangle$
    E. $\langle 30,-9 \rangle$

12

GO ON TO THE NEXT PAGE.

24. The edge of a cube is 6 cm in length. Another cube has an edge that is 3 times longer that the first cube. Which statement is true about the two cubes?

   F. The volume of the second cube is 18 times the first cube.

   G. The volume of the second cube is 27 times the first cube.

   H. The volume of the second cube is 3 times the first cube.

   J. The volume of the first cube is one–half the volume of the second cube.

   K. The volume of the first cube is one–third the volume of the second cube.

DO YOUR FIGURING HERE.

25. Which of the following expressions is a factor of $8x^3 + 125$?

   A. $4x^2 + 10x + 25$

   B. $2x^2 + 25$

   C. $2x + 25$

   D. $4x + 25$

   E. $2x + 5$

26. You randomly choose a coin from a container having 15 pennies, 10 nickels, and 22 dimes. The probability that you do not choose a penny is?

   F. 0.32

   G. 0.68

   H. 0.21

   J. 0.53

   K. 0.79

27. After painting $\frac{3}{5}$ of a wall in the backyard of her house, Marci determines she has painted 594 square feet. What is the total area of the wall in square feet?

   A. 1485

   B. 990

   C. 1584

   D. 1188

   E. 900

GO ON TO THE NEXT PAGE.

28. Which statement is true for the shaded region between $y = -x^2 + 4x + 3$ and $y = x - 4$?

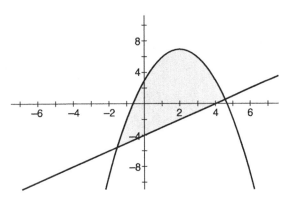

- **F.** $-x^2 - 3x + 7 \leq 0$
- **G.** $-x^2 - 3x + 7 \geq 0$
- **H.** $-x^2 + 3x + 7 \geq 0$
- **J.** $x^2 + 3x - 7 \leq 0$
- **K.** $-x^2 - 3x - 1 \geq 0$

29. The cost of 3 items, including tax, on a menu at a restaurant are fish $9.50, roast beef $11.25, and chicken $8.75. You buy one of the items and hand the cashier a $50 bill. You are still hungry, so you purchase a second item with the change the cashier gave you after your first purchase. If you received $31.75 in change after your 2nd purchased which menu items did you buy?

- **A.** Fish and chicken
- **B.** Fish and roast beef
- **C.** Chicken and roast beef
- **D.** Fish both times
- **E.** Roast beef both times

30. The volume of a right circular cone is jointly proportional to the area of its base and its height. If the volume of a cone is $\frac{20}{3}\pi$ cubic units, the area of it base is 4π cubic units, and has a height of 5 units, what is the proportionality constant of variation?

- **F.** 3
- **G.** $\frac{1}{3}$
- **H.** 4
- **J.** $\frac{4}{3}$
- **K.** 2

14

31. Line *l* contains the points $(-5, 11)$ and $(7, -4)$. Line *k* is perpendicular to line *l*. What is the slope for line *k* if its *y*-intercept is 3?

A. 3

B. $-\dfrac{5}{4}$

C. $\dfrac{4}{5}$

D. $-\dfrac{4}{5}$

E. Undefined

DO YOUR FIGURING HERE.

32. From an airport, a helicopter flies to the roof of a skyscraper. The skyscraper is 125 miles due west and 35 miles due south of the airport. To the nearest mile, how far is the skyscraper from the airport?

F. 120

G. 130

H. 100

J. 160

K. 125

33. A department store has a certain laptop computer on sale for 20% off its list price during a tax–free weekend. Zack has a coupon that takes an additional 15% off the sale price. Zack decides to buy the computer during the tax–free weekend. If the list price of the laptop computer is $425, how much does Zack pay?

A. $340

B. $361.25

C. $350.63

D. $289

E. $276.25

34. The base of a rectangular pyramid has dimensions for 12 feet by 7 feet. What is the area of the base in square inches?

F. 756

G. 108

H. 12,096

J. 6048

K. 10,498

GO ON TO THE NEXT PAGE.

35. If $a + b = 23$, and $2ab = 240$ where $a > b$, what is the value of $b - a$?

    A. -7
    B. 7
    C. 15
    D. 8
    E. -8

36. Line segment AB has its midpoint at point C. If the coordinates of A and C are (3, 5) and (9, 12) respectively, which of the following must be the coordinates for point B?

    F. $(-3, -2)$
    G. (6, 8.5)
    H. (12, 14)
    J. (15, 19)
    K. (19, 15)

37. What is the sum of the mean and mode for the set $\{7, 9, 1, 14, 2, 16, 7\}$?

    A. 7
    B. 8
    C. 15
    D. 1
    E. 9

38. Albert's car averages 25 miles per gallon of gasoline. Gas cost $2.45 per gallon. From an empty gas tank, Albert spends $36.75 to fill the tank. How far can Albert drive in his car before it runs out of gas?

    F. 375 miles
    G. 345 miles
    H. 735 miles
    J. 750 miles
    K. 500 miles

39. Arrange $\dfrac{79}{50}$, 148%, and 1.67 in ascending order.

    A. 1.67, 148%, $\dfrac{79}{50}$

    B. 1.67, $\dfrac{79}{50}$, 148%,

    C. $\dfrac{79}{50}$, 1.67, %148

    D. $\dfrac{79}{50}$, 148%, 1.67

    E. 148%, $\dfrac{79}{50}$, 1.67

DO YOUR FIGURING HERE.

GO ON TO THE NEXT PAGE.

40. Right triangle ABC has its right angle at C and the length of the hypotenuse if 10 units. If $\sin A = \dfrac{3}{4}$, which of the following is the length of the side opposite angle A?

   F. $5\sqrt{2}$

   G. 7.5

   H. $\dfrac{20}{3}\sqrt{3}$

   J. $\dfrac{20}{3}\sqrt{2}$

   K. 5

DO YOUR FIGURING HERE.

41. Which of the following transformations when applied to the graph of the parent function $y = x^3$ produces the graph of $y = (x+4)^3$?

   A. A horizontal translation to the right 4 units.

   B. A horizontal translation to the left 4 units.

   C. A vertical translation to the left 4 units.

   D. A vertical stretch by a factor of 4 units.

   E. A reflection about the line $x = 4$.

42. The square of the sum of a number and 3 is 16 times the number. Which of the following could be the number?

   F. 9

   G. 10

   H. -1

   J. -9

   K. 0

43. The length of a metal rectangular container is twice the width. The width is the same length as the container's height. If the volume is 432 cubic feet, what is the container's length in feet?

   A. 6

   B. 12

   C. 9

   D. 15

   E. 4

GO ON TO THE NEXT PAGE.

44. What is the period for the graph of $y = 3\tan(2x)$?

    F. π

    G. 2π

    H. $\dfrac{\pi}{3}$

    J. $\dfrac{\pi}{4}$

    K. $\dfrac{\pi}{2}$

DO YOUR FIGURING HERE.

45. What is the sum of the first one–thousand positive integers 1, 2,3, …, 998, 999, 1000?

    A. 500,000

    B. 500,500

    C. 1,000,000

    D. 1,001,000

    E. 750,000

46. The stem–leaf plot below shows your favorite basket-ball's team scores for the first 9 games of the season.

Stem	Leaf
5	5, 7
6	1, 3, 4, 9
7	1, 1
8	3

For example, a score of 63 is represented by stem value of 6 and a leaf value of 3.

What is the sum of the mean and mode score for the first 9 games?

    F. 129

    G. 135

    H. 137

    J. 125

    K. 150

47. Admission for a game is $2.50 for children, and $5.50 for adults. 1250 people attend the game and $6500 is collected in admission. How many adults attend the game?

    A. 750

    B. 500

    C. 1000

    D. 225

    E. 250

GO ON TO THE NEXT PAGE.

48. In the figure below, lines l and m are parallel and line n is a transversal. What is the sum of angles in degrees of x and y?

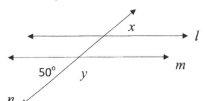

DO YOUR FIGURING HERE.

    F. 100
    G. 360
    H. 180
    J. 130
    K. 50

49. What is the range of values for $y = 3\cos x + \sin 2x$ where x is a real number?

    A. $0 \le y \le 3$
    B. $-3 \le y \le 4$
    C. $-4 \le y \le 4$
    D. $-1 \le y \le 1$
    E. $-5 \le y \le 5$

50. Out of 50 people that like candy bars or spinach or both, 42 like candy bars and 18 like spinach. If a person is selected at random from the 50 people surveyed, what is the probability that the person likes both candy bars and broccoli?

    F. 0.5
    G. 0.16
    H. 0.64
    J. 0.2
    K. 0.36

51. What will be the value of $a < 0$ if the determinant of the matrix $\begin{bmatrix} 5 & a \\ a & 3 \end{bmatrix}$ is twice the value of a?

    A. -5
    B. -3
    C. 0
    D. -1
    E. -2

GO ON TO THE NEXT PAGE.

52. The graph of a piece-wise defined function $y = f(x)$ is graphed in the standard (x,y) coordinate plane below. Which of the following describes the range for the function?

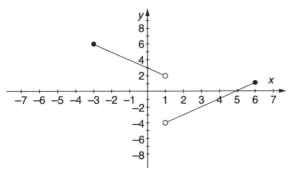

DO YOUR FIGURING HERE.

F. $-3 \leq y \leq 6$

G. $-4 \leq y \leq 6$

H. $-3 \leq y < 1$ or $1 < y \leq 6$

J. $-4 \leq y < 1$ or $2 < y \leq 6$

K. $-3 \leq y < 1$ or $1 < y \leq 6$

53. Samantha works for a company that requires her to rent a car to travel to various destinations. She rents a car for $35 per day plus $0.15 for each mile she drives. Her company allows her a budget of $85 per day to rent the car. Approximately, what is the maximum number of miles she can drive the car on the budget she is given?

A. 333

B. 800

C. 602

D. 135

E. 59

54. If $x = \dfrac{1}{yz}$, then which expression represents $y + z$ in terms of x, y, and z?

F. $\dfrac{y+z}{xyz}$

G. $\dfrac{x+y}{xyz^2}$

H. $\dfrac{2x+y}{yz}$

J. $2xy - z$

K. $2y - xz$

20

DO YOUR FIGURING HERE.

55. $\dfrac{7.2 \times 10^{-3}}{1.8 \times 10^{-8}} = ?$

   A. 4.0×10^{-5}

   B. 4.0×10^{5}

   C. 4.0×10^{-11}

   D. 4.2×10^{-5}

   E. 4.2×10^{-11}

56. Suppose you invest $1000 into an account that yields 8% interest compounded annually. Approximately how many years will it take for the investment to double in value?

   F. 10
   G. 15
   H. 12
   J. 9
   K. 6

57. What are the two inequalities used to find the solutions for $|3x - 5| < 15$?

   A. $3x - 5 < 15$ or $3x - 5 > -15$

   B. $3x - 5 < -15$ or $3x - 5 > 15$

   C. $3x - 5 < 15$ and $3x - 5 > -15$

   D. $3x - 5 < 15$ and $3x - 5 < -15$

   E. $3x - 5 > 15$ and $3x - 5 > -15$

58. A cow can produce $7\dfrac{3}{4}$ gallons of milk daily which is 992 glasses of milk. How many gallons of milk would the cow need to produce to make 1550 glasses of milk?

   F. 12
   G. 15
   H. 16
   J. 10
   K. 11

21

GO ON TO THE NEXT PAGE.

59. The sides of an isosceles triangle are 3 times the length of its base. If the height of the triangle is 12 inches and its perimeter is 63 inches, what is its area in square inches?

   A. 108
   B. 54
   C. 9
   D. 378
   E. 126

DO YOUR FIGURING HERE.

60. $x^{\frac{1}{2}}\left(x^{\frac{3}{4}}\right)^{\frac{1}{2}}$ is equivalent to which of the following expressions?

   F. $\sqrt[7]{x^8}$
   G. $\sqrt[8]{x^7}$
   H. $\sqrt[8]{x}$
   J. $\sqrt[4]{x^7}$
   K. $\sqrt[7]{x^4}$

END OF TEST

ACT Math Practice Test 2

Mark Your Answers For Test 2 Here

Date: _____

Marking Directions: Mark only one oval for each question. Fill in response completely. Erase errors cleanly without smudging.

Correct mark: ○ ◉ ○ ○ ○

1 Ⓐ Ⓑ Ⓒ Ⓓ Ⓔ	11 Ⓐ Ⓑ Ⓒ Ⓓ Ⓔ	21 Ⓐ Ⓑ Ⓒ Ⓓ Ⓔ	31 Ⓐ Ⓑ Ⓒ Ⓓ Ⓔ	41 Ⓐ Ⓑ Ⓒ Ⓓ Ⓔ	51 Ⓐ Ⓑ Ⓒ Ⓓ Ⓔ
2 Ⓕ Ⓖ Ⓗ Ⓙ Ⓚ	12 Ⓕ Ⓖ Ⓗ Ⓙ Ⓚ	22 Ⓕ Ⓖ Ⓗ Ⓙ Ⓚ	32 Ⓕ Ⓖ Ⓗ Ⓙ Ⓚ	42 Ⓕ Ⓖ Ⓗ Ⓙ Ⓚ	52 Ⓕ Ⓖ Ⓗ Ⓙ Ⓚ
3 Ⓐ Ⓑ Ⓒ Ⓓ Ⓔ	13 Ⓐ Ⓑ Ⓒ Ⓓ Ⓔ	23 Ⓐ Ⓑ Ⓒ Ⓓ Ⓔ	33 Ⓐ Ⓑ Ⓒ Ⓓ Ⓔ	43 Ⓐ Ⓑ Ⓒ Ⓓ Ⓔ	53 Ⓐ Ⓑ Ⓒ Ⓓ Ⓔ
4 Ⓕ Ⓖ Ⓗ Ⓙ Ⓚ	14 Ⓕ Ⓖ Ⓗ Ⓙ Ⓚ	24 Ⓕ Ⓖ Ⓗ Ⓙ Ⓚ	34 Ⓕ Ⓖ Ⓗ Ⓙ Ⓚ	44 Ⓕ Ⓖ Ⓗ Ⓙ Ⓚ	54 Ⓕ Ⓖ Ⓗ Ⓙ Ⓚ
5 Ⓐ Ⓑ Ⓒ Ⓓ Ⓔ	15 Ⓐ Ⓑ Ⓒ Ⓓ Ⓔ	25 Ⓐ Ⓑ Ⓒ Ⓓ Ⓔ	35 Ⓐ Ⓑ Ⓒ Ⓓ Ⓔ	45 Ⓐ Ⓑ Ⓒ Ⓓ Ⓔ	55 Ⓐ Ⓑ Ⓒ Ⓓ Ⓔ
6 Ⓕ Ⓖ Ⓗ Ⓙ Ⓚ	16 Ⓕ Ⓖ Ⓗ Ⓙ Ⓚ	26 Ⓕ Ⓖ Ⓗ Ⓙ Ⓚ	36 Ⓕ Ⓖ Ⓗ Ⓙ Ⓚ	46 Ⓕ Ⓖ Ⓗ Ⓙ Ⓚ	56 Ⓕ Ⓖ Ⓗ Ⓙ Ⓚ
7 Ⓐ Ⓑ Ⓒ Ⓓ Ⓔ	17 Ⓐ Ⓑ Ⓒ Ⓓ Ⓔ	27 Ⓐ Ⓑ Ⓒ Ⓓ Ⓔ	37 Ⓐ Ⓑ Ⓒ Ⓓ Ⓔ	47 Ⓐ Ⓑ Ⓒ Ⓓ Ⓔ	57 Ⓐ Ⓑ Ⓒ Ⓓ Ⓔ
8 Ⓕ Ⓖ Ⓗ Ⓙ Ⓚ	18 Ⓕ Ⓖ Ⓗ Ⓙ Ⓚ	28 Ⓕ Ⓖ Ⓗ Ⓙ Ⓚ	38 Ⓕ Ⓖ Ⓗ Ⓙ Ⓚ	48 Ⓕ Ⓖ Ⓗ Ⓙ Ⓚ	58 Ⓕ Ⓖ Ⓗ Ⓙ Ⓚ
9 Ⓐ Ⓑ Ⓒ Ⓓ Ⓔ	19 Ⓐ Ⓑ Ⓒ Ⓓ Ⓔ	29 Ⓐ Ⓑ Ⓒ Ⓓ Ⓔ	39 Ⓐ Ⓑ Ⓒ Ⓓ Ⓔ	49 Ⓐ Ⓑ Ⓒ Ⓓ Ⓔ	59 Ⓐ Ⓑ Ⓒ Ⓓ Ⓔ
10 Ⓕ Ⓖ Ⓗ Ⓙ Ⓚ	20 Ⓕ Ⓖ Ⓗ Ⓙ Ⓚ	30 Ⓕ Ⓖ Ⓗ Ⓙ Ⓚ	40 Ⓕ Ⓖ Ⓗ Ⓙ Ⓚ	50 Ⓕ Ⓖ Ⓗ Ⓙ Ⓚ	60 Ⓕ Ⓖ Ⓗ Ⓙ Ⓚ

This page is intentionally left blank

MATHEMATICS TEST

60 Minutes—60 Questions

DIRECTIONS: Solve each problem, choose the correct answer, and then fill in the corresponding oval on your answer document.

Do not linger over problems that take too much time. Solve as many as you can; then return to the others in the time you have left for this test.

You are permitted to use a calculator on this test. You may use your calculator for any problems you choose, but some of the problems may best be done without using a calculator.

Note: Unless otherwise stated, all of the following should be assumed.

1. Illustrative figures are NOT necessarily drawn to scale.
2. Geometric figures lie in a plane.
3. The word *line* indicates a straight line.
4. The word *average* indicates arithmetic mean.

---

1. An air conditioner repair man charges a $55 fee for a service call plus $27.50 per hour to repair an air conditioning unit. If you paid the air conditioner repair man $327.50 to repair your air conditioner, about how many hours did the repair man work on the unit?

   A. 8
   B. 20
   C. 5
   D. 12
   E. 10

DO YOUR FIGURING HERE.

2. If $f(x) = (4-x)^2 + 5$. Then $f(-2) =$?

   F. 9
   G. 41
   H. 61
   J. 14
   K. 17

25   **GO ON TO THE NEXT PAGE.**

3. Below is the graph of a function in the form $y = ax^2 + c$ where a and c are constants. Which of the following must be true for a and c?

DO YOUR FIGURING HERE.

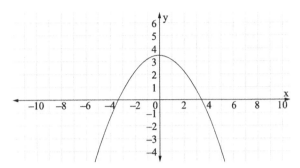

A. $a > 0$ and $c < 0$
B. $a < 0$ and $c > 0$
C. $a > 0$ and $c > 0$
D. $a < 0$ and $c < 0$
E. $a > 0$ and $c = 0$

4. Jeni's beginning hourly wage at her new job is $12.50. After 6 months, she will receive an increase in her hourly wage of 3%. Approximately how many hours did she work if she made $1850 for the 7th month of work?

F. 144
G. 148
H. 152
J. 160
K. 100

5. Let $p = qr^2 - q$. If $p = 120$ and $q = 8$, $r > 0$, then $r =$?

A. 8
B. 16
C. 4
D. 20
E. 128

6. The cost of a seedless watermelon is directly proportional to its weight. If a 25-pound watermelon costs $0.38 per pound, what is the approximate cost for a 32-pound watermelon?

F. $0.45
G. $0.37
H. $0.49
J. $0.95
K. $0.30

GO ON TO THE NEXT PAGE.

DO YOUR FIGURING HERE.

7. Which of the following statements is true about the graph of the function $y = f(x)$ shown below?

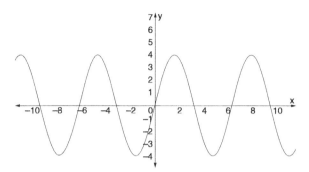

   A. Its graph has symmetry about the x-axis.
   B. The domain is for the function is $-4 \leq y \leq 4$.
   C. The graph has y-axis symmetry.
   D. The function has more positive real zeros than negative real zeros
   E. The graph has symmetry about the origin.

8. Find two consecutive integers if the sum of four times the smaller integer and three less than the larger integer is 523.

   F. 261 and 262
   G. 53 and 54
   H. 100 and 101
   J. 105 and 106
   K. 85 and 86.

9. Which expression is equivalent to $(4x^3 + 3xy - 5) - x(2x^2 - 7y + 6)$?

   A. $2x^3 - 10xy - 11$

   B. $2x^3 + 10xy - 11x$

   C. $2x^3 - 10xy + 6x - 5$

   D. $2x^3 - 4xy - 6x - 5$

   E. $2x^3 + 10xy - 6x - 5$

GO ON TO THE NEXT PAGE.

10. The table below shows how many gallons of water are poured into a 10,000-gallon pool at various times in order to fill it. There are initially 4500 gallons of water in the pool. Which equation could be used to find the time, t, in hours, it takes to fill the pool?

DO YOUR FIGURING HERE.

Time in hours, t	2	5	13	22
Gallons of water	7	17.5	45.5	77

- **F.** $4500 = 10{,}000 + 3.5t$
- **G.** $4500 = 10{,}000 - 3.5t$
- **H.** $10{,}000 = 4500 + 3.5t^2$
- **J.** $10{,}000 = 4500 - 3.5t$
- **K.** $10{,}000 = 4500 + 3.5t$

11. Let a, b, and c are constants where $a > 0$. If $x = a^{3b}$ and $y = a^{b-c}$, then $\dfrac{x}{y} = ?$

- **A.** a^{2b-c}
- **B.** a^{2b+c}
- **C.** a^{4b-c}
- **D.** $\dfrac{1}{a^{2b+c}}$
- **E.** $\dfrac{1}{a^{2b-c}}$

12. For a set of 7 numbers, the mean is 45. The median of the set is 42 and the mode is 51. What is the sum of the other four numbers in the set?

- **F.** 150
- **G.** 171
- **H.** 14
- **J.** 228
- **K.** 342

28   **GO ON TO THE NEXT PAGE.**

13. In diagram shown below, points A, C, and E are colinear. $\triangle ABC$ has an exterior angle measuring $142°$. What is the measure of angle C in degrees?

DO YOUR FIGURING HERE.

A. 38
B. 57
C. 42
D. 85
E. 48

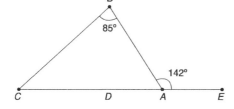

14. A rectangular garden is 15 yards long and 8 yards wide. The garden is fertilized with a blended bottle of fish emulsion that covers 360 square feet. If the garden needs to be fertilized 3 times during the spring growing season, how many bottles of fish emulsion will be needed?

F. 10
G. 12
H. 9
J. 3
K. 15

15. A piggy bank contains 12 nickels, 28 dimes, and 15 quarters. How many dimes will need to be added to the piggy bank if the probability of randomly selecting a dime will be $\frac{3}{4}$?

A. 39
B. 57
C. 10
D. 25
E. 1

16. If $|a-2b|=8$ where a and b are real numbers, which of the following is true?

F. $a = b - 8$

G. $a = 8 - 2b$

H. $a = 2b - 4$

J. $b = 4 - \dfrac{a}{2}$

K. $b = 4 + \dfrac{a}{2}$

GO ON TO THE NEXT PAGE.

17. If $f(g(x)) = (4-x)^2 + 5$ which of the following could be functions f and g?

   A. $f(x) = 4-x$ and $g(x) = x^2 + 5$
   B. $f(x) = x^2 + 5$ and $g(x) = 4-x$
   C. $f(x) = (4-x)^2$ and $g(x) = x+5$
   D. $f(x) = (4-x)^2$ and $g(x) = 5$
   E. $f(x) = 4-x$ and $g(x) = (x+5)^2$

DO YOUR FIGURING HERE.

18. From her house, Jana drives to school each morning. One morning, Jana is two-thirds of the way to school when she realizes she forgot an assignment that due. She returns home to pick up her assignment and drives back to school. If the distance from her house to school is 9 miles, how many miles did Jana drive that morning before arriving to school?

   F. 12
   G. 21
   H. 18
   J. 15
   K. 9

19. Which of the following expressions is equivalent to $(2x-1)^2 - 3x + 5$?

   A. $4x^2 - 7x + 4$
   B. $4x^2 - x + 6$
   C. $4x^2 - 7x + 6$
   D. $4x^2 - 3x + 6$
   E. $2x^2 - 7x + 6$

20. Suppose the mean of 5 numbers increases by $\frac{1}{3}$. Which of the following statements must be true?

   F. The sum of the 5 numbers must increase by $\frac{5}{3}$ of the original mean.
   G. The sum of the 5 numbers must increase by $\frac{1}{3}$ of the original mean.
   H. The sum of the 5 numbers must increase by $\frac{4}{3}$ of the original mean.
   J. The sum of the 5 numbers must increase by $\frac{1}{3}$ of the new mean.
   K. The sum of the 5 numbers must increase by $\frac{4}{3}$ of the new mean.

GO ON TO THE NEXT PAGE.

21. Which of the following is the graph of $2x - 3y = -12$ in the standard (x, y) coordinate plane?

DO YOUR FIGURING HERE.

A.
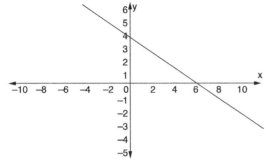

B.
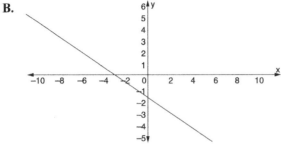

C.
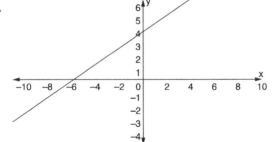

D.
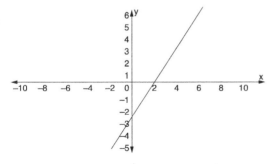

E.
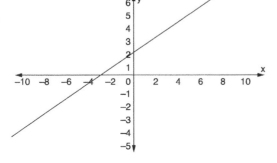

GO ON TO THE NEXT PAGE.

22. A cell phone that originally retails for $475 is on sale for 15% off its retail price. As an incentive, the retailer if offering an additional 5% off the sales price. If the tax rate is 8%, what will end up being the cost of the cell phone?

- **F.** $383.56
- **G.** 436.05
- **H.** $414.25
- **J.** $423.94
- **K.** $410.40

DO YOUR FIGURING HERE.

23. If the first and second terms in a geometric sequence are 2 and $\frac{3}{4}$ respectively, which expression represents the 10ᵗʰ term in the sequence?

- **A.** $\frac{3}{8}(2)^{10}$

- **B.** $2\left(\frac{3}{8}\right)^{10}$

- **C.** $2\left(\frac{3}{8}\right)^{9}$

- **D.** $2+\frac{5}{4}(10-1)$

- **E.** $2-\frac{5}{4}(10-1)$

24. Will needs to find the width of a pond. He determines he can best approximate the width of the pond by measuring the distance, in feet, from points E to F. To do so, he can measure the land distance from point G to E and G to F as shown in the diagram below. The angle between his two measurements is 25 degrees. To the nearest foot, what is the width of the pond?

- **F.** 36
- **G.** 44
- **H.** 73
- **J.** 43
- **K.** 38

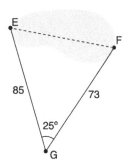

32

GO ON TO THE NEXT PAGE.

DO YOUR FIGURING HERE.

25. Arrange 152%, 1.48, and $\dfrac{8}{5}$ in descending order.

  A. 152%, 1.48, $\dfrac{8}{5}$

  B. $\dfrac{8}{5}$, 152%, 1.48

  C. $\dfrac{8}{5}$, 1.48, 152%

  D. 152%, $\dfrac{8}{5}$, 1.48

  E. 1.48, 152%, $\dfrac{8}{5}$

26. What is the slope of a line that has a y-intercept of –3 and is perpendicular to a line whose equation is $3x + 4y = -5$?

  F. –3

  G. –5

  H. $\dfrac{4}{3}$

  J. $-\dfrac{3}{4}$

  K. $-\dfrac{3}{4}$

27. Which of the following expression is a factor of $27x^3 + 64$?

  A. $9x^2 - 12x + 16$

  B. $9x^2 - 24x + 16$

  C. $9x^2 + 16$

  D. $3x - 8$

  E. $3x + 8$

GO ON TO THE NEXT PAGE.

28. Revenue generated tickets sales to a football game totaled $1,250,000. 60,000 people attended the game. People under 62 years of age paid $18 each for a ticket, and people ages 62 and over paid $15 each for a ticket. If m represents the number of people under 62, and n represents the number of people 62 years or older, which of the following set of equations could be used to find the number of people under 62 years of age that attended the football game?

F. $m + n = 60{,}000$
$18m + 15n = 1{,}250{,}000$

G. $18m + 15n = 60{,}000$
$m + n = 1{,}250{,}000$

H. $15m + 18n = 1{,}250{,}000$
$m + n = 60{,}000$

J. $15m + 18n = 60{,}000$
$m + n = 1{,}250{,}000$

K. $m + n = 60{,}000$
$m + n = 1{,}250{,}000$

DO YOUR FIGURING HERE.

29. If the ratio of a to b is 3 to 5, and c to d is 4 to 6, what is the ratio of a to c?

A. $\dfrac{9}{10}$

B. $\dfrac{10}{9}$

C. $\dfrac{9b}{10d}$

D. $\dfrac{9d}{10b}$

E. Cannot be calculated with the information given.

30. Which expression is equivalent to $\dfrac{\cos^2 x}{\sin x}$?

F. $1 - \sin x$

G. $\sin x$

H. $1 - \cos x$

J. $\csc x - \sin x$

K. $\sec x - \sin x$

34

GO ON TO THE NEXT PAGE.

31. Two cars exit an airport at the same time, one car traveling due north and the other due south. One car's speed is 4 miles an hour faster than the other car. After 3 hours, the cars are 204 miles apart. How fast, in miles per hour, is the slower car going?

    A. 34
    B. 30
    C. 32
    D. 25
    E. 20

DO YOUR FIGURING HERE.

32. The sum of 4 times a positive number and its square is 96. Which of the following value is the number?

    F. 4
    G. 16
    H. 8
    J. 12
    K. 6

33. The circle with center O containing points A, B, D, E, and F is shown below. The radius of O is 1 unit.

    If the measure of arc AFE is $\frac{1}{3}$ the circumference of the circle, what is the measure arc BGD in degrees?

    A. 76
    B. 38
    C. 60
    D. 120
    E. 44

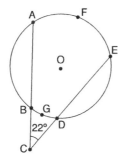

34. What is the sum of the solutions for $|2x-8|=17$?

    F. 64
    G. −32
    H. 8
    J. −8
    K. 6

35

35. Which of the following expressions is equivalent to $\dfrac{4}{1+i}$ where $i^2 = -1$?

   A. $2 + 2i$

   B. $2 - 2i$

   C. $2 + \dfrac{1}{2}i$

   D. $2 - \dfrac{1}{2}i$

   E. $4 - i$

DO YOUR FIGURING HERE.

36. Which statement is true about graphs of the functions $10x - 2y = 16$ and $y = 5x + 3$?

   F. They intersect at the point $(1, -8)$.

   G. They intersect at the point $(2, 13)$.

   H. They intersect at infinitely many points since they are the same line.

   J. They intersect at only one point since they are perpendicular to each other.

   K. They do not intersect since they are parallel and have different y-intercepts.

37. A bathtub can be filled in 15 minutes. It can be drained in 20 minutes. You begin to fill the empty bathtub with water and 8 minutes later, you realize you forgot to plug the drain. After the 8th minute, you plug the drain. How long will it take, in minutes, for the bathtub to be full of water?

   A. 13

   B. 8

   C. 17.5

   D. 21

   E. 15

GO ON TO THE NEXT PAGE.

38. If $M = a^b$ and $N = a^c$, then $\log_a (MN) =$?

    F. $b + c$

    G. $b \times c$

    H. $\dfrac{a}{c}$

    J. $a + c$

    K. $a - c$

DO YOUR FIGURING HERE.

39. The graph of a circle in the standard (x, y) coordinate plane that is tangent to the x-axis at 4 and thee y-axis at –4 is shown below. Which of the following is the equation of the circle?

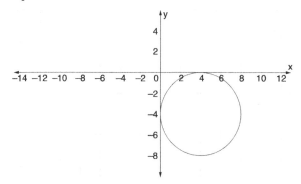

    A. $(x - 4)^2 + (y - 4)^2 = 4$

    B. $(x - 4)^2 + (y + 4)^2 = 16$

    C. $(x + 4)^2 + (y - 4)^2 = 16$

    D. $x^2 + y^2 = 16$

    E. $x^2 + y^2 = 4$

40. Which expression is equivalent to $\sqrt[4]{5^3} \cdot \sqrt{5}$?

    F. $25^{\frac{3}{2}}$

    G. $25^{\frac{3}{8}}$

    H. $5^{\frac{5}{4}}$

    J. $5^{\frac{3}{8}}$

    K. $5^{\frac{3}{8}} 4^{\frac{3}{2}}$

GO ON TO THE NEXT PAGE.

41. The pie chart given below, shows the results from a survey of percentage of people that preferred a genre for watching a movie. What are the odds of a person preferring an action movie to a preferring comedy?

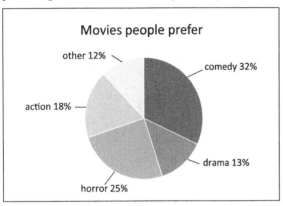

A. 9:16
B. 9:25
C. 9:41
D. 9:50
E. 9:100

DO YOUR FIGURING HERE.

42. A circular solid metal pipe 6 feet long has a radius of 2 feet. From the center of one end of the circular pipe, a circle is bored out with a drill press all the way thru the pipe. The circular bore has a radius of 6 inches. A cross section of the circular pipe and the circular bore is shown below.

After the circle is bored through, what will be the approximate volume, in cubic feet, of metal in the pipe?

F. 75
G. 66
H. 71
J. 24
K. 603

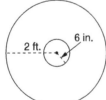

43. What is the period for the graph of $y = 4\cos\left(\dfrac{x}{2}\right)$?

A. 4π

B. $\dfrac{1}{2}$

C. 2π

D. π

E. $\dfrac{\pi}{2}$

GO ON TO THE NEXT PAGE.

44. What are the *x*-intercepts for the graph of the rational function $y = \dfrac{2x}{x^3 - 4x}$?

   F. 0

   G. −2, 0, 2

   H. −2, 0

   J. 0, 2

   K. No solution

DO YOUR FIGURING HERE.

45. If $p = -7$ is one of the roots for $p^2 + np - 28 = 0$, what must be the other root?

   A. 1

   B. 0

   C. 7

   D. −4

   E. 4

46. What is the range for the inverse of the function $h(x) = \sqrt{x - 5}$?

   F. $[\infty, 5)$

   G. $[5, \infty)$

   H. $(-5, \infty)$

   J. $(5, \infty]$

   K. All real numbers

47. Which of the following is the set of linear inequalities that satisfies the graph of the solution given below?

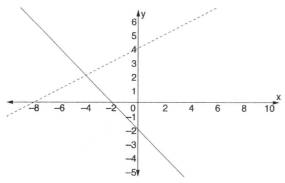

   A. $y \geq -x - 2$ and $y < \dfrac{1}{2}x + 4$

   B. $y \leq -x - 2$ and $y < \dfrac{1}{2}x + 4$

   C. $y > -x - 2$ and $y < \dfrac{1}{2}x + 4$

   D. $y \leq -x - 2$ or $y > \dfrac{1}{2}x + 4$

   E. $y < -x - 2$ or $y \geq \dfrac{1}{2}x + 4$

GO ON TO THE NEXT PAGE.

48. Miles works in the electronics department for a retailer. As an incentive for selling a stereo system, Miles receives $25 as well as 5% of the selling price of each system he sells in addition to his normal salary. If Miles sells 7 stereo systems for a total of $2520, what did he make in addition to his normal salary?

   F. $360
   G. $127.50
   H. $301
   J. $882
   K. $275

DO YOUR FIGURING HERE.

49. Which of the following equations, in matrix form, can be used to solve the system of equations below?

$$3x + y = 9$$
$$5x - 2y = 4$$

   A. $\begin{bmatrix} 3 & 5 \\ 1 & -2 \end{bmatrix}\begin{bmatrix} x \\ y \end{bmatrix} = \begin{bmatrix} 9 \\ 4 \end{bmatrix}$

   B. $\begin{bmatrix} 1 & 3 \\ -2 & 5 \end{bmatrix}\begin{bmatrix} x \\ y \end{bmatrix} = \begin{bmatrix} 9 \\ 4 \end{bmatrix}$

   C. $\begin{bmatrix} 3 & 1 \\ 5 & -2 \end{bmatrix}\begin{bmatrix} x \\ y \end{bmatrix} = \begin{bmatrix} 9 \\ 4 \end{bmatrix}$

   D. $\begin{bmatrix} x \\ y \end{bmatrix} = \begin{bmatrix} 3 & 1 \\ 5 & -2 \end{bmatrix}\begin{bmatrix} 9 \\ 4 \end{bmatrix}$

   E. $\begin{bmatrix} x \\ y \end{bmatrix} = \begin{bmatrix} 3 & 5 \\ 1 & -2 \end{bmatrix}\begin{bmatrix} 9 \\ 4 \end{bmatrix}$

50. The measure of $\angle ABC$ is $82°$. Ray $\overline{BD}$ divides $\angle ABC$ such that the measure of $\angle ABD$ is $\frac{1}{3}$ the measure of $\angle DBC$. What is the measure of $\angle DBC$?

   F. $25.3°$
   G. $56.7°$
   H. $42°$
   J. $20.5°$
   K. $61.5°$

GO ON TO THE NEXT PAGE.

51. What is the value of expression $\dfrac{2\sec^2 x - 2\tan^2 x}{5\cos^2 x + 5\sin^2 x}$ for any value of x that is in the domain of each function in the expression?

A. $\dfrac{1}{5}$

B. $\dfrac{1}{3}$

C. $\dfrac{2}{5}$

D. 0

E. Undefined

DO YOUR FIGURING HERE.

52. The change in temperature, T, in degrees Fahrenheit, from spring to summer in the middle of the country can be model by the function $T = 5\log w$, where w in weeks. Which statement is true about the temperature in the middle of the country from spring to summer?

F. The temperature is constant.
G. The temperature is decreasing at an increasing rate.
H. The temperature is increasing at a constant rate.
J. The temperature is increasing at a decreasing rate.
K. The temperature is increasing at an increasing rate.

53. What will be the coordinates if point A(3, 5) is shifted horizontally to the left 7 units and reflected across the y-axis in the standard (x, y) coordinate plane?

A. (–4, 5)
B. (–4, –5)
C. (4, 5)
D. (7, –5)
E. (–7, 5)

54. A test group of men and women are given a drug or a placebo. Forty-two percent of the group are men and it is known that thirty-five percent of the men are given a placebo. If a person from the group is chosen at random, what is the probability that it will be a man that was given a placebo?

F. 0.58
G. 0.65
H. 0.15
J. 0.77
K. 0.23

GO ON TO THE NEXT PAGE.

55. Which of the following angles, in degrees, is coterminal

to $\theta = \dfrac{21}{4}\pi$ radians?

A. 135
B. 45
C. 225
D. 270
E. 180

DO YOUR FIGURING HERE.

56. The stem–leaf plot below shows the grades of each assignment in your math class for a grading period. For example, grade of 94 is represented by stem value of 9 and a leaf value of 4.

If each assignment carries an equal weight, what must the value for n be for your average to be an 80?

Stem	Leaf
5	2
6	n, 8
7	3, 9, 9
8	1, 5, 5, 5, 8
9	2, 4, 8

$$9 \mid 4 = 94$$

F. 0
G. 1
H. 3
J. 5
K. 7

57. A mixture containing 4% orange oil is mixed with 3 quarts of another mixture that contains 12% orange oil. How many quarts of the 4% mixture should be used to produce a mixture that is 8% orange oil?

A. 3
B. 1
C. 2
D. 4
E. 5

GO ON TO THE NEXT PAGE.

58. In the figure below, $\triangle ABC \sim \triangle EFG$, $a = 12$ units, $c = 5$ units, and $e = 8$ units. What is the length of g in units?

DO YOUR FIGURING HERE.

F. $\dfrac{3}{10}$

G. $\dfrac{10}{3}$

H. $\dfrac{96}{5}$

J. $\dfrac{15}{2}$

K. $\dfrac{5}{2}$

59. In the same tomato garden, Sophia can plant 16 tomato plants in one hour and Noah can plant 12 tomato plants in one and a half hours. If they work together, how many hours will it take them to plant 84 tomato plants?

A. 6
B. 1.5
C. 3.5
D. 5.25
E. 2.5

60. C, F, and E lie on the same ray as shown in the diagram below. The ratio of CF to FE is 3:1. Which of the following statements must be true?

F. CE = 4FE

G. FE = $\dfrac{1}{3}$CE

H. FE = $\dfrac{3}{4}$CE

J. CF = $\dfrac{4}{3}$FE

K. CF = $\dfrac{3}{4}$CE

END OF TEST

This page is intentionally left blank

ACT Math Practice Test 3

Mark Your Answers For Test 3 Here

Date: _____

Marking Directions: Mark only one oval for each question. Fill in response completely. Erase errors cleanly without smudging.

Correct mark: ○ ● ○ ○ ○

1 Ⓐ Ⓑ Ⓒ Ⓓ Ⓔ   11 Ⓐ Ⓑ Ⓒ Ⓓ Ⓔ   21 Ⓐ Ⓑ Ⓒ Ⓓ Ⓔ   31 Ⓐ Ⓑ Ⓒ Ⓓ Ⓔ   41 Ⓐ Ⓑ Ⓒ Ⓓ Ⓔ   51 Ⓐ Ⓑ Ⓒ Ⓓ Ⓔ
2 Ⓕ Ⓖ Ⓗ Ⓙ Ⓚ   12 Ⓕ Ⓖ Ⓗ Ⓙ Ⓚ   22 Ⓕ Ⓖ Ⓗ Ⓙ Ⓚ   32 Ⓕ Ⓖ Ⓗ Ⓙ Ⓚ   42 Ⓕ Ⓖ Ⓗ Ⓙ Ⓚ   52 Ⓕ Ⓖ Ⓗ Ⓙ Ⓚ
3 Ⓐ Ⓑ Ⓒ Ⓓ Ⓔ   13 Ⓐ Ⓑ Ⓒ Ⓓ Ⓔ   23 Ⓐ Ⓑ Ⓒ Ⓓ Ⓔ   33 Ⓐ Ⓑ Ⓒ Ⓓ Ⓔ   43 Ⓐ Ⓑ Ⓒ Ⓓ Ⓔ   53 Ⓐ Ⓑ Ⓒ Ⓓ Ⓔ
4 Ⓕ Ⓖ Ⓗ Ⓙ Ⓚ   14 Ⓕ Ⓖ Ⓗ Ⓙ Ⓚ   24 Ⓕ Ⓖ Ⓗ Ⓙ Ⓚ   34 Ⓕ Ⓖ Ⓗ Ⓙ Ⓚ   44 Ⓕ Ⓖ Ⓗ Ⓙ Ⓚ   54 Ⓕ Ⓖ Ⓗ Ⓙ Ⓚ
5 Ⓐ Ⓑ Ⓒ Ⓓ Ⓔ   15 Ⓐ Ⓑ Ⓒ Ⓓ Ⓔ   25 Ⓐ Ⓑ Ⓒ Ⓓ Ⓔ   35 Ⓐ Ⓑ Ⓒ Ⓓ Ⓔ   45 Ⓐ Ⓑ Ⓒ Ⓓ Ⓔ   55 Ⓐ Ⓑ Ⓒ Ⓓ Ⓔ
6 Ⓕ Ⓖ Ⓗ Ⓙ Ⓚ   16 Ⓕ Ⓖ Ⓗ Ⓙ Ⓚ   26 Ⓕ Ⓖ Ⓗ Ⓙ Ⓚ   36 Ⓕ Ⓖ Ⓗ Ⓙ Ⓚ   46 Ⓕ Ⓖ Ⓗ Ⓙ Ⓚ   56 Ⓕ Ⓖ Ⓗ Ⓙ Ⓚ
7 Ⓐ Ⓑ Ⓒ Ⓓ Ⓔ   17 Ⓐ Ⓑ Ⓒ Ⓓ Ⓔ   27 Ⓐ Ⓑ Ⓒ Ⓓ Ⓔ   37 Ⓐ Ⓑ Ⓒ Ⓓ Ⓔ   47 Ⓐ Ⓑ Ⓒ Ⓓ Ⓔ   57 Ⓐ Ⓑ Ⓒ Ⓓ Ⓔ
8 Ⓕ Ⓖ Ⓗ Ⓙ Ⓚ   18 Ⓕ Ⓖ Ⓗ Ⓙ Ⓚ   28 Ⓕ Ⓖ Ⓗ Ⓙ Ⓚ   38 Ⓕ Ⓖ Ⓗ Ⓙ Ⓚ   48 Ⓕ Ⓖ Ⓗ Ⓙ Ⓚ   58 Ⓕ Ⓖ Ⓗ Ⓙ Ⓚ
9 Ⓐ Ⓑ Ⓒ Ⓓ Ⓔ   19 Ⓐ Ⓑ Ⓒ Ⓓ Ⓔ   29 Ⓐ Ⓑ Ⓒ Ⓓ Ⓔ   39 Ⓐ Ⓑ Ⓒ Ⓓ Ⓔ   49 Ⓐ Ⓑ Ⓒ Ⓓ Ⓔ   59 Ⓐ Ⓑ Ⓒ Ⓓ Ⓔ
10 Ⓕ Ⓖ Ⓗ Ⓙ Ⓚ   20 Ⓕ Ⓖ Ⓗ Ⓙ Ⓚ   30 Ⓕ Ⓖ Ⓗ Ⓙ Ⓚ   40 Ⓕ Ⓖ Ⓗ Ⓙ Ⓚ   50 Ⓕ Ⓖ Ⓗ Ⓙ Ⓚ   60 Ⓕ Ⓖ Ⓗ Ⓙ Ⓚ

This page is intentionally left blank

MATHEMATICS TEST

60 Minutes—60 Questions

DIRECTIONS: Solve each problem, choose the correct answer, and then fill in the corresponding oval on your answer document.

Do not linger over problems that take too much time. Solve as many as you can; then return to the others in the time you have left for this test.

You are permitted to use a calculator on this test. You may use your calculator for any problems you

choose, but some of the problems may best be done without using a calculator.

Note: Unless otherwise stated, all of the following should be assumed.

1. Illustrative figures are NOT necessarily drawn to scale.
2. Geometric figures lie in a plane.
3. The word *line* indicates a straight line.
4. The word *average* indicates arithmetic mean.

---

1. Which expression is equivalent to $(a^3 - 2ab + 5b) - a(2a^2 - 7b) - b(2b + 3)$?

   A. $-a^3 - 9ab - 2b^2 + 2b$
   B. $-a^3 + 5ab - 2b^2 + 2b$
   C. $-a^3 - 9ab - 2b^2 + 8b$
   D. $3a^3 + 5ab - 2b^2 + 2b$
   E. $3a^3 - 9ab - 2b^2 + 2b$

2. Which of the following equations is a parabola that has its vertex at (–2, 4) and contains the point (1, 22)?

   F. $y = (x - 2)^2 + 4$
   G. $y = (x - 1)^2 + 22$
   H. $y = 2(x + 2)^2 - 4$
   J. $y = 2(x + 2)^2 + 4$
   K. $y = 6(x + 2)^2 + 4$

3. While driving her car along a highway, Marci counted 5 road signs every 2 minutes. If she travels along the highway for 24 minutes, how many road signs will she count?

   A. 48
   B. 120
   C. 60
   D. 72
   E. 50

DO YOUR FIGURING HERE.

GO ON TO THE NEXT PAGE.

DO YOUR FIGURING HERE.

4. In the diagram below, $\angle ABC = 137°$ and BD divides $\angle ABC$ so that $\angle CBD$ is 11 degrees less than 3 times $\angle ABD$. What is the measure of $\angle CBD$ in degrees?

   F. 85
   G. 37
   H. 100
   J. 80
   K. 90

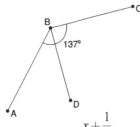

5. If $x = 3$ and $y = 6$, what is the value of $\dfrac{x + \dfrac{1}{y}}{\dfrac{1}{x}}$?

   A. $\dfrac{19}{2}$

   B. $\dfrac{2}{19}$

   C. $\dfrac{19}{18}$

   D. $\dfrac{3}{2}$

   E. $\dfrac{1}{6}$

6. Two perpendicular lines intersect at (3,4). If one of the lines contains (5, 10), which of the following is a point on the other line?

   F. (6, 3)
   G. (3, 6)
   H. (0, –5)
   J. (4, 7)
   K. (1, –2)

7. What is the value of $2f(3) - g(3)$ if $f(x) = 3x^2 - 18$ and $g(x) = 4x - 2(5 - x)$?

   A. 26
   B. 5
   C. 10
   D. 82
   E. 0

8. What is the length of the line segment joining the midpoints of $\overline{AC}$ and $\overline{BC}$ in right triangle $\triangle ABC$ shown below?

   F. 6
   G. 4.5
   H. 15
   J. 30
   K. 21

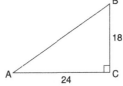

GO ON TO THE NEXT PAGE.

9. The 1st and 3rd terms in a geometric sequence are 3, 48 respectively. What is the 10th term?

- **A.** 262,144
- **B.** 786,432
- **C.** 3,145,728
- **D.** 147
- **E.** 163

DO YOUR FIGURING HERE.

10. Which of the following expressions is a factor of $16x^2 - 49$?

- **F.** $8x + 7$
- **G.** $8x - 7$
- **H.** $4x^2 + 7$
- **J.** $4x^2 - 7$
- **K.** $4x - 7$

11. The storage capacity of a rectangular shed is 1080 cubic feet. What is the volume of the shed in cubic yards?

- **A.** 360
- **B.** 3240
- **C.** 120
- **D.** 29,160
- **E.** 90

12. Which of the following expressions is equivalent to $2x^{\frac{5}{3}}$?

- **F.** $\frac{2}{3}x^5$
- **G.** $x^{\frac{10}{3}}$
- **H.** $\frac{2\sqrt{x^5}}{3}$
- **J.** $2\sqrt[3]{x^5}$
- **K.** $2\sqrt[5]{x^3}$

13. Julian is a salesman in the kitchen appliance department at a retail store. The department sells refrigerators, ranges, and dishwashers. He receives a weekly base salary of $350 each week plus $25 for each refrigerator, range or dishwasher he sells. If his gross salary for a given week is $1250, how many appliances did he sell?

- **A.** 36
- **B.** 50
- **C.** 7
- **D.** 72
- **E.** 4015

GO ON TO THE NEXT PAGE.

14. In a survey at an elementary school, it was found that 4 out of every 5 students do not like spinach. If two students at the school are chosen at random where the first student chosen can be chosen again, what is the probability that they both like spinach?

F. $\dfrac{16}{25}$

G. $\dfrac{1}{25}$

H. $\dfrac{2}{5}$

J. $\dfrac{3}{5}$

K. $\dfrac{4}{25}$

15. What is the slope of a line that has an x-intercept of 4 and a y-intercept of –9?

A. $\dfrac{4}{9}$

B. $-\dfrac{4}{9}$

C. $\dfrac{9}{4}$

D. $\dfrac{5}{9}$

E. $-\dfrac{9}{5}$

16. The temperature of oil in a car is recorded in the table below for the first 5 minutes after the car is turned off.

Time (minutes)	Temperature (°F)
0	275
1	262
2	242
3	202
4	152
5	91

Which of the following statements is true about the temperature?

F. The temperature of the oil is decreasing at an increasing rate.

G. The temperature of the oil is decreasing at a decreasing rate.

H. The temperature of the oil is decreasing at a constant rate.

J. The temperature of the oil is inversely proportional to time.

K. The temperature of the oil varies directly with time.

DO YOUR FIGURING HERE.

GO ON TO THE NEXT PAGE.

17. If $u = \langle 5, 11 \rangle$, $v = \langle -8, 16 \rangle$ and $u - v + w = \langle 9, 15 \rangle$ which of the following is w?

   A. $\langle 12, -6 \rangle$

   B. $\langle -6, 12 \rangle$

   C. $\langle -4, 20 \rangle$

   D. $\langle -4, 12 \rangle$

   E. $\langle 12, -12 \rangle$

DO YOUR FIGURING HERE.

18. A horizontal line intersects the center of a circle whose equation is $(x-4)^2 + (y+5)^2 = 121$. The horizontal line contains which of the following points?

   F. (15, 5)

   G. (−7, 5)

   H. (15, −5)

   J. (4, 6)

   K. (4, −16)

19. Which of the following expressions is equivalent to $x^2 + 16x$?

   A. $(x-4)^2 - 64$

   B. $(x+8)^2 - 64$

   C. $(x-8)^2 - 64$

   D. $(x+8)^2 - 64$

   E. $(x+8)^2 + 64$

20. Let $z = yx^2 - y$ where $y, z > 0$. Which expression gives the value for x?

   F. $\sqrt{\dfrac{z+y}{z}}$

   G. $\sqrt{\dfrac{z+y}{y}}$

   H. $\sqrt{\dfrac{z-y}{y}}$

   J. $\sqrt{\dfrac{y}{z+y}}$

   K. $\sqrt{\dfrac{y}{z-y}}$

GO ON TO THE NEXT PAGE.

21. A square is inscribed in a circle centered at O at shown below. If the area of the circle is 9π square inches, what is the length of a side of the square?

A. $3\sqrt{3}$
B. $3\sqrt{2}$
C. $\dfrac{3}{2}$
D. 6
E. $\dfrac{5}{2}$

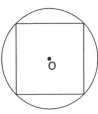

DO YOUR FIGURING HERE.

22. What is $\dfrac{4}{7}$ of 41% of 249?

F. 5.83
G. 58.29
H. 71.14
J. 249.87
K. 10.62

23. If Jonathan increases his caloric intake, he hopes to gain the weight he needs to be able to play football. Below is a table of values for the increase in daily calories each week for a five-week period in Johnathan's diet and the weight he has gained each week. What appears to be the relationship for the weight gained each week in terms of the calories added to his diet?

Increase in Calories	Weight gained (lbs.)
200	0.4
400	0.8
800	1.6
1500	3.0
2000	4.0

A. The relationship is exponential.
B. The relationship is quadratic.
C. The relationship is linear.
D. The relationship is sinusoidal.
E. There is no relationship.

24. Let f be an invertible function where $f(3) = 7$ and $f(7) = 3$. If g is the inverse function for f, then $f(g(7)) = ?$

F. 9
G. 7
H. 21
J. $\dfrac{1}{7}$
K. $\dfrac{1}{3}$

GO ON TO THE NEXT PAGE.

25. What is the sum of the mode and the median for the set containing $\{5x, 2x, x, 6x, x, 7x, 3x, 10x\}$?

   A. $6x$
   B. $7x$
   C. $4x$
   D. $5x$
   E. $8x$

26. Which of the following functions transforms the parent function $y = \sqrt{x}$ three units to the left and five units down?

   F. $y = 5\sqrt{x+3}$
   G. $y = 3\sqrt{x} - 5$
   H. $y = \sqrt{x-3} - 5$
   J. $y = \sqrt{x-3} + 5$
   K. $y = \sqrt{x+3} - 5$

27. Which of the following is the equation of the circle graphed in the standard (x, y) coordinate plane shown below?

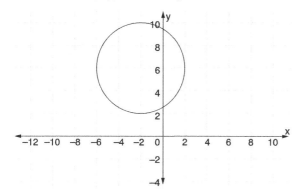

   A. $(x+2)^2 + (y-6)^2 = 16$
   B. $(x-2)^2 + (y+6)^2 = 16$
   C. $(x-2)^2 + (y-6)^2 = 16$
   D. $(x+2)^2 + (y+6)^2 = 4$
   E. $(x-2)^2 + (y+6)^2 = 4$

28. What amount of ounces of frozen peas costing \$0.03 for each ounce should be added to 14 ounces of diced frozen carrots costing \$0.06 for each ounce to make a bag of frozen peas and carrots which costs \$0.05 for each ounce?

   F. 14
   G. 28
   H. 7
   J. 20
   K. 42

DO YOUR FIGURING HERE.

GO ON TO THE NEXT PAGE.

29. Simplify $\left(4+\sqrt{-2}\right)\left(4-\sqrt{-2}\right)$ where $i^2 = -1$.

  A. $16-4i$
  B. $16+4i$
  C. 14
  D. 12
  E. 18

DO YOUR FIGURING HERE.

30. What is the solution for $|3x-7| < 11$?

  F. $-\dfrac{4}{3} < x < 6$
  G. $6 < x < -\dfrac{4}{3}$
  H. $x < 6$ or $x > -\dfrac{4}{3}$
  J. $x < -\dfrac{4}{3}$ or $x > 6$
  K. No solution exists

31. A circle with center O contains points A, C, D, and E shown below. If $\angle ACE = 82°$, what is the measure, in degrees, of $\overarc{ADE}$?

  A. $82°$
  B. $164°$
  C. $41°$
  D. $180°$
  E. $90°$

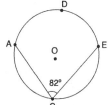

32. A swimming pool that holds 10,000 gallons of water is one-quarter full. You begin to fill the pool with water from your water hose that pours 20 gallons of water each minute. Ten minutes later, your next-door neighbor helps fill the pool with his hose that pours 30 gallons of water each minute. How many minutes will it take until the pool is full of water?

  F. 206
  G. 156
  H. 50
  J. 44
  K. 60

33. What is $\log_a\left(\dfrac{M^2}{N}\right)$ if $M = a^b$ and $N = a^c$?

  A. $b - c$
  B. $2b - c$
  C. $2b + c$
  D. $\dfrac{2b}{c}$
  E. $\dfrac{b}{2c}$

GO ON TO THE NEXT PAGE.

34. Which of the following statements is true about the graphs of the functions $y = 6x - 5$ and $y = (x+1)^2 - 2$?

    F. The graphs of the two functions intersect at 2 points.

    G. The graphs of the two functions are tangent at (2, 7).

    H. The graphs of the two functions are tangent at (−1, −2).

    J. The graphs of the two functions are perpendicular at (2, 7).

    K. The graphs of the two functions do not intersect.

DO YOUR FIGURING HERE.

35. Which expression is equivalent to $\dfrac{\sin x}{\cos x} + \dfrac{\cos x}{\sin x}$?

    A. 1

    B. 2

    C. $\sin x + \cos x$

    D. $\sin^2 x + \cos^2 x$

    E. $\dfrac{1}{\sin x \cos x}$

36. A hotel logs the number of days a hotel patron spends the night in one of their rooms. The distribution table is given below.

No. of nights spent	Frequency
2	59
3	45
4	32
5	18
6	9

What is the probability that a person spends the night in one of their rooms for more than 4 days?

    F. 0.17

    G. 0.36

    H. 0.64

    J. 0.20

    K. 0.15

37. How many terms are in an arithmetic sequence which has a sum of 264 and whose first and last terms are 9 and 39 respectively?

    A. 24

    B. 9

    C. 11

    D. 10

    E. 18

GO ON TO THE NEXT PAGE.

38. The sum of three numbers is 348. The first number is 4 more than the second, while the third number is the average of the first two numbers. Which of the following is the set of numbers?

   A. 120, 116, 118
   B. 126, 106, 116
   C. 118, 114, 116
   D. 115, 111, 113
   E. 136, 132, 74

DO YOUR FIGURING HERE.

39. The graph of $y = a\sin(bx)$ is given below in the standard (x, y) coordinate plane. What is the value of b?

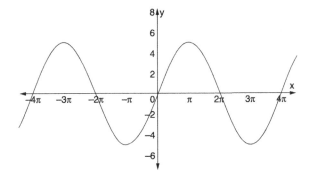

   A. -2
   B. 4π
   C. 2π
   D. $-\dfrac{1}{2}$
   E. $\dfrac{1}{2}$

40. Sid wants to build a rectangular dog pen using an existing stone wall for one of the sides. The other three sides of the pen will be built using 200 feet of a fencing material. What will be the maximum area, in square feet, of the pen Sid can build?

   F. 50
   G. 100
   H. 4950
   J. 9900
   K. 2000

GO ON TO THE NEXT PAGE.

41. Rationalize $\dfrac{2}{3+\sqrt{5}}$.

DO YOUR FIGURING HERE.

- **A.** $\dfrac{3}{2}-\dfrac{\sqrt{10}}{4}$
- **B.** $\dfrac{3}{2}-\dfrac{\sqrt{5}}{2}$
- **C.** $\dfrac{3}{2}+\dfrac{\sqrt{5}}{2}$
- **D.** $\dfrac{6}{13}-\dfrac{2\sqrt{5}}{13}$
- **E.** $\dfrac{6}{13}+\dfrac{2\sqrt{5}}{13}$

42. In the standard (x, y) coordinate system, a line containing $(7, 13)$ intersects the x-axis at 4. What is the measure of the smallest angle formed, in degrees, between the line and the x-axis?

- **F.** 103
- **G.** 77
- **H.** 13
- **J.** 167
- **K.** 54

43. If $(x+a)(x+b) = x^2 - 2x - 15$, what is the average of a and b?

- **A.** 8
- **B.** 1
- **C.** −8
- **D.** −1
- **E.** 0

44. What is the solution set for the graph below?

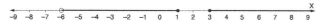

- **F.** $-6 < x \le 1$ or $x \ge 3$
- **G.** $1 < x \le -6$ or $x \ge 3$
- **H.** $-6 < x$ or $x \le 1$ or $x \ge 3$
- **J.** $-6 > x$ or $x \ge 1$ or $x \ge 3$
- **K.** $-6 \le x$ or $x < 1$ or $x \ge 3$

57

GO ON TO THE NEXT PAGE.

45. $\dfrac{2}{x-1}+(x-2)^{-1} =$

    A. $\dfrac{2x-3}{(x-1)(x-2)}$

    B. $\dfrac{3}{(x-1)(x-2)}$

    C. $\dfrac{3x-5}{(x-1)(x-2)}$

    D. $\dfrac{3}{(x-2)}$

    E. $\dfrac{2}{(x-1)}$

DO YOUR FIGURING HERE.

46. From home, Karen walks to the grocery store at a rate of 3 miles per hour. Ten minutes later, her brother Nick rides his bicycle to the grocery store at a rate of 15 miles per hour. Nick catches up with Karen before reaching the grocery store. How many minutes did it take Nick to catch up with his sister?

    F. 5
    G. 12.5
    H. 33.3
    J. 10
    K. 22.5

47. The graph of f is transformed to produce the graph of g shown below. Which of the following statements best describes the transformation?

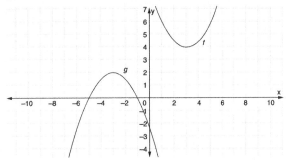

    A. The graph of f is reflected across the x-axis, then shifted horizontally to the left 3 units.

    B. The graph of f is reflected across the y-axis, then shifted vertically down 2 units.

    C. The graph of f is reflected across the y-axis, shifted horizontally to the left 3 units, then shifted vertically up 6 units.

    D. The graph of f is reflected across the x-axis, shifted horizontally to the left 6 units, then shifted vertically up 6 units.

    E. The graph of f is reflected across the x-axis, shifted horizontally to the left 6 units, then shifted vertically up 2 units.

GO ON TO THE NEXT PAGE.

48. What is the range for the graph of the function $y = -\sqrt{x} + 3$?

    F. $[3, -\infty)$
    G. $(-\infty, 3]$
    H. $(-\infty, 0]$
    J. $[0, \infty)$
    K. All real numbers

DO YOUR FIGURING HERE.

49. In radians, a coterminal angle for $765°$ is?

    A. $\dfrac{5\pi}{4}$

    B. $-\dfrac{\pi}{4}$

    C. $\dfrac{\pi}{4}$

    D. $\dfrac{\pi}{6}$

    E. $-\dfrac{2}{3}\pi$

50. If the diagonals of a parallelogram are perpendicular to each other, the parallelogram will also be a?

    F. Square
    G. Rhombus
    H. Rectangle
    J. Circle
    K. None of the above

51. The number of minutes, m, it takes a packing machine to package n packages varies jointly with the number of packages and the size of a package, s. If 3 is the constant of variation, which of the following is true about m?

    A. $m = \dfrac{ns}{3}$

    B. $m = 3(n + s)$

    C. $m = \dfrac{3n}{s}$

    D. $m = \dfrac{3s}{n}$

    E. $m = 3ns$

GO ON TO THE NEXT PAGE.

52. If $\dfrac{2p-q}{p+2q}=\dfrac{8}{9}$, what is the product of p and q?

    F. 5
    G. 2
    H. 10
    J. 3
    K. 7

DO YOUR FIGURING HERE.

53. In scientific notation, $1,000,000 \times 3,200,000 = ?$

    A. 32,000,000,000,000
    B. 3,200,000,000,000
    C. 3.2×10^{12}
    D. 32×10^{11}
    E. 0.32×10^{13}

54. Find the length of $\overline{BC}$ for $\triangle ABC$ shown below.

    F. 12.8
    G. 14.7
    H. 21.5
    J. 35.9
    K. 19

55. What is the sum of the horizontal and vertical asymptotes for $y=\dfrac{(x+3)(x-4)}{x^2-16}$?

    A. 1
    B. 3
    C. -3
    D. -17
    E. 17

56. Which of the following expressions has the greatest value if n is a proper fraction?

    F. n
    G. n^2
    H. n^3
    J. $\dfrac{1}{n}$
    K. $\sqrt{n}$

GO ON TO THE NEXT PAGE.

57. If $\sin\theta = -\dfrac{1}{2}$ and $\dfrac{1}{2}\pi < \theta < \dfrac{3}{2}\pi$, then $\cos\theta = ?$

DO YOUR FIGURING HERE.

- **A.** $\dfrac{1}{2}$
- **B.** $\dfrac{\sqrt{3}}{2}$
- **C.** $-\dfrac{\sqrt{3}}{2}$
- **D.** $\dfrac{\sqrt{2}}{2}$
- **E.** $-\dfrac{\sqrt{2}}{2}$

58. Set A = {7, 21, 11, 9, 1, 3, 11}. If the mean, median, and mode are the same for set B and set B contains 13 numbers, then the sum of the numbers in set B is?

- **F.** 117
- **G.** 63
- **H.** 143
- **J.** 81
- **K.** 130

59. Let $\triangle ABC \sim \triangle DEF$. If side $a = 4$, $b = 9$, and $d = 2$. What is the length of side e?

- **A.** 18
- **B.** $\dfrac{9}{2}$
- **C.** $\dfrac{2}{9}$
- **D.** $\dfrac{9}{4}$
- **E.** $\dfrac{4}{9}$

60. Which quadratic equation has roots of –3 and 4?

- **F.** $x^2 + x - 12$
- **G.** $x^2 - x - 12$
- **H.** $x^2 - x - 1$
- **J.** $x^2 - x + 1$
- **K.** $x^2 - 7x - 12$

END OF TEST

This page is intentionally left blank

ACT Math Practice Test 4

Mark Your Answers For Test 4 Here

Date: _____

Marking Directions: Mark only one oval for each question. Fill in response completely. Erase errors cleanly without smudging.

Correct mark: ○ ◉ ○ ○ ○

1 Ⓐ Ⓑ Ⓒ Ⓓ Ⓔ	11 Ⓐ Ⓑ Ⓒ Ⓓ Ⓔ	21 Ⓐ Ⓑ Ⓒ Ⓓ Ⓔ	31 Ⓐ Ⓑ Ⓒ Ⓓ Ⓔ	41 Ⓐ Ⓑ Ⓒ Ⓓ Ⓔ	51 Ⓐ Ⓑ Ⓒ Ⓓ Ⓔ
2 Ⓕ Ⓖ Ⓗ Ⓙ Ⓚ	12 Ⓕ Ⓖ Ⓗ Ⓙ Ⓚ	22 Ⓕ Ⓖ Ⓗ Ⓙ Ⓚ	32 Ⓕ Ⓖ Ⓗ Ⓙ Ⓚ	42 Ⓕ Ⓖ Ⓗ Ⓙ Ⓚ	52 Ⓕ Ⓖ Ⓗ Ⓙ Ⓚ
3 Ⓐ Ⓑ Ⓒ Ⓓ Ⓔ	13 Ⓐ Ⓑ Ⓒ Ⓓ Ⓔ	23 Ⓐ Ⓑ Ⓒ Ⓓ Ⓔ	33 Ⓐ Ⓑ Ⓒ Ⓓ Ⓔ	43 Ⓐ Ⓑ Ⓒ Ⓓ Ⓔ	53 Ⓐ Ⓑ Ⓒ Ⓓ Ⓔ
4 Ⓕ Ⓖ Ⓗ Ⓙ Ⓚ	14 Ⓕ Ⓖ Ⓗ Ⓙ Ⓚ	24 Ⓕ Ⓖ Ⓗ Ⓙ Ⓚ	34 Ⓕ Ⓖ Ⓗ Ⓙ Ⓚ	44 Ⓕ Ⓖ Ⓗ Ⓙ Ⓚ	54 Ⓕ Ⓖ Ⓗ Ⓙ Ⓚ
5 Ⓐ Ⓑ Ⓒ Ⓓ Ⓔ	15 Ⓐ Ⓑ Ⓒ Ⓓ Ⓔ	25 Ⓐ Ⓑ Ⓒ Ⓓ Ⓔ	35 Ⓐ Ⓑ Ⓒ Ⓓ Ⓔ	45 Ⓐ Ⓑ Ⓒ Ⓓ Ⓔ	55 Ⓐ Ⓑ Ⓒ Ⓓ Ⓔ
6 Ⓕ Ⓖ Ⓗ Ⓙ Ⓚ	16 Ⓕ Ⓖ Ⓗ Ⓙ Ⓚ	26 Ⓕ Ⓖ Ⓗ Ⓙ Ⓚ	36 Ⓕ Ⓖ Ⓗ Ⓙ Ⓚ	46 Ⓕ Ⓖ Ⓗ Ⓙ Ⓚ	56 Ⓕ Ⓖ Ⓗ Ⓙ Ⓚ
7 Ⓐ Ⓑ Ⓒ Ⓓ Ⓔ	17 Ⓐ Ⓑ Ⓒ Ⓓ Ⓔ	27 Ⓐ Ⓑ Ⓒ Ⓓ Ⓔ	37 Ⓐ Ⓑ Ⓒ Ⓓ Ⓔ	47 Ⓐ Ⓑ Ⓒ Ⓓ Ⓔ	57 Ⓐ Ⓑ Ⓒ Ⓓ Ⓔ
8 Ⓕ Ⓖ Ⓗ Ⓙ Ⓚ	18 Ⓕ Ⓖ Ⓗ Ⓙ Ⓚ	28 Ⓕ Ⓖ Ⓗ Ⓙ Ⓚ	38 Ⓕ Ⓖ Ⓗ Ⓙ Ⓚ	48 Ⓕ Ⓖ Ⓗ Ⓙ Ⓚ	58 Ⓕ Ⓖ Ⓗ Ⓙ Ⓚ
9 Ⓐ Ⓑ Ⓒ Ⓓ Ⓔ	19 Ⓐ Ⓑ Ⓒ Ⓓ Ⓔ	29 Ⓐ Ⓑ Ⓒ Ⓓ Ⓔ	39 Ⓐ Ⓑ Ⓒ Ⓓ Ⓔ	49 Ⓐ Ⓑ Ⓒ Ⓓ Ⓔ	59 Ⓐ Ⓑ Ⓒ Ⓓ Ⓔ
10 Ⓕ Ⓖ Ⓗ Ⓙ Ⓚ	20 Ⓕ Ⓖ Ⓗ Ⓙ Ⓚ	30 Ⓕ Ⓖ Ⓗ Ⓙ Ⓚ	40 Ⓕ Ⓖ Ⓗ Ⓙ Ⓚ	50 Ⓕ Ⓖ Ⓗ Ⓙ Ⓚ	60 Ⓕ Ⓖ Ⓗ Ⓙ Ⓚ

This page is intentionally left blank

MATHEMATICS TEST

60 Minutes — 60 Questions

DIRECTIONS: Solve each problem, choose the correct answer, and then fill in the corresponding oval on your answer document.

Do not linger over problems that take too much time. Solve as many as you can; then return to the others in the time you have left for this test.

You are permitted to use a calculator on this test. You may use your calculator for any problems you choose, but some of the problems may best be done without using a calculator.

Note: Unless otherwise stated, all of the following should be assumed.

1. Illustrative figures are NOT necessarily drawn to scale.
2. Geometric figures lie in a plane.
3. The word *line* indicates a straight line.
4. The word *average* indicates arithmetic mean.

---

1. Simplify $(x^3 - 2xy + 4x) - x(3x^2 - 2xy) - y(2x^2 - 7)$.

   A. $-2x^3 - 2xy + 4x - 7y$

   B. $-2x^3 - 2xy + 4x + 7y$

   C. $-2x^3 - 4x^2y - 2xy + 4x - 7y$

   D. $4x^3 - 4xy + 4x + 7y$

   E. $-2x^3 - 6x^2y + 4x + 7y$

2. What is the slope of the line containing $(4, -7)$ that is parallel to $2x - 3y = 7$?

   F. $-\dfrac{7}{8}$

   G. $-\dfrac{7}{4}$

   H. $-\dfrac{3}{2}$

   J. $\dfrac{2}{3}$

   K. $-\dfrac{7}{2}$

3. What is the solution set for the graph shown below?

   A. $-3 < x < -\infty$ and $6 \leq x < 1$

   B. $-3 < x < -\infty$ or $6 \leq x < 1$

   C. $-\infty \leq x < -3$ or $1 \leq x < 6$

   D. $-\infty < x < -3$ or $1 \leq x < 6$

   E. $-\infty < x < -3$ and $1 \leq x < 6$

DO YOUR FIGURING HERE.

GO ON TO THE NEXT PAGE.

4. Which of the following is the area of a square in terms of its perimeter, P?

DO YOUR FIGURING HERE.

   F. $\dfrac{P^2}{16}$

   G. $\dfrac{P^2}{4}$

   H. $\dfrac{P^2}{8}$

   J. $\dfrac{\sqrt{P}}{2}$

   K. $\dfrac{\sqrt{P}}{16}$

5. Let $g(x) = 2x^2 - 3x + 5$. If $g(x) = 19$, which of the following could be a value for x?

   A. $-\dfrac{7}{2}$

   B. $-\dfrac{2}{7}$

   C. -2

   D. 2

   E. There are no values of x.

6. What is the measure of $\angle CAE$ if A is the intersection of $\overline{CD}$ and $\overline{BE}$ for the figure shown below?

   F. 31
   G. 149
   H. 124
   J. 25
   K. 56

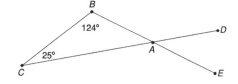

7. Your car's gasoline tank is one-half full of gasoline when you decide to take a trip. You drive one-third of the gasoline out of your car before filling the tank at a gas station. If the tank holds 18 gallons of gasoline full, how much gasoline did you put into the tank?

   A. 3
   B. 9
   C. 15
   D. 18
   E. 12

GO ON TO THE NEXT PAGE.

8. If $m = 4$ and $n = \dfrac{2}{3}$, what is the value of $\dfrac{\frac{1}{m}}{m+n}$?

DO YOUR FIGURING HERE.

   F. $\dfrac{3}{32}$

   G. $\dfrac{32}{3}$

   H. $\dfrac{3}{56}$

   J. $\dfrac{7}{6}$

   K. $\dfrac{9}{28}$

9. A high school's graduating class has 250 people. Sixty percent of the graduating class are male, and eighty-two percent of the graduating class will go to a four-year college. What is the probability that a person chosen in the graduating class will be male that attends a four-year college?

   A. 0.51

   B. 0.49

   C. 0.22

   D. 0.78

   E. 0.13

10. If $f(2) = -6$ and $f(5) = 9$ where f is a linear function, then $f(10) = ?$

   F. 34

   G. 40

   H. $-\dfrac{23}{5}$

   J. $\dfrac{3}{56}$

   K. 18

11. Which of the following transformations takes the graph of the parent function $f(x) = \log_2(x), x > 0$ to the graph of $g(x) = \log_2(x-4), x > 4$?

   A. Translation up 4 units.

   B. Translation down 4 units.

   C. Translation right 4 units.

   D. Translation left 4 units.

   E. Vertical stretch by a factor of 4 units.

GO ON TO THE NEXT PAGE.

DO YOUR FIGURING HERE.

12. What is 32% of $\frac{1}{5}$ of 152?

    F. 972.8
    G. 9.73
    H. 152.5
    J. 97.28
    K. 243.2

13. Which expression is **not** a factor of $x^5 - 16x$?

    A. x
    B. $x + 2$
    C. $x - 2$
    D. $x^2 + 4$
    E. $x^2 - 4$

14. The graph for a system of three equations of a circle, an ellipse, and a line are shown below. How many solutions are there for the system?

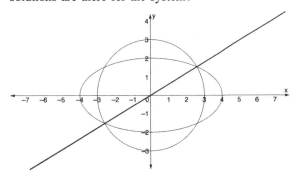

    F. 1
    G. 2
    H. 3
    J. 4
    K. none

15. The total cost for a company that produces x number of 3-ringed binders is $C = 1.15x + 475$, where C is the cost, in dollars. A 3-ringed binder sells for $1.53. A profit is realized when the income generated from selling x 3-ringed binders is greater than the total cost of producing them. Which of the following statements is true about the company realizing a profit for selling x 3-ringed binders?

    A. $475 - 0.38x > 0$
    B. $475 + 0.38x > 0$
    C. $0.38x - 475 > 0$
    D. $0.38x - 475 < 0$
    E. $-0.38x - 475 < 0$

GO ON TO THE NEXT PAGE.

16. Which of the following intervals is $\sin x > \cos x$?

DO YOUR FIGURING HERE.

   F. $0 < x < \dfrac{\pi}{4}$

   G. $\dfrac{\pi}{4} < x < \dfrac{\pi}{2}$

   H. $\pi < x < \dfrac{5\pi}{4}$

   J. $\dfrac{3\pi}{2} < x < \dfrac{7\pi}{4}$

   K. $0 < x < \dfrac{\pi}{3}$

17. Rationalize $\dfrac{3+i}{2-i}$ where $i^2 = -1$?

   A. $\dfrac{7}{5} + i$

   B. $\dfrac{7}{5} - i$

   C. $\dfrac{5+5i}{3+4i}$

   D. $1+i$

   E. $5+5i$

18. Below is a stem-leaf plot for the temperature, in degrees Fahrenheit, taken at various times during a day. For example, a temperature of 43 is represented by stem value of 4 and a leaf value of 3. What is the difference, in degrees Fahrenheit, between the mean temperature and the mode for that day?

Stem	Leaf
4	2, 4, 7
5	1, 1, 4
6	0, 2, 4, 5
7	1, 3

   F. 6

   G. 4

   H. 1

   J. 7

   K. 0

19. If $f(x) = \sqrt{x^2 + 4}$ and $g(x) = 2x + 1$, what is the value of $f(g(-3))$?

   A. $\sqrt{29}$

   B. $-5i\sqrt{5}$

   C. $-5\sqrt{29}$

   D. $1 + 2\sqrt{29}$

   E. $-5 + i\sqrt{5}$

GO ON TO THE NEXT PAGE.

20. In the standard (x, y) coordinate system the graph of which of the following equations is parallel to the graph of the line $y = 2$?

F. $y = 2x$

G. $y = -\dfrac{1}{2}x$

H. $y = 3$

J. $x = 2$

K. $x = -\dfrac{1}{2}$

21. Which of the following is a point on the circle in the standard (x, y) coordinate system whose center is $(3, 5)$ and radius is 4?

A. $(7, 5)$

B. $(1, 5)$

C. $(7, 9)$

D. $(-1, -1)$

E. $(3, 5)$

22. Which expression is equivalent to $\dfrac{\sin x \cot x}{\cos^2 x}$?

F. $\csc x$

G. $\sec x$

H. $\tan x$

J. $\dfrac{\sin^2 x}{\cos^3 x}$

K. $\dfrac{\sin^2 x}{\cos^2 x}$

23. Of 155 students that were surveyed, 125 took an English course, 75 took an advanced math course, and 45 took both an English course and an advanced math course. If a student that was surveyed was chosen at random, what is the probability the student only took an advanced math class?

A. 0.52

B. 0.29

C. 0.48

D. 0.19

E. 0.81

24. Which expression has a factor of $(x + 3)$?

F. $x^2 - 3x + 9$

G. $x^2 + 9$

H. $x^3 + 27$

J. $x^3 - 27$

K. $2x^2 - 7x - 9$

DO YOUR FIGURING HERE.

GO ON TO THE NEXT PAGE.

25. Bacteria is grown in a petri dish. Initially, the petri dish is $\frac{1}{10}$ full of the bacteria. Every hour the bacteria is fed a solution and the amount in the petri dish doubles in value. Which equation represents how full, F, the petri dish is of bacteria where h is time, in hours?

A. $F = \frac{1}{10} + (2)^h$

B. $F = 2 + \frac{1}{10}^{\,h}$

C. $\left(2 + \frac{1}{10}\right)^h$

D. $F = 2\left(\frac{1}{10}\right)^h$

E. $F = \frac{1}{10}(2)^h$

DO YOUR FIGURING HERE.

26. Chords $\overline{AC}$ and $\overline{BE}$ intersect the circle with center O at F in the figure shown below. What is the measure of $\angle BFC$, in degrees, given the measures of $\overset{\frown}{ADE}$ and $\overset{\frown}{BGC}$?

F. 82

G. 104

H. 11

J. 93

K. 87

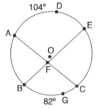

27. If $x^n = \left(x^2 \cdot x^3\right)^{-1}\left(x^4\right)^3$, then $n = \,?$

A. 2

B. 1

C. 7

D. 17

E. 13

28. The first and fourth term in an arithmetic sequence are 4, and −5. What is the 10th term?

F. −20

G. −23

H. −26

J. 31

K. 28

71

GO ON TO THE NEXT PAGE.

29. Arrange $\frac{11}{6}$, 173%, and 1.80 in ascending order?

   A. $\frac{11}{6}$, 173%, 1.80

   B. 173%, 1.80, $\frac{11}{6}$

   C. $\frac{11}{6}$, 1.80, 173%

   D. 173%, $\frac{11}{6}$, 1.80

   E. 1.80, $\frac{11}{6}$, 173%

DO YOUR FIGURING HERE.

30. What is the difference of the absolute value of the solutions for $|2x-6|=18$?

   F. 18
   G. 6
   H. −18
   J. −24
   K. 0

31. Let the set shown below be a sequence that continues in the pattern. What is the 12th term in the sequence?

   {1, 1, 2, 3, 5, 8, 13, 21, 34, ...}

   A. 89
   B. 233
   C. 144
   D. 226
   E. 272

32. A shipping company ships packages locally for $0.55 per kilogram. How much does the shipping company charge to ship a package locally that weighs 103 pounds?

   F. $46.71
   G. $56.56
   H. $84.93
   J. $25.71
   K. $59.24

GO ON TO THE NEXT PAGE.

33. What is the system for the two inequalities that is graphed below? The equation for the graphs of the two lines is $y = -\dfrac{1}{2}x + 3$ and $y = x - 2$.

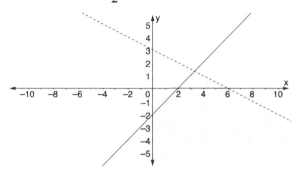

DO YOUR FIGURING HERE.

A. $y < -\dfrac{1}{2}x + 3$ and $y \geq x - 2$

B. $y < -\dfrac{1}{2}x + 3$ and $y \leq x - 2$

C. $y > -\dfrac{1}{2}x + 3$ and $y \leq x - 2$

D. $y \leq -\dfrac{1}{2}x + 3$ and $y < x - 2$

E. $y \geq -\dfrac{1}{2}x + 3$ and $y < x - 2$

34. Which expression is equivalent to $\dfrac{x}{1 - \sqrt{2}}$?

F. $-\dfrac{x}{3} - \dfrac{x\sqrt{2}}{3}$

G. $\dfrac{x}{3} - \dfrac{x\sqrt{2}}{3}$

H. $-x - x\sqrt{2}$

J. $x + x\sqrt{2}$

K. $x - x\sqrt{2}$

35. Points A, B, and C are collinear in the figure shown below. What is the measure of the smaller angle in degrees?

A. $\angle ACE = 29°$
B. $\angle ACE = 42°$
C. $\angle ACE = 151°$
D. $\angle ECB = 151°$
E. $\angle ECB = 120°$

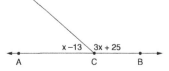

73

GO ON TO THE NEXT PAGE.

36. If $x = 2$ is one x-intercepts for the graph of $y = x^2 + bx - 12$, what must be the value for b?

    F. −2
    G. −6
    H. 6
    J. 4
    K. −4

DO YOUR FIGURING HERE.

37. The graph of $y = f(x)$ is shown below. What is the value for $g(0)$ if $g(x) = f(x + 4) - 1$?

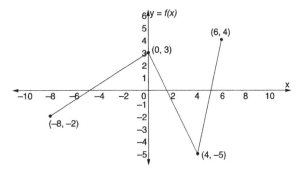

    A. 3
    B. −5
    C. −2
    D. 4
    E. −6

38. What is the period for the graph of $y = 2\cos\left(\dfrac{x}{4}\right) + 1$?

    F. π
    G. 2π
    H. 8π
    J. 4π
    K. $\dfrac{\pi}{2}$

39. What is the perimeter of the triangle shown in the figure below with the given dimensions?

    A. 35.27
    B. 34.01
    C. 27.78
    D. 26.08
    E. 29

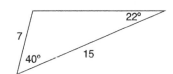

74

GO ON TO THE NEXT PAGE.

40. The inverse of function f is function g. If $f(2) = 3$, $f(3) = 5$, and $f(4) = 2$, then $f(g(3)) = ?$

    F. 6

    G. 8

    H. 3

    J. 10

    K. Can not be determined with the given values.

DO YOUR FIGURING HERE.

41. What is the probability of making a perfect score on a 5-question multiple choice quiz that has 4 answer choices?

    A. $\dfrac{1}{20}$

    B. $\dfrac{1}{625}$

    C. $\dfrac{1}{1024}$

    D. $\dfrac{1}{120}$

    E. $\dfrac{1}{240}$

42. In the standard (x, y) coordinate plane, what is the image for the point $(4, 8)$ that is reflected across the y-axis then translated up 3 units?

    F. $(4, -5)$

    G. $(7, -8)$

    H. $(-5, 4)$

    J. $(-4, 11)$

    K. $(-4, 5)$

43. You push a wheelbarrow that has a single wheel straight across a driveway. The radius of the wheel is 6 inches. If the wheel rotated 20 times, approximately how many feet did you push the wheelbarrow?

    A. 63

    B. 31

    C. 189

    D. 120

    E. 126

GO ON TO THE NEXT PAGE.

44. Let $V = \langle v_1, v_2 \rangle$. What is the sum of the component for V if $2\langle 5,3 \rangle - \langle v_1, v_2 \rangle = \langle 7, -2 \rangle$?

   F. 3
   G. 8
   H. -5
   J. 11
   K. 13

DO YOUR FIGURING HERE.

45. Adults and children are swimming in a public swimming pool. The entrance fee to the pool is $1.75 for each child and $2.75 for each adult. The pool collects $271.75 in entrance fees on a single day when there were 130 people swimming. Which of the following system of equations can be used to determine how many adults, a, and how many children, c, were at the swimming pool?

   A. $2.75a + 1.75c = 130$
              $a + c = 271.75$
   B. $2.75a + 1.75c = 271.75$
              $a + c = 130$
   C. $a + 1.75c = 271.75$
       $2.75a + c = 130$
   D. $1.75a + 2.75c = 271.75$
              $a + c = 130$
   E. $1.75a + 2.75c = 130$
              $a + c = 271.75$

46. Which expression is a factor of $8x^3 - 125$?

   F. $2x + 5$
   G. $x + 5$
   H. $4x^2 - 10x + 25$
   J. $4x^2 + 10x + 25$
   K. $4x^2 + 25$

47. A solution containing water and 5% sugar is added to 2 quarts of a second solution containing water and 8% sugar. How many quarts of the 5% sugar solution should be added to the 8% sugar solution to make a solution that is 7% sugar?

   A. 7
   B. 1
   C. 3
   D. 5.2
   E. 2.6

GO ON TO THE NEXT PAGE.

48. The graph of which of the following lines passes through the center of the graph of a circle whose equation is $(x-5)^2 + (y-3)^2 = 36$?

   F. $y = 2x - 7$

   G. $y = x + 2$

   H. $y = \dfrac{3}{5}x + 1$

   J. $y = \dfrac{3}{5}x - 1$

   K. $y = x$

DO YOUR FIGURING HERE.

49. A wood deck is in the shape of a right triangle and a square as shown in the composite figure below. The side lengths of the triangle are 9 feet and 12 feet. What is the perimeter of the deck, in feet?

   A. 279

   B. 333

   C. 84

   D. 66

   E. 81

50. If $\log_x 16 = 4$ and $\log_2 32 = y$, then $y^x = ?$

   F. 25

   G. 32

   H. 10

   J. 20

   K. 2

51. Let $|m+1| < n$. If $n = 5$, which of the following expressions is true for m?

   A. $m < 4$

   B. $m < -6$

   C. $0 < m < 4$

   D. $-6 < m < 4$

   E. $4 < m < -6$

52. Andrew wants an 84 average for the grading period in his math class. There are 5 assignments for the class each having equal weight. If Andrew scored an 85, 85, 75, and 92 on his first 4 assignments, what must he make on his fifth assignment to have an 84 average for the grading period?

   F. 84

   G. 83

   H. 85

   J. 67

GO ON TO THE NEXT PAGE.

53. Which is true for x if $3^{x^2-x} = 3^6$?

   A. $x = -3$ or 2
   B. $x = -2$ or 3
   C. $x = -2$ only
   D. $x = 3$ only
   E. $x = -2$ only

DO YOUR FIGURING HERE.

54. The geometric mean for three numbers is 12. If two of the numbers are 4 and 16, what must the third number be?

   F. 8
   G. 27
   H. 64
   J. 10
   K. 2.25

55. Thirty people are surveyed to determine their preference for one of 4 fruits. The results are in the bar graph displayed below. What is the probability that a person chosen at random prefers bananas or apples as their preferred fruit?

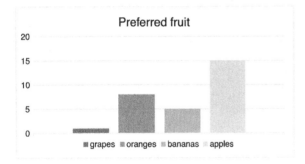

   A. 0.45
   B. 0.55
   C. 0.67
   D. 0.98
   E. 0.25

56. If $0 < x < 1$, which expression has the smallest value?

   F. x^2
   G. $\sqrt{x}$
   H. $\dfrac{x}{2}$
   J. $x - x$
   K. x

GO ON TO THE NEXT PAGE.

57. What are the dimensions, in feet, that will maximize the area of a rectangle that has a perimeter of 16 feet?

    A. 4 feet by 4 feet
    B. 2 feet by 8 feet
    C. 8 feet by 8 feet
    D. 2 feet by 6 feet
    E. 1 foot by 5 feet

58. If one of the interior angles in a dodecagon measures 55 degrees, what is the sum of the rest of the interior angles in degrees?

    F. 1385
    G. 1745
    H. 1025
    J. 495
    K. 1440

59. The number of drive-thru restaurants, y, from 1998 to 2005 can be modeled by $y = 8200 - 940\ln x$ where x is in years. Approximately how many years will it take for the number of drive-thru restaurants reach 6250?

    A. 12
    B. 8
    C. 9
    D. 6
    E. 2

60. $\dfrac{7.5 \times 10^8}{2.5 \times 10^{-5}} = ?$

    F. 3×10^3
    G. 3×10^{-3}
    H. 3×10^{13}
    J. 5×10^3
    K. 5×10^{-13}

DO YOUR FIGURING HERE.

END OF TEST

This page is intentionally left blank

ACT Math Practice Test 5

Mark Your Answers For Test 5 Here

Date: _____

Marking Directions: Mark only one oval for each question. Fill in response completely. Erase errors cleanly without smudging.

Correct mark: ○ ◐ ○ ○ ○

1 Ⓐ Ⓑ Ⓒ Ⓓ Ⓔ	11 Ⓐ Ⓑ Ⓒ Ⓓ Ⓔ	21 Ⓐ Ⓑ Ⓒ Ⓓ Ⓔ	31 Ⓐ Ⓑ Ⓒ Ⓓ Ⓔ	41 Ⓐ Ⓑ Ⓒ Ⓓ Ⓔ	51 Ⓐ Ⓑ Ⓒ Ⓓ Ⓔ
2 Ⓕ Ⓖ Ⓗ Ⓙ Ⓚ	12 Ⓕ Ⓖ Ⓗ Ⓙ Ⓚ	22 Ⓕ Ⓖ Ⓗ Ⓙ Ⓚ	32 Ⓕ Ⓖ Ⓗ Ⓙ Ⓚ	42 Ⓕ Ⓖ Ⓗ Ⓙ Ⓚ	52 Ⓕ Ⓖ Ⓗ Ⓙ Ⓚ
3 Ⓐ Ⓑ Ⓒ Ⓓ Ⓔ	13 Ⓐ Ⓑ Ⓒ Ⓓ Ⓔ	23 Ⓐ Ⓑ Ⓒ Ⓓ Ⓔ	33 Ⓐ Ⓑ Ⓒ Ⓓ Ⓔ	43 Ⓐ Ⓑ Ⓒ Ⓓ Ⓔ	53 Ⓐ Ⓑ Ⓒ Ⓓ Ⓔ
4 Ⓕ Ⓖ Ⓗ Ⓙ Ⓚ	14 Ⓕ Ⓖ Ⓗ Ⓙ Ⓚ	24 Ⓕ Ⓖ Ⓗ Ⓙ Ⓚ	34 Ⓕ Ⓖ Ⓗ Ⓙ Ⓚ	44 Ⓕ Ⓖ Ⓗ Ⓙ Ⓚ	54 Ⓕ Ⓖ Ⓗ Ⓙ Ⓚ
5 Ⓐ Ⓑ Ⓒ Ⓓ Ⓔ	15 Ⓐ Ⓑ Ⓒ Ⓓ Ⓔ	25 Ⓐ Ⓑ Ⓒ Ⓓ Ⓔ	35 Ⓐ Ⓑ Ⓒ Ⓓ Ⓔ	45 Ⓐ Ⓑ Ⓒ Ⓓ Ⓔ	55 Ⓐ Ⓑ Ⓒ Ⓓ Ⓔ
6 Ⓕ Ⓖ Ⓗ Ⓙ Ⓚ	16 Ⓕ Ⓖ Ⓗ Ⓙ Ⓚ	26 Ⓕ Ⓖ Ⓗ Ⓙ Ⓚ	36 Ⓕ Ⓖ Ⓗ Ⓙ Ⓚ	46 Ⓕ Ⓖ Ⓗ Ⓙ Ⓚ	56 Ⓕ Ⓖ Ⓗ Ⓙ Ⓚ
7 Ⓐ Ⓑ Ⓒ Ⓓ Ⓔ	17 Ⓐ Ⓑ Ⓒ Ⓓ Ⓔ	27 Ⓐ Ⓑ Ⓒ Ⓓ Ⓔ	37 Ⓐ Ⓑ Ⓒ Ⓓ Ⓔ	47 Ⓐ Ⓑ Ⓒ Ⓓ Ⓔ	57 Ⓐ Ⓑ Ⓒ Ⓓ Ⓔ
8 Ⓕ Ⓖ Ⓗ Ⓙ Ⓚ	18 Ⓕ Ⓖ Ⓗ Ⓙ Ⓚ	28 Ⓕ Ⓖ Ⓗ Ⓙ Ⓚ	38 Ⓕ Ⓖ Ⓗ Ⓙ Ⓚ	48 Ⓕ Ⓖ Ⓗ Ⓙ Ⓚ	58 Ⓕ Ⓖ Ⓗ Ⓙ Ⓚ
9 Ⓐ Ⓑ Ⓒ Ⓓ Ⓔ	19 Ⓐ Ⓑ Ⓒ Ⓓ Ⓔ	29 Ⓐ Ⓑ Ⓒ Ⓓ Ⓔ	39 Ⓐ Ⓑ Ⓒ Ⓓ Ⓔ	49 Ⓐ Ⓑ Ⓒ Ⓓ Ⓔ	59 Ⓐ Ⓑ Ⓒ Ⓓ Ⓔ
10 Ⓕ Ⓖ Ⓗ Ⓙ Ⓚ	20 Ⓕ Ⓖ Ⓗ Ⓙ Ⓚ	30 Ⓕ Ⓖ Ⓗ Ⓙ Ⓚ	40 Ⓕ Ⓖ Ⓗ Ⓙ Ⓚ	50 Ⓕ Ⓖ Ⓗ Ⓙ Ⓚ	60 Ⓕ Ⓖ Ⓗ Ⓙ Ⓚ

This page is intentionally left blank

MATHEMATICS TEST

60 Minutes — 60 Questions

DIRECTIONS: Solve each problem, choose the correct answer, and then fill in the corresponding oval on your answer document.

Do not linger over problems that take too much time. Solve as many as you can; then return to the others in the time you have left for this test.

You are permitted to use a calculator on this test. You may use your calculator for any problems you choose, but some of the problems may best be done without using a calculator.

Note: Unless otherwise stated, all of the following should be assumed.

1. Illustrative figures are NOT necessarily drawn to scale.
2. Geometric figures lie in a plane.
3. The word *line* indicates a straight line.
4. The word *average* indicates arithmetic mean.

---

1. What is the value of the expression $3x^2 - (x + 4y^2)$ when $x = 2$ and $y = -5$?

   A. −86
   B. −90
   C. 108
   D. 32
   E. 100

DO YOUR FIGURING HERE.

2. Every 3 minutes you can answer 4 questions on a multiple-choice test. How long will it take to answer an 84 multiple-choice test?

   F. 63 minutes
   G. 112 minutes
   H. 49 minutes
   J. 84 minutes
   K. 36 minutes

3. Order $\frac{7}{4}$, 1.79, $\sqrt{3}$, and 171% from least to greatest.

   A. $\frac{7}{4}$, 1.79, $\sqrt{3}$, 171%

   B. 171%, $\sqrt{3}$, $\frac{7}{4}$, 1.79

   C. 171%, $\sqrt{3}$, 1.79, $\frac{7}{4}$

   D. $\sqrt{3}$, 171%, 1.79, $\frac{7}{4}$

   E. 1.79, $\frac{7}{4}$, $\sqrt{3}$, 171%

GO ON TO THE NEXT PAGE.

4. What is the perimeter of the right triangle shown below?

   F. 26
   G. 120
   H. 60
   J. 34
   K. 76

DO YOUR FIGURING HERE.

5. Simplify $(3 + 2i)(1 - 4i) + 2i(5i)$ where $i^2 = -1$.

   A. $-15 - 10i$
   B. $21 + 10i$
   C. $21 - 10i$
   D. $1 + 10i$
   E. $1 - 10i$

6. What is the value of $\dfrac{x+2}{\dfrac{3}{y}}$ if $x = \dfrac{2}{3}$ and $y = 2$?

   F. 4
   G. $\dfrac{16}{9}$
   H. $\dfrac{8}{9}$
   J. 4
   K. 5

7. What is the sum of the mean and the median for the set $\{9, 5, 2, 6, 13\}$?

   A. 7
   B. 6
   C. 13
   D. 42
   E. 1

8. Which of the following equations is a parabola that has its vertex at $(3, -5)$ and contains the point $(6, 4)$?

   F. $y = (x-2)^2 - 12$
   G. $y = 2(x-3)^2 - 5$
   H. $y = 2(x-6)^2 + 4$
   J. $y = (x-3)^2 - 5$
   K. $y = (x+5)^2 + 3$

84

GO ON TO THE NEXT PAGE.

9. Brittney drives 240 miles in her car each week. Her car averages 21 miles per gallon of fuel and fuel costs $2.25 per gallon. She also spends $45 for lunch each week. She budgets $75 each week to spend on fuel and lunch. Which statement is true about Brittney's budget for each week?

   A. She is under her budget by $4.29.
   B. She is over her budget by $4.29.
   C. She is under her budget by $17.25.
   D. She is over her budget by $17.25.
   E. She meets her budget each week.

10. What is the 10th term of a geometric sequence whose 1st and 2nd terms are 3, –6 respectively?

   F. 3072
   G. –6144
   H. –1536
   J. –78
   K. 84

11. If a square is rotated about one of its sides, which of the following figures is produced?

   A. Cone
   B. Cylinder
   C. Cube
   D. Prism
   E. Sphere

12. What is the equation of the circle graph below in the standard (x, y) coordinate system?

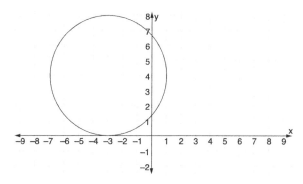

   F. $(x+3)^2 + (y-4)^2 = 4$

   G. $(x-3)^2 + (y+4)^2 = 4$

   H. $(x-4)^2 + (y+4)^2 = 16$

   J. $(x-3)^2 + (y+4)^2 = 16$

   K. $(x+3)^2 + (y-4)^2 = 16$

DO YOUR FIGURING HERE.

GO ON TO THE NEXT PAGE.

13. What is the GCF (greatest common factor) for $24x^2yz^3$ and $8xz$?

   A. $8xyz$
   B. $8xz$
   C. $8x^2z^3$
   D. $2\,xyz$
   E. $2\,xz$

DO YOUR FIGURING HERE.

14. Which of the following expressions is a factor of $2x^2 + 9x - 18$?

   F. $x - 6$
   G. $2x + 3$
   H. $x - 3$
   J. $2x - 3$
   K. $2x + 6$

15. What is the slope of a line that is perpendicular to the graph of a line whose equation is $3x - 5y = 4$?

   A. $\dfrac{3}{5}$

   B. $-\dfrac{3}{5}$

   C. $\dfrac{5}{3}$

   D. $-\dfrac{5}{3}$

   E. $-\dfrac{4}{5}$

16. The equation $\dfrac{(x+1)^2}{9} + \dfrac{(y-2)^2}{4} = 1$ is the graph of a?

   F. Line
   G. Parabola
   H. Ellipse
   J. Circle
   K. Hyperbola

17. In the figure given below, the circle with center O is inscribed into square $ABCD$. If $AB = 10$, what is the area of the region that is outside of the circle but inside of the square?

   A. $100 - 100\pi$
   B. $25\pi + 100$
   C. $25\pi - 100$
   D. $100 - 25\pi$
   E. $100 + 25\pi$

GO ON TO THE NEXT PAGE.

18. The table below shows the distance, d, in miles, a car has travelled for various times, t, in hours.

t	1	3	6	7
d	45	141	285	333

Which is the equation of best fit where d is written in terms of t?

   F. $t = 4d^3 + 33$
   G. $d = 4t^3 + 33$
   H. $d = 48t - 3$
   J. $t = 48d - 3$
   K. $d = 32t + 13$

19. You spend 35% of one day studying for a test. During the rest of the day, 60% is spent sleeping. What percent of your day remains for doing other things?

   A. 26%
   B. 14%
   C. 24%
   D. 40%
   E. 65%

20. If $x < -1$, which of the following expressions has the greatest value?

   F. $\dfrac{x}{2}$
   G. $2x$
   H. x^3
   J. $-x^2$
   K. x

21. Which of the following is equivalent to the expression $\dfrac{2}{\sqrt{-8}}$ where $i = -1$?

   A. $\dfrac{\sqrt{2}}{2}i$
   B. $-\dfrac{\sqrt{2}}{2}i$
   C. $\dfrac{\sqrt{2}}{4}i$
   D. $-\dfrac{\sqrt{2}}{4}i$
   E. $-\dfrac{1}{2}i$

DO YOUR FIGURING HERE.

87

GO ON TO THE NEXT PAGE.

22. If 3 of the vertices for a rectangle that is graphed in the standard (x, y) coordinate plane are $(-7, 2)$, $(5, -2)$, and $(-7, -2)$, what must be the coordinates of the 4th vertex?

   F. $(-5, 2)$
   G. $(5, 2)$
   H. $(7, 2)$
   J. $(7, -2)$
   K. $(5, -7)$

DO YOUR FIGURING HERE.

23. Simplify $\dfrac{x^3 y^4 z}{xyz^2} \cdot \dfrac{1}{xz^{-2}}$.

   A. $\dfrac{x^2 y^3}{z^3}$
   B. $\dfrac{xy^3}{z^3}$
   C. $xy^3 z$
   D. $x^2 y^2 z$
   E. $xy^2 z$

24. Which of the following expressions is equivalent to $\tan\theta$ if θ is in the 1st quadrant?

   F. $1 - \sec\theta$
   G. $\sec\theta - 1$
   H. $\sec^2\theta - 1$
   J. $\sqrt{\sec^2\theta - 1}$
   K. $\dfrac{1}{1 - \sec^2\theta}$

25. A food stand sells hotdogs and hamburgers. Together, the food stand sold 250 hotdogs and hamburgers in a day. A hotdog sold for \$1.75 and a hamburger is sold for \$3.50. If the food stand made \$612.50 in a given day, which system of equations can be used to find the number of hotdogs, x and hamburgers, y sold?

   A. $\begin{aligned} x + y &= 612.50 \\ 1.75x + 3.50y &= 250 \end{aligned}$

   B. $\begin{aligned} x + y &= 250 \\ 1.75x + 3.50y &= 612.50 \end{aligned}$

   C. $\begin{aligned} x + y &= 250 \\ 3.50x + 1.75y &= 612.50 \end{aligned}$

   D. $\begin{aligned} x + y &= 612.50 \\ 3.50x + 1.75y &= 250 \end{aligned}$

   E. $\begin{aligned} 1.75x + y &= 612.50 \\ x + 3.50y &= 250 \end{aligned}$

GO ON TO THE NEXT PAGE.

26. To estimate the length of a pond, you measure the distance from a fixed point to each end of the pond. The angle between the 2 distances you measure, in feet, from the fixed point are shown in the diagram below. Which of the following is the best estimate for the length of the pond, in feet?

    F. 45.43
    G. 48.79
    H. 84.05
    J. 52.55
    K. 72.12

DO YOUR FIGURING HERE.

27. What is the value for $f(g(-2))$ if $f(x) = x^2 + 2$ and $g(x) = 3x + 4$?

    A. −12
    B. 4
    C. −8
    D. 22
    E. 6

28. Selma is working on a school project. When she is $\frac{2}{3}$ of the way done with the project, she realizes she has worked for 120 minutes on her project. If she continues in this way, how many more minutes will she need to work to complete the project?

    F. 180
    G. 60
    H. 20
    J. 40
    K. 90

29. If the graph of $y = f(x)$ is vertically stretched by a factor of 2, translated 3 units to the left, then 4 units upwards, the translated graph has an equation of?

    A. $y = 2f(x - 3) + 4$
    B. $y = -2f(x + 3) + 4$
    C. $y = 2f(x + 3) + 4$
    D. $y = -2f(x + 4) - 3$
    E. $y = 2f(x - 4) + 3$

30. Line l contains the points (2, 5) and (−6, 3). Line k is perpendicular to line l. What is the slope for line k if its y-intercept is 7?

    F. $\frac{1}{4}$
    G. $-\frac{1}{4}$
    H. −4
    J. 4
    K. $-\frac{1}{7}$

GO ON TO THE NEXT PAGE.

31. If $\log_5 M = 2$ and $\log_a 64 = 3$, then $M - a = ?$

    DO YOUR FIGURING HERE.

    A. $-\dfrac{34}{3}$
    B. -49
    C. 21
    D. 29
    E. 1

32. The base of a rectangular prism has dimensions of 15 feet by 13 feet. What is the area, in square yards, of the base of the prism?

    F. 585
    G. 168
    H. 18.67
    J. 21.67
    K. 67

33. Points A, B, and C are colinear. The coordinates for A and B are (3, 4) and (28, 4) respectively. Which of the following are the coordinates of C that is three-fifths of the way from A to B?

    A. (25, 4)
    B. (13, 4)
    C. (3, 17)
    D. (18, 17)
    E. (18, 4)

34. The equations $y = 4 - \dfrac{1}{2}(x-2)^2$ and $y = x - 2$ are graphed in the standard (x, y) coordinate plane below. Which of the following is the solution set for the system of the given equations?

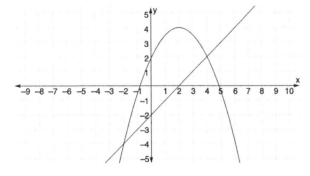

    F. (0, –2) and (0, 2)
    G. (–2, –4) and (4, 2)
    H. (–4, –2) and (2, 4)
    J. (–1, 0), (2, 0) and (5, 0)
    K. (2, 4) and (2, 0)

GO ON TO THE NEXT PAGE.

35. Cayden has 3 shirts, 2 pair of pants, and one pair of shoes. An outfit consists of 1 of the shirts worn with one pair of paints, and one pair of shoes. How many distinct outfits can Cayden wear?

  A. 5
  B. 24
  C. 6
  D. 12
  E. 3

DO YOUR FIGURING HERE.

36. If $\dfrac{a}{b} = 30$ and $5a + b = 15$, then $\dfrac{b}{a} = ?$

  F. $\dfrac{6b}{3-a}$

  G. $\dfrac{3-a}{6b}$

  H. $\dfrac{2b}{1-a}$

  J. $2a - 6b$
  K. $3a + b$

37. Which of the following expressions yields a rational number?

  A. $\sqrt{-9}$
  B. $i\sqrt{9}$
  C. $i\sqrt{9} \cdot i\sqrt{3}$
  D. $(3 - i)(3 + i)$
  E. $(3 + i)(3 + i)$

38. Which expression is equivalent to $x^2 - 18x$?

  F. $(x + 9)^2 - 81$
  G. $(x - 9)^2 - 81$
  H. $(x - 9)^2 + 81$
  J. $(x + 9)^2 + 81$
  K. $(x + 9)^2$

39. Right triangle ABC has its right angle at C and the length of the hypotenuse is 39 units. If $\cos A = \dfrac{5}{13}$, which of the following is the length of the side opposite angle A?

  A. 15
  B. 36
  C. 39
  D. 12
  E. 10

GO ON TO THE NEXT PAGE.

DO YOUR FIGURING HERE.

40. The sale price for a laptop computer has been discounted to $485. If the normal sale price for the laptop computer is $550, what is the discount expressed as a percent?

F. 88

G. 13

H. 12

J. 15

K. 20

41. $\triangle ABC$ is an isosceles triangle that is inscribed in the circle with center O shown in the figure below. What are the measures of the base angles B and C, in degrees, if $\overset{\frown}{BEC} = 210°$?

A. 35

B. 105

C. 37.5

D. 75

E. 30.5

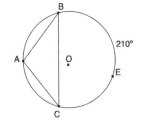

42. An object is dropped from the top of a bridge that is 190 feet high. If $h = -16t^2 + 190$ represents the height, h of the object, in feet, at time t, in seconds, approximately how many seconds does it take for the object to hit the ground?

F. 3.45

G. 4.50

H. 11.88

J. 144

K. 190

43. For what values of θ is $|\sin\theta| \leq 1$ if θ is an angle in the first or second quadrant?

A. $0° < \theta < 90°$

B. $90° < \theta < 180°$

C. $0° < \theta < 180°$

D. $180° < \theta < 270°$

E. $270° < \theta < 360°$

44. Which expression is the value for M if $5 = \log\dfrac{M}{3}$?

F. $3 \cdot 10^5$

G. $-3 \cdot 10^5$

H. $5 \cdot 10^3$

J. $-5 \cdot 10^3$

K. $10^{\frac{3}{5}}$

GO ON TO THE NEXT PAGE.

45. What is the value for k if the determinant for the matrix $\begin{bmatrix} 6 & k \\ k & 4 \end{bmatrix}$ is 3 times k?

   A. 8
   B. −3
   C. 4
   D. −6
   E. −8

DO YOUR FIGURING HERE.

46. If the graph of $y = x^2$ is reflected across the x-axis then shifted horizontally right 3 units, the transformed graph has which of the following equations?

   F. $y = -(x+3)^2$
   G. $y = (x-3)^2$
   H. $y = -(x \boxminus 3)^2$
   J. $y = -x^2 + 3$
   K. $y = x^2 - 3$

47. What is the period for the graph of $y = 4\cos\left(\dfrac{\pi}{2}x\right)$?

   A. 4π
   B. 2π
   C. $\dfrac{\pi}{2}$
   D. 4
   E. 2

48. Patricia's grade for her statistics class is determined by her test average, quiz average, and homework average. The test average carries a weight of 50% of her grade, quiz average has a weight of 30%, and homework accounts for 20% of her grade. If her test and quiz averages are 86 and 88 respectively, what needs to be her homework average if she is to have a grade of 85 for the class?

   F. 87
   G. 78
   H. 81
   J. 90
   K. 85

49. The expression $\dfrac{12}{\sqrt{3}}$ is a ?

   A. Rational number
   B. Irrational number
   C. Integer
   D. Imaginary number
   E. not a real number

GO ON TO THE NEXT PAGE.

50. The graphs of the lines $y = -x - 2$ and $y = \frac{1}{2}x - 1$ are graphed in the standard (x, y) coordinate plane below. Which of the following is the set of inequalities that has the shaded region graphed as its solution set?

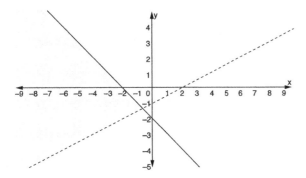

F. $y \geq -x - 2$
$y < \frac{1}{2}x - 1$

G. $y \leq -x - 2$
$y < \frac{1}{2}x - 1$

H. $y > -x - 2$
$y \leq \frac{1}{2}x - 1$

J. $y \leq -x - 2$
$y > \frac{1}{2}x - 1$

K. $y \leq -x - 2$
$y \leq \frac{1}{2}x - 1$

DO YOUR FIGURING HERE.

51. What are the zeros for $y = \frac{x^2 - 81}{x^2 - 9x}$?
   A. $x = -9$ or 9
   B. $x = 0, -9,$ or 9
   C. $x = -9$
   D. $x = 0$ or 9
   E. $x = -9$ or 0

52. Which expression if equivalent to $\cos(-\theta)$?
   F. $-\sin(\theta)$
   G. $-\cos(\theta)$
   H. $\cos(\theta)$
   J. $-\sin(-\theta)$
   K. $-\cos(-\theta)$

GO ON TO THE NEXT PAGE.

53. Most states in the United States have license plate numbers that contain 7 values. If there are 3 letters from the alphabet followed by 4 digits from 0 thru 9, how many combinations of license plate numbers can a state have if the letters and digits can be repeated?

   A. 175,760,000

   B. 78,624,000

   C. 11,232,000

   D. 2,600

   E. 260

   F. 1820

DO YOUR FIGURING HERE.

54. If $x = 6$ is a root for $y = x^2 - bx - 24$, which of the follow could be the value for b?

   G. –2

   H. 2

   J. 4

   K. –4

   K. –6

55. What is the domain for the inverse of $y = \sqrt{x+5} + 3$?

   A. $x \geq -5$

   B. $x \geq -3$

   C. $x \geq 3$

   D. $x \leq -5$

   E. $x \leq 3$

56. Let $\triangle ABC \sim \triangle DEF$. If sides $a = 18$, $d = 3$, and $c = 42$, what is the length of side f?

   F. 14

   G. 7

   H. 6

   J. 252

   K. $\dfrac{7}{9}$

57. In the figure below, $\angle ABC = 130°$. If $\angle CBD = x$ and $\angle ABD = x + 10$, what is the measure of $\angle ABD$ in degrees?

   A. 130

   B. 230

   C. 100

   D. 110

   E. 120

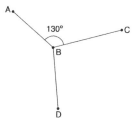

GO ON TO THE NEXT PAGE.

58. If $\left(3x^4y\right)^2 = 9x^m y^n$, what is the value of $m + n$?

F. 11
G. 9
H. 10
J. 16
K. 6

DO YOUR FIGURING HERE.

59. What is $\dfrac{7.2\times10^{12}}{2.4\times10^{-5}}$?

A. 3×10^7
B. 3×10^{17}
C. 3×10^{-60}
D. 4.8×10^7
E. 4.8×10^{17}

60. What is the length of the side opposite angle C in the right triangle $\triangle ABC$ shown in the figure below?

F. 13.27
G. 2.27
H. 5.62
J. 1.52
K. 12.52

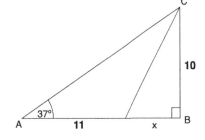

96

END OF TEST

ACT Math
Practice Test 6

Mark Your Answers For Test 6 Here

Date: _____

Marking Directions: Mark only one oval for each question. Fill in response completely. Erase errors cleanly without smudging.

Correct mark: ○ ◉ ○ ○ ○

1 Ⓐ Ⓑ Ⓒ Ⓓ Ⓔ	11 Ⓐ Ⓑ Ⓒ Ⓓ Ⓔ	21 Ⓐ Ⓑ Ⓒ Ⓓ Ⓔ	31 Ⓐ Ⓑ Ⓒ Ⓓ Ⓔ	41 Ⓐ Ⓑ Ⓒ Ⓓ Ⓔ	51 Ⓐ Ⓑ Ⓒ Ⓓ Ⓔ
2 Ⓕ Ⓖ Ⓗ Ⓙ Ⓚ	12 Ⓕ Ⓖ Ⓗ Ⓙ Ⓚ	22 Ⓕ Ⓖ Ⓗ Ⓙ Ⓚ	32 Ⓕ Ⓖ Ⓗ Ⓙ Ⓚ	42 Ⓕ Ⓖ Ⓗ Ⓙ Ⓚ	52 Ⓕ Ⓖ Ⓗ Ⓙ Ⓚ
3 Ⓐ Ⓑ Ⓒ Ⓓ Ⓔ	13 Ⓐ Ⓑ Ⓒ Ⓓ Ⓔ	23 Ⓐ Ⓑ Ⓒ Ⓓ Ⓔ	33 Ⓐ Ⓑ Ⓒ Ⓓ Ⓔ	43 Ⓐ Ⓑ Ⓒ Ⓓ Ⓔ	53 Ⓐ Ⓑ Ⓒ Ⓓ Ⓔ
4 Ⓕ Ⓖ Ⓗ Ⓙ Ⓚ	14 Ⓕ Ⓖ Ⓗ Ⓙ Ⓚ	24 Ⓕ Ⓖ Ⓗ Ⓙ Ⓚ	34 Ⓕ Ⓖ Ⓗ Ⓙ Ⓚ	44 Ⓕ Ⓖ Ⓗ Ⓙ Ⓚ	54 Ⓕ Ⓖ Ⓗ Ⓙ Ⓚ
5 Ⓐ Ⓑ Ⓒ Ⓓ Ⓔ	15 Ⓐ Ⓑ Ⓒ Ⓓ Ⓔ	25 Ⓐ Ⓑ Ⓒ Ⓓ Ⓔ	35 Ⓐ Ⓑ Ⓒ Ⓓ Ⓔ	45 Ⓐ Ⓑ Ⓒ Ⓓ Ⓔ	55 Ⓐ Ⓑ Ⓒ Ⓓ Ⓔ
6 Ⓕ Ⓖ Ⓗ Ⓙ Ⓚ	16 Ⓕ Ⓖ Ⓗ Ⓙ Ⓚ	26 Ⓕ Ⓖ Ⓗ Ⓙ Ⓚ	36 Ⓕ Ⓖ Ⓗ Ⓙ Ⓚ	46 Ⓕ Ⓖ Ⓗ Ⓙ Ⓚ	56 Ⓕ Ⓖ Ⓗ Ⓙ Ⓚ
7 Ⓐ Ⓑ Ⓒ Ⓓ Ⓔ	17 Ⓐ Ⓑ Ⓒ Ⓓ Ⓔ	27 Ⓐ Ⓑ Ⓒ Ⓓ Ⓔ	37 Ⓐ Ⓑ Ⓒ Ⓓ Ⓔ	47 Ⓐ Ⓑ Ⓒ Ⓓ Ⓔ	57 Ⓐ Ⓑ Ⓒ Ⓓ Ⓔ
8 Ⓕ Ⓖ Ⓗ Ⓙ Ⓚ	18 Ⓕ Ⓖ Ⓗ Ⓙ Ⓚ	28 Ⓕ Ⓖ Ⓗ Ⓙ Ⓚ	38 Ⓕ Ⓖ Ⓗ Ⓙ Ⓚ	48 Ⓕ Ⓖ Ⓗ Ⓙ Ⓚ	58 Ⓕ Ⓖ Ⓗ Ⓙ Ⓚ
9 Ⓐ Ⓑ Ⓒ Ⓓ Ⓔ	19 Ⓐ Ⓑ Ⓒ Ⓓ Ⓔ	29 Ⓐ Ⓑ Ⓒ Ⓓ Ⓔ	39 Ⓐ Ⓑ Ⓒ Ⓓ Ⓔ	49 Ⓐ Ⓑ Ⓒ Ⓓ Ⓔ	59 Ⓐ Ⓑ Ⓒ Ⓓ Ⓔ
10 Ⓕ Ⓖ Ⓗ Ⓙ Ⓚ	20 Ⓕ Ⓖ Ⓗ Ⓙ Ⓚ	30 Ⓕ Ⓖ Ⓗ Ⓙ Ⓚ	40 Ⓕ Ⓖ Ⓗ Ⓙ Ⓚ	50 Ⓕ Ⓖ Ⓗ Ⓙ Ⓚ	60 Ⓕ Ⓖ Ⓗ Ⓙ Ⓚ

This page is intentionally left blank

MATHEMATICS TEST

60 Minutes—60 Questions

DIRECTIONS: Solve each problem, choose the correct answer, and then fill in the corresponding oval on your answer document.

Do not linger over problems that take too much time. Solve as many as you can; then return to the others in the time you have left for this test.

You are permitted to use a calculator on this test. You may use your calculator for any problems you choose, but some of the problems may best be done without using a calculator.

Note: Unless otherwise stated, all of the following should be assumed.

1. Illustrative figures are NOT necessarily drawn to scale.
2. Geometric figures lie in a plane.
3. The word *line* indicates a straight line.
4. The word *average* indicates arithmetic mean.

---

1. Simplify $3x - (y^2 + 2xy) + 4(x - y)$ if $x = 5$ and $y = -2$.
   - **A.** 43
   - **B.** 59
   - **C.** 67
   - **D.** -49
   - **E.** -52

2. If $\dfrac{4}{mn} = 24$, then the value of mn is?
   - **F.** 96
   - **G.** 6
   - **H.** $\dfrac{1}{96}$
   - **J.** $\dfrac{1}{4}$
   - **K.** $\dfrac{1}{6}$

3. For $\triangle ABC$ in the figure below, segments $\overline{AD}$ and $\overline{CE}$ intersect at B. What is the sum, in degrees, of angles A, C, and $\angle CBD$?
   - **A.** 120
   - **B.** 60
   - **C.** 180
   - **D.** 240
   - **E.** 300

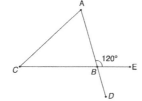

4. If $4x + 7 = 43$, then what is the value of $2x - 5$?
   - **F.** 24
   - **G.** 21
   - **H.** 13
   - **J.** 85
   - **K.** 108

DO YOUR FIGURING HERE.

GO ON TO THE NEXT PAGE.

5. Which of the following expressions is a factor of $2x^2 - x - 15$?

   A. $2x - 5$
   B. $x + 3$
   C. $2x + 5$
   D. $2x - 3$
   E. $x + 5$

DO YOUR FIGURING HERE.

6. Jeanette wants to get an accurate reading on how many miles per gallon her car gets on a tank of fuel. She does 5 trials and finds that her car gets 23.1, 23.8, 23.7, 23.8, and 23.1 miles per gallon for each tank of fuel used. What is the sum of the median and mean of the 5 trials?

   F. 47.3
   G. 47.2
   H. 46.6
   J. 23.5
   K. 23.8

7. Let $g(x) = x^2 + 1$. If $f(g(2)) = 25$, which of the following could be function f?

   A. $4x + 5$
   B. $5x + 4$
   C. $5x - 1$
   D. $10x$
   E. $5x$

8. The graph of a line in the standard (x, y) coordinate plane has an x-intercept of 8 and a slope of $-\dfrac{3}{4}$ has which y-intercept?

   F. $(0, 8)$
   G. $(0, -8)$
   H. $(0, 6)$
   J. $(0, 0)$
   K. $(0, -6)$

9. One-half of a number is 54. One-fourth of one-half of another number is 12. What is the sum of the two numbers?

   A. 66
   B. 30
   C. 123
   D. 204
   E. 180

GO ON TO THE NEXT PAGE.

10. Which expression is equivalent to $\dfrac{6xy^2 - 12x^5y}{2xy^3}$?

    F. $\dfrac{3 - 4x^4}{y}$

    G. $\dfrac{3y - 6x^4}{y^2}$

    H. $\dfrac{3x - 6x^4}{y}$

    J. $3 - 6x^4$

    K. $3y - 6x^4$

DO YOUR FIGURING HERE.

11. For the circle centered at O in the figure below, $\overline{AC}$ is a diameter and the measure of $\overset{\frown}{ACE}$ is 290 degrees. What is the measure of $\angle ACE$, in degrees?

    A. 290
    B. 140
    C. 70
    D. 35
    E. 30

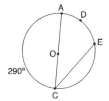

12. Which of the following represents the area, A of an equilateral triangle having sides s, in terms of its perimeter?

    F. $A = \dfrac{\sqrt{3}}{2}s^2$

    G. $A = \dfrac{\sqrt{3}}{4}s^2$

    H. $A = \dfrac{\sqrt{3}}{2}P^2$

    J. $A = \dfrac{\sqrt{3}}{18}P^2$

    K. $P = \dfrac{\sqrt{3}}{18}A^2$

13. One-fifth of the students in a math class made a grade of 90 or above for the semester, and two-sevenths made a grade between an 80 and 89. What fraction of the students in the class made a grade of an 80 or below?

    A. $\dfrac{18}{35}$

    B. $\dfrac{1}{2}$

    C. $\dfrac{1}{4}$

    D. $\dfrac{17}{35}$

    E. $\dfrac{3}{4}$

101

GO ON TO THE NEXT PAGE.

14. Which of the following could be the equation of a parabola whose graph has x-intercepts of -3 and 4 and opens downward?

    A. $y = -x^2 + x + 12$
    B. $y = x^2 - x - 12$
    C. $y = 2x^2 - 2x + -24$
    D. $y = -x^2 + 2x - 7$
    E. $y = -x^2 + 16$

DO YOUR FIGURING HERE.

15. A plumber charges \$55 per hour for a service call plus a \$40 fee to drive to the destination. How many hours will the plumber work if he is paid a total of \$425 to complete a service call?

    A. 7.7
    B. 7
    C. 9.25
    D. 9
    E. 10.63

16. Simplify $\sqrt{-36} - \sqrt{-8}$ where $i^2 = -1$.

    F. $6i - 4\sqrt{2}i$
    G. $6i + 2\sqrt{2}i$
    H. $6i - 2\sqrt{2}i$
    J. $-4\sqrt{2}i$
    K. $8\sqrt{2}i$

17. Which of the following statements is true about the graph of the function $y = f(x)$ shown below?

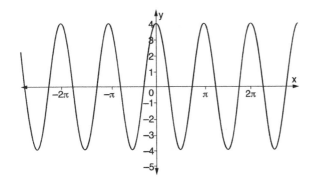

    A. It has a period of 2π.
    B. It has a period of π.
    C. It has a period of $\dfrac{\pi}{2}$.
    D. It is an odd function.
    E. It has x-axis symmetry.

GO ON TO THE NEXT PAGE.

18. Let $f(x) = x^2 - 6x + 2$. If $f(x) = -7$, what is the value for x?

   F. 83
   G. 9
   H. 3
   J. −3
   K. 5

DO YOUR FIGURING HERE.

19. Which expression has a factor of $x + 2$?

   A. $x^3 - 8$
   B. $x^3 + 8$
   C. $x^2 + x + 2$
   D. $x^2 + 3x + 1$
   E. $3x - 6$

20. Let functions f and g be inverses of each other. If $f(2) = 5$, $f(5) = 3$, and $f(3) = 6$, then what must be the value of $f(g(5))$?

   F. 6
   G. 5
   H. 3
   J. 2
   K. Can not be determined with the given values.

21. What is the value for a if the determinant for the matrix $\begin{bmatrix} 4 & 5 \\ 6 & -a \end{bmatrix}$ has a value of 14?

   A. $\dfrac{13}{2}$
   B. $-\dfrac{13}{2}$
   C. 11
   D. −11
   E. −19

22. You and a friend are among 6 people that are chosen at random for an experiment that requires 2 people. What is the probability that both you and your friend are chosen?

   F. $\dfrac{1}{6}$
   G. $\dfrac{1}{30}$
   H. $\dfrac{1}{5}$
   J. $\dfrac{1}{15}$
   Z. $\dfrac{11}{30}$

GO ON TO THE NEXT PAGE.

23. 152 is 8 less than 4 times some number. What must be the number?

A. 19.5
B. 40
C. 36
D. 160
E. −36

DO YOUR FIGURING HERE.

24. Which of the following functions is **not** odd?

F. $y = \sin x$
G. $y = \tan x$
H. $y = \cos x$
J. $y = x^3$
K. $y = x$

25. Two perpendicular lines intersect at $(4, -1)$. If the slope of one of the lines is $-\dfrac{1}{5}$, which of the following is the equation of the other line?

A. $y + 1 = 5(x - 4)$
B. $y - 1 = 5(x + 4)$
C. $y + 1 = -5(x - 4)$
D. $y - 1 = -5(x + 4)$
E. $y + 1 = \dfrac{1}{5}(x - 4)$

26. Which of the following expressions is equivalent to $\dfrac{\sin^2 x \csc^2 x}{\cos^2 x}$?

F. $\tan^2 x$
G. $\sec^2 x$
H. $\csc^2 x$
J. $\sec x$
K. $\csc x$

27. Water leaks out of a faucet at 54 ounces each minute. A lawn sprinkler waters a yard using 30 gallons per hour. At the given rates, which statement is true?

A. Water leaks out of the faucet at 10 more ounces each minute.
B. The lawn sprinkler waters the yard at 10 more ounces each minute.
C. Water leaks out of the faucet at 14 more ounces each minute.
D. The lawn sprinkler waters the yard at 14 more ounces each minute.
E. The rates at which both are using water each minute is the same.

GO ON TO THE NEXT PAGE.

28. What is the sum of the x and y-intercepts for the graph of $y = \dfrac{x^2 - 9}{x + 3}$?

F. −6
G. 6
H. −3
J. 3
K. 0

29. In the standard (x, y) coordinate system, $B(-5, 4)$ and $C(2, -1)$. If segment $\overline{BC}$ is reflected across the origin then shifted 6 units to the right, what will be the transformed coordinates for B?

A. (5, 2)
B. (5, −10)
C. (11, −4)
D. (−1, −4)
E. (−11, −4)

30. The graph of the lines $y = x + 2$ and $y = -x + 3$ along with the solution set for the set of inequalities is shown in the standard (x, y) coordinate system below. Which of the following system of inequalities satisfies the solution?

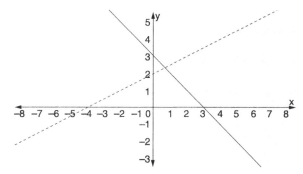

F. $y \geq -x + 3$ and $y < x + 2$
G. $y > -x + 3$ and $y \leq x + 2$
H. $y \leq -x + 3$ and $y > x + 2$
J. $y \geq -x + 3$ and $y > x + 2$
K. $y > -x + 3$ and $y \geq x + 2$

31. Kylie is training for a marathon. The first day she runs 3 miles. Each day afterwards she runs $\dfrac{3}{7}$ a mile more than she did the day before. Approximately how many miles will Kyle have run on day 30?

A. 15.9
B. 15.4
C. 31.3
D. 33
E. 42.9

DO YOUR FIGURING HERE.

GO ON TO THE NEXT PAGE.

32. If $\dfrac{x}{y} = -3$ then what is the value for $4\left(\dfrac{y}{x}\right)^2$?

   DO YOUR FIGURING HERE.

   F. 36
   G. −36
   H. $\dfrac{4}{9}$
   J. $-\dfrac{4}{9}$
   K. $\dfrac{9}{4}$

33. What type of solutions are there for the equation $x^3 - 27 = 0$?

   A. One real number and two complex numbers
   B. Two real numbers and one complex number
   C. Three complex numbers
   D. Three real numbers
   E. One real number

34. If A(4, −1) and B(m, 3) are 5 units from each other in the standard (x, y) coordinate plane, which number could be the value for m?

   F. −7
   G. −1
   H. 7
   J. 0
   K. 5

35. A fabricating machine cuts out an ellipse from a piece of sheet metal to make an emblem for a product. The length of the major axis, k, of the ellipse that is cut out must be within 0.001 inches of the desired length of 8 inches. Which of the following statements is true about the length of the major axis?

   A. $|k - 0.001| \leq 8$
   B. $|k + 0.001| \leq 8$
   C. $|k + 8| \leq 0.001$
   D. $|k - 8| \leq 0.001$
   E. $|k| \leq 0.001$

GO ON TO THE NEXT PAGE.

36. For the right triangle shown in the figure below, which statement is true about angles α and θ?

DO YOUR FIGURING HERE.

A. $\dfrac{\tan\alpha}{\tan\theta} = \dfrac{a}{y}$

B. $\dfrac{\tan\alpha}{\tan\theta} = \dfrac{y}{a}$

C. $\dfrac{\tan\theta}{\tan\alpha} = \dfrac{y}{a}$

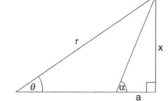

D. $\tan\alpha\tan\theta = ay$

E. $y\tan\alpha = a\tan\theta$

37. The mean for a set of 7 numbers is 24. What must be the value of an eighth number added to the set that changes the mean to 27?

A. 24
B. 7
C. 48
D. 3
E. 27

38. The graph of 2 distinct lines in the standard (x, y) are parallel. One line has its x and y-intercepts at −7 and 12 respectively. What is the slope of the other line?

F. $-\dfrac{7}{12}$

G. $\dfrac{12}{7}$

H. $-\dfrac{12}{7}$

J. −5
K. 5

39. Which expression is equivalent to $2x^{\frac{3}{5}}$?

A. $2\sqrt[3]{x^5}$

B. $2\sqrt[5]{x^3}$

C. $2\sqrt{x^{\frac{3}{5}}}$

D. $\sqrt[5]{2x^3}$

E. $\sqrt[3]{2x^5}$

GO ON TO THE NEXT PAGE.

40. An initial investment of $1200 grows at a rate of 8% annually. The amount, A, of the investment after t years is modeled by the function $A = 1200(1 + 0.08)^t$. Approximately how long will it take, in years, for the investment to have a value of $24,000$?

    F. 39
    G. 20
    H. 19
    J. 25
    K. 33

41. Which function is the inverse of $y = \sqrt[3]{x+2}$?

    F. $y = x^3 - 2$
    G. $y = (x-2)^3$
    H. $y = x^3 + 2$
    J. $x = (y+2)^3$
    K. $x = 2y^3$

42. What is the value for all the coterminal angles of $32°$ where n is an integer?

    F. $32° + 180°n$
    G. $32° - 180°n$
    H. $32° + 360°n$
    J. $32° - 270°n$
    K. $32° + 900°n$

43. Which is the matrix equivalence for the system of equations,

    $3x + 2y = 5$
    $6x - y = 14$

    A. $\begin{bmatrix} 3 & 2 \\ 6 & -1 \end{bmatrix} \begin{bmatrix} x \\ y \end{bmatrix} = \begin{bmatrix} 14 \\ 5 \end{bmatrix}$

    B. $\begin{bmatrix} 3 & 6 \\ 2 & -1 \end{bmatrix} \begin{bmatrix} x \\ y \end{bmatrix} = \begin{bmatrix} 14 \\ 5 \end{bmatrix}$

    C. $\begin{bmatrix} 3 & 6 \\ 2 & -1 \end{bmatrix} \begin{bmatrix} x \\ y \end{bmatrix} = \begin{bmatrix} 5 \\ 14 \end{bmatrix}$

    D. $\begin{bmatrix} 6 & 2 \\ 3 & -1 \end{bmatrix} \begin{bmatrix} x \\ y \end{bmatrix} = \begin{bmatrix} 5 \\ 14 \end{bmatrix}$

    E. $\begin{bmatrix} 3 & 2 \\ 6 & -1 \end{bmatrix} \begin{bmatrix} x \\ y \end{bmatrix} = \begin{bmatrix} 5 \\ 14 \end{bmatrix}$

DO YOUR FIGURING HERE.

GO ON TO THE NEXT PAGE.

44. What is the length of side f for $\triangle$DEF shown in the figure below?

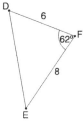

F. 54.9
G. 15.2
H. 3.9
J. 10
K. 7.4

DO YOUR FIGURING HERE.

45. Let P be some point on the graph of $y = \sqrt{x-4}$. Which expression represents the distance that P is from the origin in terms of the x-coordinate of P?

A. $x - \sqrt{x-4}$
B. $x + \sqrt{x-4}$
C. $\sqrt{x^2 + x + 4}$
D. $\sqrt{x^2 + x - 4}$
E. $\sqrt{x^2 + (x-4)^2}$

46. One of the sides of a square, measuring 8 units, is adjacent to one of the sides of an equilateral triangle. What is the area of the polygon, in square units, formed by the square and the equilateral triangle?

A. $64 + 4\sqrt{3}$
B. $64 + 16\sqrt{3}$
C. 96
D. 32
E. 108

47. The graph of a quadratic function in the form $y = ax^2 + bx + c$ in the standard (x, y) coordinate system is shown below. Which statement is true about a and c?

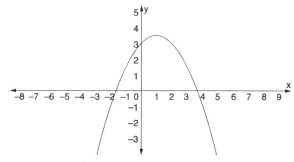

A. $a > 0$ and $c < 0$
B. $a < 0$ and $c > 0$
C. $a < 0$ and $c < 0$
D. $a > 0$ and $c > 0$
E. $a > 0$ and $c = 0$

GO ON TO THE NEXT PAGE.

48. To build a playscape you need lumber consisting of 2×4 and 2×6 pieces of wood. Together you need 54 pieces of wood. Each 2×4 cost \$4 and each 2×6 cost \$7. If you pay \$288 for the pieces of wood, how many 2×4 and 2×6 pieces did you buy?

   F. 27 of the 2×4 pieces and 27 of the 2×6 pieces
   G. 24 of the 2×4 pieces and 30 of the 2×6 pieces
   H. 30 of the 2×4 pieces and 24 of the 2×6 pieces
   J. 30 of the 2×4 pieces and 22 of the 2×6 pieces
   K. 30 of the 2×4 pieces and 26 of the 2×6 pieces

49. $\triangle ABC \sim \triangle DEF$. If $\angle A = 32°$, $\angle E = 47°$, then the measure of $\angle C$, in degrees, is ?

   A. 101
   B. 79
   C. 32
   D. 47
   E. 119

50. What is the radius of a circle given by the equation $x^2 + 8x + (y - 6)^2 = 36$?

   F. 18
   G. 36
   H. $2\sqrt{13}$
   J. $4\sqrt{13}$
   K. 16

51. If $\log_M 64 = \dfrac{2}{3}$ and $e^{lnN} = 7$, then $M + N = $?

   A. 64
   B. 23
   C. 17
   D. 57
   E. $\dfrac{64}{7}$

52. What is the area of a circle, in square units, that has a circumference of 100 units?

   F. 2500π
   G. $\dfrac{2500}{\pi}$
   H. $2500\pi^3$
   J. 100π
   K. $\dfrac{100}{\pi}$

DO YOUR FIGURING HERE.

GO ON TO THE NEXT PAGE.

53. Let $y = f(x)$ be a linear function. What is the slope of f if $f(2) = 5$ and $f(7) = -9$?

A. $-\dfrac{5}{14}$

B. $\dfrac{14}{5}$

C. $-\dfrac{14}{5}$

D. $-\dfrac{11}{2}$

E. $\dfrac{2}{11}$

DO YOUR FIGURING HERE.

54. If $n < -1$ which expression has the greatest value?

F. n^2

G. $2n$

H. $\dfrac{1}{n}$

J. $\sqrt{-n}$

K. n^3

55. Hudson can finish an assigned work project in 6 hours. Kaden can complete the same project in 4 hours. If they work together, how many hours will it take Hudson and Kaden to finish the work project?

A. 5

B. 12

C. $\dfrac{1}{10}$

D. $\dfrac{12}{5}$

E. $\dfrac{5}{12}$

56. If $sin\theta = \dfrac{12}{13}$ and $\dfrac{\pi}{2} < \theta < \pi$ then $cos\theta =$?

F. $\dfrac{5}{13}$

G. $\dfrac{5}{12}$

H. $-\dfrac{5}{13}$

J. $-\dfrac{5}{12}$

K. $-\dfrac{12}{13}$

111

GO ON TO THE NEXT PAGE.

57. The graph of 2 vertices of a right triangle are M(3, 4) and N(–5, 8). If P is the 3rd vertex of the triangle and $\angle NMP$ is the right angle for the triangle, what must be the slope of side MP?

A. $\dfrac{1}{2}$

B. $-\dfrac{1}{2}$

C. 2

D. –2

E. Can not be determined with the given information

58. If you roll a 6-sided die where each side is numbered 1 through 6, and flip a two-headed coin labeled heads and tail respectively, at the same time, what is the probability the you roll a 4 with the die and get a tails with the coin flip?

F. $\dfrac{1}{6}$

G. $\dfrac{1}{2}$

H. $\dfrac{1}{2}$

J. $\dfrac{1}{12}$

K. $\dfrac{2}{3}$

59. For 3 consecutive integers, the sum of twice the second and three times the first is 82. What is the third integer?

A. 14

B. 18

C. 16

D. 32

E. 34

60. If $1 < m < 3 < n$, what can always be said about the relationship between m and n?

F. $m > 3 > n$

G. $m > n$

H. $n > m > 3$

J. $n > m$

K. $1 > m > n$

DO YOUR FIGURING HERE.

END OF TEST

ACT Math Practice Test 7

Mark Your Answers For Test 7 Here

Date: _____

Marking Directions: Mark only one oval for each question. Fill in response completely. Erase errors cleanly without smudging.

Correct mark: ○ ● ○ ○ ○

1 Ⓐ Ⓑ Ⓒ Ⓓ Ⓔ	11 Ⓐ Ⓑ Ⓒ Ⓓ Ⓔ	21 Ⓐ Ⓑ Ⓒ Ⓓ Ⓔ	31 Ⓐ Ⓑ Ⓒ Ⓓ Ⓔ	41 Ⓐ Ⓑ Ⓒ Ⓓ Ⓔ	51 Ⓐ Ⓑ Ⓒ Ⓓ Ⓔ
2 Ⓕ Ⓖ Ⓗ Ⓙ Ⓚ	12 Ⓕ Ⓖ Ⓗ Ⓙ Ⓚ	22 Ⓕ Ⓖ Ⓗ Ⓙ Ⓚ	32 Ⓕ Ⓖ Ⓗ Ⓙ Ⓚ	42 Ⓕ Ⓖ Ⓗ Ⓙ Ⓚ	52 Ⓕ Ⓖ Ⓗ Ⓙ Ⓚ
3 Ⓐ Ⓑ Ⓒ Ⓓ Ⓔ	13 Ⓐ Ⓑ Ⓒ Ⓓ Ⓔ	23 Ⓐ Ⓑ Ⓒ Ⓓ Ⓔ	33 Ⓐ Ⓑ Ⓒ Ⓓ Ⓔ	43 Ⓐ Ⓑ Ⓒ Ⓓ Ⓔ	53 Ⓐ Ⓑ Ⓒ Ⓓ Ⓔ
4 Ⓕ Ⓖ Ⓗ Ⓙ Ⓚ	14 Ⓕ Ⓖ Ⓗ Ⓙ Ⓚ	24 Ⓕ Ⓖ Ⓗ Ⓙ Ⓚ	34 Ⓕ Ⓖ Ⓗ Ⓙ Ⓚ	44 Ⓕ Ⓖ Ⓗ Ⓙ Ⓚ	54 Ⓕ Ⓖ Ⓗ Ⓙ Ⓚ
5 Ⓐ Ⓑ Ⓒ Ⓓ Ⓔ	15 Ⓐ Ⓑ Ⓒ Ⓓ Ⓔ	25 Ⓐ Ⓑ Ⓒ Ⓓ Ⓔ	35 Ⓐ Ⓑ Ⓒ Ⓓ Ⓔ	45 Ⓐ Ⓑ Ⓒ Ⓓ Ⓔ	55 Ⓐ Ⓑ Ⓒ Ⓓ Ⓔ
6 Ⓕ Ⓖ Ⓗ Ⓙ Ⓚ	16 Ⓕ Ⓖ Ⓗ Ⓙ Ⓚ	26 Ⓕ Ⓖ Ⓗ Ⓙ Ⓚ	36 Ⓕ Ⓖ Ⓗ Ⓙ Ⓚ	46 Ⓕ Ⓖ Ⓗ Ⓙ Ⓚ	56 Ⓕ Ⓖ Ⓗ Ⓙ Ⓚ
7 Ⓐ Ⓑ Ⓒ Ⓓ Ⓔ	17 Ⓐ Ⓑ Ⓒ Ⓓ Ⓔ	27 Ⓐ Ⓑ Ⓒ Ⓓ Ⓔ	37 Ⓐ Ⓑ Ⓒ Ⓓ Ⓔ	47 Ⓐ Ⓑ Ⓒ Ⓓ Ⓔ	57 Ⓐ Ⓑ Ⓒ Ⓓ Ⓔ
8 Ⓕ Ⓖ Ⓗ Ⓙ Ⓚ	18 Ⓕ Ⓖ Ⓗ Ⓙ Ⓚ	28 Ⓕ Ⓖ Ⓗ Ⓙ Ⓚ	38 Ⓕ Ⓖ Ⓗ Ⓙ Ⓚ	48 Ⓕ Ⓖ Ⓗ Ⓙ Ⓚ	58 Ⓕ Ⓖ Ⓗ Ⓙ Ⓚ
9 Ⓐ Ⓑ Ⓒ Ⓓ Ⓔ	19 Ⓐ Ⓑ Ⓒ Ⓓ Ⓔ	29 Ⓐ Ⓑ Ⓒ Ⓓ Ⓔ	39 Ⓐ Ⓑ Ⓒ Ⓓ Ⓔ	49 Ⓐ Ⓑ Ⓒ Ⓓ Ⓔ	59 Ⓐ Ⓑ Ⓒ Ⓓ Ⓔ
10 Ⓕ Ⓖ Ⓗ Ⓙ Ⓚ	20 Ⓕ Ⓖ Ⓗ Ⓙ Ⓚ	30 Ⓕ Ⓖ Ⓗ Ⓙ Ⓚ	40 Ⓕ Ⓖ Ⓗ Ⓙ Ⓚ	50 Ⓕ Ⓖ Ⓗ Ⓙ Ⓚ	60 Ⓕ Ⓖ Ⓗ Ⓙ Ⓚ

This page is intentionally left blank

MATHEMATICS TEST

60 Minutes—60 Questions

DIRECTIONS: Solve each problem, choose the correct answer, and then fill in the corresponding oval on your answer document.

Do not linger over problems that take too much time. Solve as many as you can; then return to the others in the time you have left for this test.

You are permitted to use a calculator on this test. You may use your calculator for any problems you

choose, but some of the problems may best be done without using a calculator.

Note: Unless otherwise stated, all of the following should be assumed.

1. Illustrative figures are NOT necessarily drawn to scale.
2. Geometric figures lie in a plane.
3. The word *line* indicates a straight line.
4. The word *average* indicates arithmetic mean.

---

1. If $3x - 9y^2 = 81$, then what is the value of $3y^2 - x$?
   A. 27
   B. −27
   C. 81
   D. 9
   E. −9

2. If $f(x) = x^2 - 5x$ and $g(x) = 4x - 1$, then what is the value of $f(g(2))$?
   F. 14
   G. −13
   H. −25
   J. 25
   K. −42

3. What is the length of side a for right triangle ΔABC shown in the figure below?
   A. 32
   B. 16
   C. $\dfrac{16}{3}\sqrt{3}$
   D. $\dfrac{\sqrt{3}}{16}$
   E. 8

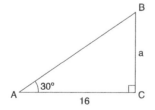

4. Derrick has scores of 73, 93, 87, and 91 on 4 of his quizzes in science. What is the difference in his median score and mean score?
   F. 1
   G. 2
   H. 0
   J. 4
   K. 3

DO YOUR FIGURING HERE.

GO ON TO THE NEXT PAGE.

5. What is the rate of change for the graph of the function $3x + 5y = 6$?

   A. 5
   B. 6
   C. 2
   D. $\dfrac{6}{5}$
   E. $-\dfrac{3}{5}$

DO YOUR FIGURING HERE.

6. Which expression is equivalent to $(3x + 1)(x - 4)$?

   F. $3x^2 + 3x - 4$
   G. $3x^2 - 11x - 4$
   H. $3x^2 - x - 4$
   J. $3x^2 - 4$
   K. $3x^2 + 4$

7. If one-half of 40 is n, what is $\dfrac{2}{5}$ of n?

   A. 12
   B. 32
   C. 8
   D. 16
   E. 20

8. Which of the following functions is **not** an even function?

   F. $y = cosx$
   G. $y = x^4 + x^2$
   H. $y = |x|$
   J. $y = sinx$
   K. $y = \sqrt{4 - x^2}$

9. Which equation best represents the domain and range values given in the table below?

x	y
3	4
5	10
10	25
11	28

   A. $y = 2x - 2$
   B. $y = 4x - 10$
   C. $y = 3x - 5$
   D. $y = x^2 - 15$
   E. $y = 2x^2 - 14$

116

GO ON TO THE NEXT PAGE.

10. What is the center for the graph of the circle whose equation is $x^2 - 10x + y^2 + 6x + 9 = 0$?

   F. $(-5, 3)$
   G. $(5, -3)$
   H. $(3, 5)$
   J. $(3, -5)$
   K. $(-3, 5)$

DO YOUR FIGURING HERE.

11. What is the value of x if $3(27)^x = 9$?

   A. $-\dfrac{1}{3}$
   B. $\dfrac{1}{3}$
   C. 3
   D. -3
   E. 0

12. Let $\triangle ABC \sim \triangle DEF$ If side $a = 4$, $b = 9$, $c = 2$, and $d = 8$, what is the perimeter of $\triangle DEF$?

   F. 14
   G. 16
   H. 26
   J. 19
   K. 30

13. The sum of 3 consecutive odd integers is 159. What is the value of the smallest integer?

   A. 55
   B. 53
   C. 50
   D. 51
   E. 52

.or the nth term, a_n, in the sequence
$, -1, \dots\}$?

   $4n$
   $\cdot\ 4n$
   $\ - 4n$
   $11(4^n)$
   $= 11(-4^n)$

117

GO ON TO THE NEXT PAGE.

15. The graph of the quadratic function in the form $y = ax^2 + bx + c$ where a, b, and c are constants is shown in the standard (x, y) coordinate plane below. Which statement is true about the constants?

DO YOUR FIGURING HERE.

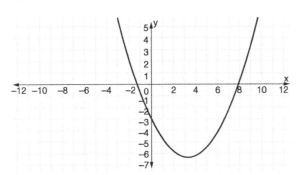

- **A.** $a > 0$ and $c > 0$
- **B.** $a < 0$ and $c < 0$
- **C.** $a > 0$ and $c < 0$
- **D.** $a > 0$ and $b = 0$
- **E.** $c < 0$ and $b = 0$

16. An equation for the graph of which of the following lines is parallel to the x-axis?

- **F.** $x = 5$
- **G.** $y = x$
- **H.** $y = 5$
- **J.** $y = x + 5$
- **K.** $x = 5y$

17. What is the domain for the inverse of $y = \sqrt{x+4}$?

- **A.** $[0, \infty]$
- **B.** $[0, \infty)$
- **C.** $(0, \infty)$
- **D.** $[-4, \infty)$
- **E.** $[\infty, -4)$

18. The probability of randomly choosing a green marble from a bag containing green, red, and blue marbles is $\frac{1}{5}$. If there are 11 red marbles and 5 blue marbles, how many green marbles must be in the bag?

- **F.** 16
- **G.** 20
- **H.** 15
- **J.** 4
- **K.** 5

GO ON TO THE NEXT PAGE.

19. Which of the following expressions is a factor of $8x^3 + 125$?

  A. $x + 5$
  B. $x - 5$
  C. $2x + 5$
  D. $x^2 - 10x + 5$
  E. $x^2 + 10x + 25$

DO YOUR FIGURING HERE.

20. If $u = \langle 5, 4 \rangle$ and $u - v = \langle 4, 11 \rangle$ which of the following is v?

  A. $\langle 0, -6 \rangle$
  B. $\langle -6, 0 \rangle$
  C. $\langle -1, -7 \rangle$
  D. $\langle 1, -7 \rangle$
  E. $\langle 1, 7 \rangle$

21. A plane departs from an airport travelling at an average of 400 miles per hour. One hour later, a second plane departs the same airport travelling in the opposite direction at an average of 475 miles per hour. How long will it take, in hours after the first plane leaves, for the 2 planes to be 2150 miles from each other?

  A. 3.7
  B. 3
  C. 19
  D. 10.7
  E. 5

22. What is the solution for $x = \sqrt{8 - 2x}$?

  F. $x = -4$ or 2
  G. $x = -4$
  H. $x = 2$
  J. $x = 0$
  K. there is no solution

23. Which of the following expressions simplifies to a rational number?

  A. $\sqrt{1} + 1$
  B. $\frac{4}{\sqrt{2}}$

24. For the circle with center O shown in the diagram below, $\overline{CE}$ is tangent to circle O at B. If $\overset{\frown}{ADB} = 245°$ and $\overset{\frown}{AB} = 115°$, what must be the measure of $\angle ACE$, in degrees?

DO YOUR FIGURING HERE.

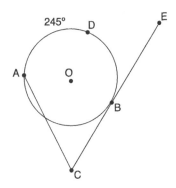

- **F.** 245
- **G.** 115
- **H.** 122.5
- **J.** 65
- **K.** 90

25. Line l contains $(3, 4)$ and $(5, 8)$ and line p contains $(-5, -3)$ and $(k, 5)$ where k is some constant. If l and p are parallel, then what must be the value for k?

- **A.** 2
- **B.** −21
- **C.** 18
- **D.** −15
- **E.** −1

26. If $\dfrac{a}{b+3} = 2$, then $\dfrac{a}{2+\dfrac{6}{b}} = ?$

- **F.** $2b + 6$
- **G.** $6b + 2$
- **H.** a
- **J.** b
- **K.** 6

27. The graph of which of the following functions has the largest maximum value?

- **A.** $y = -3x^2 + 3$
- **B.** $y = -x^2 + 7$
- **C.** $y = |x + 2| + 9$
- **D.** $y = 4\sin x$
- **E.** $y = \cos x$

28. The half-life of a radio-active isotope initially containing 25 gm of material can be described by the function, $A = 26\left(\dfrac{1}{2}\right)^{\frac{t}{1350}}$, where A is the amount, in grams, left after t years. What does 1350 mean for the function?

F. The amount of the isotope left after 1350 years.
G. The amount of the isotope left after 2700 years.
H. The time it takes for one-half of the isotope to be left.
J. The time it takes for twice the initial amount of the isotope to be left.

29. Fill in the blank with the operator that makes the following equality true: $5 - 2(8 \_\_ 15 + 1) = 17$.

A. Addition
B. Subtraction
C. Multiplication
D. Division
E. Square

Use the graph of $y = f(x)$, shown below, to answer questions 30 and 31.

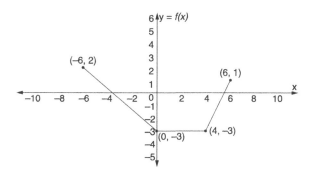

30. What is the range for f?

F. $[-3, 1]$
G. $[-6, 6]$
H. $[-3, 2]$
J. $[-3, 6]$
K. $[-6, 2]$

31. What is the value of $g(4)$ if $g(x) = f(x - 2) + 1$?

A. -3
B. -2
C. 0
D. 1
E. 2

DO YOUR FIGURING HERE.

GO ON TO THE NEXT PAGE.

32. What are all the solutions for $x^4 - 5x^2 - 36 = 0$?

   F. $-3, 3, -2i, 2i$
   G. $-3, 3$
   H. $-2, 2, -3i, 3i$
   J. $-2, 2$
   K. No solutions exist

DO YOUR FIGURING HERE.

33. Let $3^y(3^2) = 81$ and $5^{x-y} = 125$, what must be the value of x?

   A. 4
   B. 1
   C. 5
   D. 3
   E. 0

34. The diameter of a car's tires are 32 inches. If the tires rotate at 100 revolutions per minute, how many feet has the car travelled in 10 minutes?

   F. 100,531
   G. 67,021
   H. 16,755
   J. 5585
   K. 4500

35. If the graph of $y = \sqrt[3]{x}$ is reflected about the x-axis then translated horizontally to the right 3 units, which of the following represents the transformed graph?

   A. $y = \sqrt[3]{-x+3}$
   B. $y = -\sqrt[3]{x} - 3$
   C. $y = -\sqrt[3]{x-3}$
   D. $y = \sqrt[3]{-x+3}$
   E. $y = -3\sqrt[3]{x}$

36. What is the equation of a circle that has a diameter of 16 units and has a center that is the intersection of the lines $y = x$ and $y = 2x - 4$?

   F. $(x+4)^2 + (y+4)^2 = 16$
   G. $(x+4)^2 + (y+4)^2 = 64$
   H. $(x-4)^2 + (y-4)^2 = 8$
   J. $(x-4)^2 + (y-4)^2 = 256$
   K. $(x-4)^2 + (y-4)^2 = 64$

GO ON TO THE NEXT PAGE.

37. An initial investment of $10,000 has an amount, *A*, that is modeled by the function $A = 10,000e^{0.08t}$ where *t* is time in years. Approximately how many years will it take for the initial investment to double in value?

 A. 9
 B. 20
 C. 18
 D. 5
 E. 15

DO YOUR FIGURING HERE.

38. What is the ratio of the area of a circle to its circumference if the diameter is 9 inches?

 F. 4 to 9
 G. 9 to 4
 H. 9 to 8
 J. 8 to 9
 K. 9 to 2

39. Customer reviews for a product that is rated with a score of 1−5 are given in the table below. What is the mean score of the customer reviews?

Score	Number of customers
1	25
2	100
3	52
4	17
5	115

 A. 3
 B. 5
 C. 4.7
 D. 3.6
 E. 4.2

40. For the right triangle shown in the diagram below, find the length of a, the distance of the segment whose endpoints are the vertices of the 30-degree and 60-degree angles.

 F. 8.66
 G. 25.98
 H. 34.64
 J. 17.32
 K. 12.68

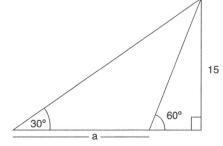

GO ON TO THE NEXT PAGE.

41. If $0 < n < 1$, which of the following expressions has the greatest value?

 A. n^2

 B. $\sqrt{n}$

 C. $\dfrac{1}{n}$

 D. n

 E. $n - 1$

DO YOUR FIGURING HERE.

42. In function notation, the set $\{(x,y)|3x+2y-4(x-y)=12\}$ is which of the following?

 F. $f(x) = \dfrac{x}{6} + 12$

 G. $f(x) = \dfrac{x}{6} + 2$

 H. $f(x) = -x + 6y = 12$

 J. $x - 6y = -12$

 K. $-x + 6y = 12$

43. If $x^2 - 16x + c$ is a perfect square trinomial, what is the value for c?

 A. 8

 B. -8

 C. -64

 D. 64

 E. 32

44. If $(4, 3)$ is a solution to the system, $ax + by = 5$ and $ax - by = 11$ where a and b are constants, then which of the following must be the values for a and b?

 F. $a = 4, b = 3$

 G. $a = 5, b = 11$

 H. $a = 2, b = -1$

 J. $a = -1, b = 2$

 K. $a = 1, b = -2$

45. The graphs of lines l and k are perpendicular and intersect at $(3, 5)$ in the standard (x, y) coordinate plane. If $(1, 9)$ is also on line l, which of the following points is also on line k?

 A. $(7, 3)$

 B. $(3, 7)$

 C. $(1, 1)$

 D. $(11, 9)$

 E. $(9, 11)$

GO ON TO THE NEXT PAGE.

46. Simplify $\dfrac{8.4 \times 10^{12}}{2.8 \times 10^{-3}}$.

    F. 3×10^{9}

    G. 3×10^{15}

    H. 3×10^{-4}

    J. 5.6×10^{9}

    K. 5.6×10^{15}

47. Which expression is equivalent to $\dfrac{\sin x \cdot \cot x}{\sec x}$?

    A. $cosx$

    B. $cos^2 x$

    C. $sin^2 x$

    D. $sin^2 x cos^2 x$

    E. 1

48. What is the sum of the asymptotes for the graph of $y = \dfrac{4x - 12}{2x + 6}$?

    F. 0

    G. 5

    H. -1

    J. 3

    K. 1

49. The stem-leaf plot given below shows the grades for a test in Andrew's science class. Andrew's score is the median score for the class. What grade did Andrew make on the test?

Stem	Leaf
5	0
6	1, 8, 9
7	0, 4, 4, 5, 5
8	2, 6, 6, 6, 6, 8
9	0, 1, 5, 5

    A. 86

    B. 79

    C. 75

    D. 82

    E. 86

DO YOUR FIGURING HERE.

DO YOUR FIGURING HERE.

50. The graph of a polynomial function is shown in the standard (x, y) coordinate system below. Which of the following equations best represents the graph of the polynomial?

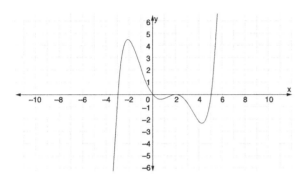

   F. $y = x(x+3)(x-2)^2(x-5)$

   G. $y = x(x+3)(x-2)(x-5)$

   H. $y = x(x-3)(x+2)^2(x+5)$

   J. $y = (x+3)(x-2)^2(x-5)$

   K. $y = x(x+3)(x-2)(x-5)^2$

51. The perimeter of a rectangle is 182 inches. If the length of the rectangle is two and one-half times the width, what is the area of the rectangle in square inches?

   A.   676

   B.   1690

   C.   8281

   D.   4225

   E.   5300

52. If $f(g(x)) = 3x^2 - 3x - 1$ and $g(x) = x^2 - x$, which of the following could be $f(x)$?

   F. $3x$

   G. $x - 1$

   H. $3x - x$

   J. $3x - 1$

   K. $2x^2 - 4x - 1$

GO ON TO THE NEXT PAGE.

DO YOUR FIGURING HERE.

53. For the graphs of $y = f(x)$ and $y = g(x)$ shown in the standard (x, y) coordinate plane below, which of the following values of x is $g(x) - f(x) = 9$?

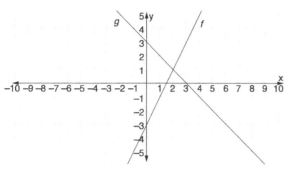

- **A.** 2
- **B.** −1
- **C.** 0
- **D.** 3
- **E.** 4

54. What is the sum of the following geometric sequence, {1, 3, 27, ..., 6561}?

- **F.** 29,524
- **G.** 9841
- **H.** 2046
- **J.** 3281
- **K.** 6562

55. Todd can rake the leaves in his yard in 4 hours. Patty can rake the leaves in Todd's yard in 7 hours. Working together, how many hours will it take them to rake the leaves in Todd's yard?

- **A.** 5.5
- **B.** 2.5
- **C.** 3.5
- **D.** 6
- **E.** 4

56. Which of the following angles, in degrees, is coterminal to $\dfrac{25}{6}\pi$?

- **F.** 30°
- **G.** −30°
- **H.** 60°
- **J.** 150°
- **K.** −60°

GO ON TO THE NEXT PAGE.

57. Twelve more than the square of some number is eight times the number. Which of the following could be the number?

 A. −6
 B. −2
 C. 4
 D. 3
 E. 6

DO YOUR FIGURING HERE.

58. A mixture containing 5% of an insecticide is mixed with 3 quarts of another mixture that contains 9% of the same insecticide. How many quarts of the 5% mixture should be used to produce a mixture that is 8% of the insecticide?

 F. 3
 G. 4
 H. 1
 J. 5
 K. 2

59. Given △ABC in the diagram below. What is the measure of angle A?

 A. 53.9
 B. 35.8
 C. 50.1
 D. 78.9
 E. 27.5

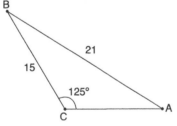

60. Which expression is equivalent to $\dfrac{42x - 3x^2}{6x}$?

 F. $\dfrac{42 - x}{3}$
 G. $7 - 3x$
 H. $\dfrac{14 - x^2}{2x}$
 J. $7 - \dfrac{x}{2}$
 K. $\dfrac{42 - 3x}{6}$

END OF TEST

ACT Math
Practice Test 8

Mark Your Answers For Test 8 Here

Date: _____

Marking Directions: Mark only one oval for each question. Fill in response completely. Erase errors cleanly without smudging.

Correct mark: ◯ ◉ ◯ ◯ ◯

1 Ⓐ Ⓑ Ⓒ Ⓓ Ⓔ	11 Ⓐ Ⓑ Ⓒ Ⓓ Ⓔ	21 Ⓐ Ⓑ Ⓒ Ⓓ Ⓔ	31 Ⓐ Ⓑ Ⓒ Ⓓ Ⓔ	41 Ⓐ Ⓑ Ⓒ Ⓓ Ⓔ	51 Ⓐ Ⓑ Ⓒ Ⓓ Ⓔ
2 Ⓕ Ⓖ Ⓗ Ⓙ Ⓚ	12 Ⓕ Ⓖ Ⓗ Ⓙ Ⓚ	22 Ⓕ Ⓖ Ⓗ Ⓙ Ⓚ	32 Ⓕ Ⓖ Ⓗ Ⓙ Ⓚ	42 Ⓕ Ⓖ Ⓗ Ⓙ Ⓚ	52 Ⓕ Ⓖ Ⓗ Ⓙ Ⓚ
3 Ⓐ Ⓑ Ⓒ Ⓓ Ⓔ	13 Ⓐ Ⓑ Ⓒ Ⓓ Ⓔ	23 Ⓐ Ⓑ Ⓒ Ⓓ Ⓔ	33 Ⓐ Ⓑ Ⓒ Ⓓ Ⓔ	43 Ⓐ Ⓑ Ⓒ Ⓓ Ⓔ	53 Ⓐ Ⓑ Ⓒ Ⓓ Ⓔ
4 Ⓕ Ⓖ Ⓗ Ⓙ Ⓚ	14 Ⓕ Ⓖ Ⓗ Ⓙ Ⓚ	24 Ⓕ Ⓖ Ⓗ Ⓙ Ⓚ	34 Ⓕ Ⓖ Ⓗ Ⓙ Ⓚ	44 Ⓕ Ⓖ Ⓗ Ⓙ Ⓚ	54 Ⓕ Ⓖ Ⓗ Ⓙ Ⓚ
5 Ⓐ Ⓑ Ⓒ Ⓓ Ⓔ	15 Ⓐ Ⓑ Ⓒ Ⓓ Ⓔ	25 Ⓐ Ⓑ Ⓒ Ⓓ Ⓔ	35 Ⓐ Ⓑ Ⓒ Ⓓ Ⓔ	45 Ⓐ Ⓑ Ⓒ Ⓓ Ⓔ	55 Ⓐ Ⓑ Ⓒ Ⓓ Ⓔ
6 Ⓕ Ⓖ Ⓗ Ⓙ Ⓚ	16 Ⓕ Ⓖ Ⓗ Ⓙ Ⓚ	26 Ⓕ Ⓖ Ⓗ Ⓙ Ⓚ	36 Ⓕ Ⓖ Ⓗ Ⓙ Ⓚ	46 Ⓕ Ⓖ Ⓗ Ⓙ Ⓚ	56 Ⓕ Ⓖ Ⓗ Ⓙ Ⓚ
7 Ⓐ Ⓑ Ⓒ Ⓓ Ⓔ	17 Ⓐ Ⓑ Ⓒ Ⓓ Ⓔ	27 Ⓐ Ⓑ Ⓒ Ⓓ Ⓔ	37 Ⓐ Ⓑ Ⓒ Ⓓ Ⓔ	47 Ⓐ Ⓑ Ⓒ Ⓓ Ⓔ	57 Ⓐ Ⓑ Ⓒ Ⓓ Ⓔ
8 Ⓕ Ⓖ Ⓗ Ⓙ Ⓚ	18 Ⓕ Ⓖ Ⓗ Ⓙ Ⓚ	28 Ⓕ Ⓖ Ⓗ Ⓙ Ⓚ	38 Ⓕ Ⓖ Ⓗ Ⓙ Ⓚ	48 Ⓕ Ⓖ Ⓗ Ⓙ Ⓚ	58 Ⓕ Ⓖ Ⓗ Ⓙ Ⓚ
9 Ⓐ Ⓑ Ⓒ Ⓓ Ⓔ	19 Ⓐ Ⓑ Ⓒ Ⓓ Ⓔ	29 Ⓐ Ⓑ Ⓒ Ⓓ Ⓔ	39 Ⓐ Ⓑ Ⓒ Ⓓ Ⓔ	49 Ⓐ Ⓑ Ⓒ Ⓓ Ⓔ	59 Ⓐ Ⓑ Ⓒ Ⓓ Ⓔ
10 Ⓕ Ⓖ Ⓗ Ⓙ Ⓚ	20 Ⓕ Ⓖ Ⓗ Ⓙ Ⓚ	30 Ⓕ Ⓖ Ⓗ Ⓙ Ⓚ	40 Ⓕ Ⓖ Ⓗ Ⓙ Ⓚ	50 Ⓕ Ⓖ Ⓗ Ⓙ Ⓚ	60 Ⓕ Ⓖ Ⓗ Ⓙ Ⓚ

This page is intentionally left blank

MATHEMATICS TEST

60 Minutes — 60 Questions

DIRECTIONS: Solve each problem, choose the correct answer, and then fill in the corresponding oval on your answer document.

Do not linger over problems that take too much time. Solve as many as you can; then return to the others in the time you have left for this test.

You are permitted to use a calculator on this test. You may use your calculator for any problems you

choose, but some of the problems may best be done without using a calculator.

Note: Unless otherwise stated, all of the following should be assumed.

1. Illustrative figures are NOT necessarily drawn to scale.
2. Geometric figures lie in a plane.
3. The word *line* indicates a straight line.
4. The word *average* indicates arithmetic mean.

---

1. If $4a - 16b^3 = 48$, then what is the value of $4b^3 - a$?
   - **A.** 12
   - **B.** −48
   - **C.** −12
   - **D.** 4
   - **E.** −4

DO YOUR FIGURING HERE.

2. If $f(x) = 5x - 3$, then what is the value of $f(f^{-1}(2))$?
   - **F.** 7
   - **G.** 1
   - **H.** $\dfrac{1}{2}$
   - **J.** −2
   - **K.** 2

3. Which of the following statements is always true about real numbers x and y?
   - **A.** If $x > 0 > y$ then, $y - x > 0$.
   - **B.** If $x > y$ then, $x - y > 0$.
   - **C.** If $x > y > 0$ then, $\dfrac{y}{x} > 1$.
   - **D.** If $x > 0 > y$ then, $x \cdot y > 0$.
   - **E.** If $x > 0 > y$ then, $x \cdot y < 0$.

4. Which statement is false about parallelogram ABCD shown below?
   - **F.** $AC = BD$
   - **G.** $AD = BC$
   - **H.** $\angle A = \angle C$
   - **J.** $\angle C + \angle D = 180°$
   - **K.** $AB \parallel DC$

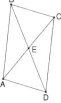

GO ON TO THE NEXT PAGE

5. Completely factor $16x^4 - 81$.

   A. $(4x^2 - 9)^2$
   B. $(2x - 3)(2x + 3)(4x^2 + 9)$
   C. $(2x - 3)^2(2x + 3)^2$
   D. $(4x - 9)(4x + 9)$
   E. $(4x - 9)^2$

DO YOUR FIGURING HERE.

6. The product of some number and the sum of the number and 7 is 60. Which of the following could be the number?

   F. 12
   G. −5
   H. −12
   J. 3
   K. −3

7. A plumber charges $45 per hour to repair a leaky water pipe in a house plus a fee of $75 to travel to the destination. If the home-owners budgeted $480 to have the drain repaired, how many hours will the plumber have to repair the problem?

   A. 10
   B. 9
   C. 4
   D. 6.4
   E. 10.7

8. What is the y-intercept for the graph of a line that contains $(5, 0)$ and $(3, 8)$?

   F. 5
   G. 0
   H. −4
   J. $\dfrac{5}{4}$
   K. 20

9. Which of the following is the equation of a circle with a diameter of 8 units and center is the intersection of the y-axis and the parabola $y = x^2 - 5$?

   A. $(x-5)^2 + y^2 = 64$
   B. $x^2 + (y-5)^2 = 64$
   C. $(x+5)^2 + y^2 = 8$
   D. $x^2 + (y-5)^2 = 16$
   E. $x^2 + (y+5)^2 = 16$

132

GO ON TO THE NEXT PAGE.

10. Jason asked 7 of his classmates if they passed or failed the most recent test in science class. Three of the seven students said they failed the test. How many students can Jason predict passed the test if the class has 42 students?

    F. 18

    G. 21

    H. 24

    J. 10

    K. 39

11. What is the value of $3x(x - 4y) - y^2$ if $x = 2$ and $y = -5$?

    A. −1

    B. −79

    C. 170

    D. 107

    E. 25

12. The graph of the quadratic function in the form $y = ax^2 + bx + c$ where a, b, and c are constants is shown in the standard (x, y) coordinate plane below. Which statement is true about the constants?

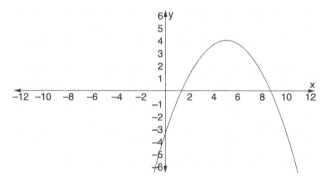

    F. $a > 0$ and $c > 0$

    G. $a < 0$ and $c < 0$

    H. $a > 0$ and $c < 0$

    J. $a > 0$ and $b = 0$

    K. $a < 0$ and $b = 0$

13. 25% of 156 is 3 less than twice some number. What is the number?

    A. 75

    B. 18

    C. 21

    D. 42

    E. 38

DO YOUR FIGURING HERE.

GO ON TO THE NEXT PAGE.

14. The 1st term in an arithmetic sequence is 9 and the 5th term is -7. What is the 10th term in the sequence?

   F. -27
   G. 27
   H. 30
   J. -43
   K. -135

DO YOUR FIGURING HERE.

15. The time is takes to heat an object is modeled by the function $t = 2\sqrt{c-15}$ where is time, in seconds and C is temperature in degrees Celsius. What will be the temperature of the object if it is heated for 20 seconds?

   A. 415
   B. 329
   C. 115
   D. 25
   E. 215

16. What is the factored form of $3x^2 - 5x - 12$?

   F. $(3x-4)(x+3)$
   G. $(3x+4)(x-3)$
   H. $(3x+4)(x+3)$
   J. $(3x-2)(x+6)$
   K. $(3x+2)(x-6)$

17. Which of the following sets of numbers are the lengths of sides for a right triangle?

   A. 1, 2, 4
   B. 0.2, 0.5, 0.8
   C. 10, 24, 26
   D. 6, 12, 18
   E. 2, 6, 9

18. Zack spends 30% if his day at school. Of the other 70% of his day, Zack spends 20% doing homework. How many hours are left in Zack's day that is not spent in school or doing homework?

   F. 3.36
   G. 13.44
   H. 16.80
   J. 5.04
   K. 8.25

GO ON TO THE NEXT PAGE.

19. Which of the following is the equation for a parabola that has its vertex at (4, 3) and passes through (6, –1)?

A. $y = -(x-6)^2 - 1$

B. $y = -(x+6)^2 - 1$

C. $y = (x-6)^2 + 1$

D. $y = -(x-4)^2 + 3$

E. $y = (x-4)^2 - 3$

DO YOUR FIGURING HERE.

20. What is the measure of $\overset{\frown}{EFC}$ if $\overset{\frown}{ADB} = 120°$ and $\angle AGB = 74°$ for the circle with center O in the figure below?

F. 37 degrees

G. 97 degrees

H. 28 degrees

J. 56 degrees

K. 60 degrees

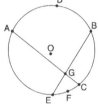

21. The graph of the function $y = f(x)$ has a period of 14 units. What is the period for the graph of $y = g(x)$ if $g(x) = f(x-7)$?

A. 7

B. 2

C. –2

D. 14

E. –14

22. An initial investment of $2500 that earns 6% annually is modeled by $A = 2500(1 + 0.06)^t$ where A is the amount of the investment, in dollars, after t years. What is the amount of the investment after 20 years?

F. $8018

G. $26,500

H. $4000

J. $25,000

K. $1500

23. What is the value of $\dfrac{x+2}{\frac{1}{y}}$ if $x = 3$ and $y = 4$?

A. 12

B. $\dfrac{5}{4}$

C. $\dfrac{4}{5}$

D. 20

E. 2

Use the graph of $y = f(x)$ below to answer questions 24 and 25.

GO ON TO THE NEXT PAGE.

24. Over which of the following intervals if the graph of f constant?

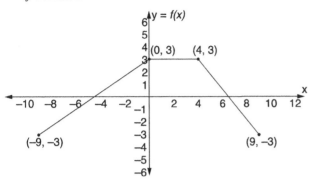

F.   [−9, 0]
G.   [0, 9]
H.   [−3, 3]
J.   [0, 4]
K.   [4, 9]

DO YOUR FIGURING HERE.

25. Which of the following has the greatest function value?

A. $f(8)$
B. $f(−7)$
C. $f(2)$
D. $f(−9)$
E. $f(6)$

26. What is the coefficient for the 3rd degree term if $(2x − 4)^5$ is expanded?

F.   −1280
G.   1280
H.   −640
J.   320
K.   −256

27. What is the volume of a right circular cone whose base has an area of 6π square units and a height of $4h$ units?

A. $24\pi h$
B. $3\pi h^2$
C. $8\pi h$
D. $216\pi^2 h$
E. $12\pi h$

136

GO ON TO THE NEXT PAGE.

28. The vertex and y-intercept for the graph of a parabola in the form $y = f(x)$ are (2, 3) and (0, 5) respectively. Which statement is true for the graph of $x = f(y)$?

    F. The vertex is (5, 0) and the y-intercept is (3, 2).
    G. The vertex is (3, 2) and the x-intercept is (5, 0).
    H. The vertex (3, 2) and the y-intercept is (0, 5).
    J. The vertex is (5, 0) and the x-intercept is (3, 2).
    K. The vertex is (2, 3) and the x-intercept is (5, 0).

DO YOUR FIGURING HERE.

29. The x and y-intercepts for the graph of a line are (−4, 0) and (0, 10) respectively. Which of the following points are on the graph of the line?

    A. (2, 15)
    B. (−15, −10)
    C. (5, 8)
    D. (11, −6)
    E. (1, 25)

30. Vaughn rides a bicycle with tires that have a radius of 15 inches. If the tires are rotating at 2 revolutions per second, what is the linear distance, in feet, Vaughn travels on the bicycle in 10 seconds?

    F. 1885
    G. 943
    H. 79
    J. 157
    K. 1178

31. What is the probability of making a perfect score on a 4-question multiple choice quiz that has 5 answer choices, if you answer each question randomly?

    A. $\dfrac{4}{625}$

    B. $\dfrac{1}{625}$

    C. $\dfrac{5}{625}$

    D. $\dfrac{20}{625}$

    E. $\dfrac{49}{625}$

GO ON TO THE NEXT PAGE

32. What is the period for the sinusoidal graph shown in the standard (x, y) coordinate system below?

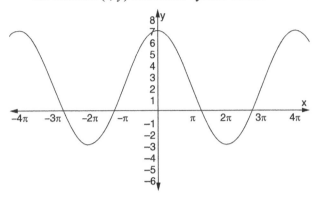

DO YOUR FIGURING HERE.

- **F.** 2π
- **G.** π
- **H.** 4π
- **J.** 7
- **K.** 10

33. Which expression is equivalent to $\dfrac{\sqrt{-9}}{1-4i^2}$ where $i=-1$?

- **A.** $\dfrac{3}{5}i$
- **B.** $-i$
- **C.** $-3i$
- **D.** $-\dfrac{3}{5}$
- **E.** $-\dfrac{3}{5}i$

34. What is $\dfrac{2}{5}$ of 45% of 235?

- **F.** 21.2
- **G.** 84.6
- **H.** 84.6
- **J.** 42.3
- **K.** 13.1

35. Let $u=\langle-3,7\rangle$. If $u-v=\langle12,-16\rangle$, what are the components for v?

- **A.** $\langle-9, 9\rangle$
- **B.** $\langle-15, 23\rangle$
- **C.** $\langle-5, 13\rangle$
- **D.** $\langle-5, -13\rangle$
- **E.** $\langle-4, -4\rangle$

138

GO ON TO THE NEXT PAGE.

36. What are the coordinates of the point $\frac{2}{3}$ of the way from point A to point B on line segment $\overline{AB}$ if $A(5,\ 6)$ and $B(5,\ 27)$?

    F. (5, 21)
    G. (5, 13)
    H. (5, 20)
    J. (20, 5)
    K. (21, 5)

37. What is the maximum value of $7\sin(2A) - 3\cos(B) + 1$ where A and B are real numbers?

    A. 5
    B. 12
    C. 18
    D. 10
    E. 11

38. What is the ratio of the area of a rectangle to its perimeter if its base is 8 units and height is 5 units?

    F. 13 to 20
    G. 40 to 13
    H. 13 to 40
    J. 20 to 13
    K. 32 to 13

39. Which system of inequalities is true for the shaded region between the graphs of the lines $y = -x - 2$ and $y = \frac{1}{2}x + 1$?

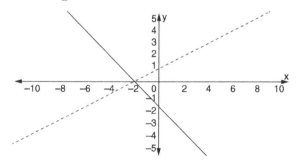

    A. $y > -x - 2$ and $y < \frac{1}{2}x + 1$

    B. $y < -x - 2$ and $y > \frac{1}{2}x + 1$

    C. $y \le -x - 2$ and $y \ge \frac{1}{2}x + 1$

    D. $y \ge x - 2$ and $y < \frac{1}{2}x + 1$

    E. $y \le -x - 2$ and $y \le \frac{1}{2}x + 1$

GO ON TO THE NEXT PAGE.

40. Which of the following transformations when applied to the graph of the parent function?

    $y = lnx$ produces the graph of $y = \ln(x+4)$?

    F. A vertical translation up 4 units.
    G. A vertical translation down 4 units.
    H. A horizontal translation right 4 units.
    J. A horizontal translation left 4 units.
    K. A vertical stretch by a factor of 4.

DO YOUR FIGURING HERE.

41. If $x = 3$ is a zero for the graph of $y = 2x^2 + bx - 6$, which of the following is the value for b?

    A. -4
    B. 4
    C. 1
    D. -1
    E. 0

42. One hundred thirty people were surveyed about their preference for certain kinds of fruit. One hundred of them preferred apples, 50 of them preferred oranges, and 20 of them preferred both apples and oranges. What is the probability that a person chosen at random only prefers apples?

    F. 0.23
    G. 0.15
    H. 0.62
    J. 0.77
    K. 0.38

43. Which expression is equivalent to $\dfrac{\cos x \tan x}{\sin^2 x}$?

    A. $\sec x$
    B. $\csc x$
    C. $\cot^2 x \cdot \sin x$
    D. $\tan^2 x \cdot \sin x$
    E. $\cos x$

44. If $x^n = \left(x^4 \cdot x^{-1}\right)^3$ and $y^m = \left(\dfrac{y^5}{y^2}\right)^{-1}$, then $m + n =$?

    F. -15
    G. -4
    H. 6
    J. -27
    K. 17

GO ON TO THE NEXT PAGE.

45. Points A and C lie on line segment $\overline{DE}$. What is the measure of $\angle BCD$, in degrees?

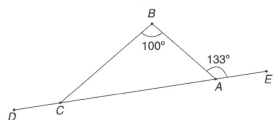

DO YOUR FIGURING HERE.

A. 133
B. 100
C. 33
D. 147
E. 135

46. Which expression is a rational number when simplified?

F. $\left(3+\sqrt{5}\right)\left(3+\sqrt{5}\right)$

G. $\left(3+\sqrt{5}\right)\left(3-\sqrt{5}\right)$

H. $\left(3+\sqrt{5}\right)^2$

J. $\dfrac{1}{3+\sqrt{5}}$

K. $\dfrac{3}{\sqrt{5}}$

47. In the standard (x, y) coordinate plane, what is the image for the point $(-5, 7)$ that is reflected across the x-axis then, translated horizontally right 4 units?

A. $(5, 11)$
B. $(5, 3)$
C. $(-1, -7)$
D. $(-1, 7)$
E. $(-5, -3)$

48. The graph of which of the following equations passes through the center of a circle with the equation $(x+4)^2+(y-5)^2=64$?

F. $y=2(x-4)^2+5$
G. $y=2(x+5)^2-4$
H. $y=2(x-4)^2+8$
J. $y=-x+1$
K. $y=x-1$

GO ON TO THE NEXT PAGE.

49. What is the measure of an exterior angle for a regular dodecagon, in degrees?

    A. 150
    B. 30
    C. 120
    D. 60
    E. 45

DO YOUR FIGURING HERE.

50. If $log_2 32 = M$ and $3 ln e = N$, what is sum of M and N?

    F. 8
    G. 19
    H. 5
    J. 2
    K. 15

51. There are 165 adults and children at an event. The cost for an adult to attend the event is $10 and $7 for a child. If the event made $1455 for the costs of tickets, how many adults attended the event?

    A. 65
    B. 100
    C. 82
    D. 120
    E. 95

52. What are the coordinates for the head of a vector that is the sum of the 2 vectors graphed in the standard (x, y) coordinate plane below with the given head coordinates?

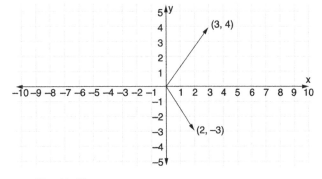

    F. (1, 7)
    G. (5, 1)
    H. (0, 6)
    J. (3, 4)
    K. (2, –3)

142

GO ON TO THE NEXT PAGE.

53. A machine can bottle 50 gallons of juice every 2 hours. One gallon of juice is equivalent to 16 glasses of juice. How many hours will it take for the machine to bottle 6400 glasses of juice?

DO YOUR FIGURING HERE.

A. 8
B. 400
C. 16
D. 64
E. 10

54. Which of the following is true for the inequality $|x-16| < 4$?

F. $x < 20$
G. $x > -4$
H. $20 < x < 12$
J. $12 < x < 20$
K. $-4 < x < 20$

55. The graph of which equation has its zeros at -2 and 3?

A. $y = 2x - 6$
B. $y = x^3 + 8$
C. $y = 2x^2 - 2x - 12$
D. $y = x + 2$
E. $y = \sqrt{x - 3}$

56. If $\cos\theta = -\dfrac{1}{2}$ and $\pi < \theta < \dfrac{3}{2}\pi$, what is the value of $\sin\theta$?

F. $\dfrac{\sqrt{3}}{2}$

G. $-\dfrac{1}{2}$

H. $\dfrac{\sqrt{2}}{2}$

J. $\dfrac{-\sqrt{2}}{2}$

K. $\dfrac{-\sqrt{3}}{2}$

GO ON TO THE NEXT PAGE.

57. What is the perimeter of $\triangle ABC$ shown in the figure below?

DO YOUR FIGURING HERE.

A. 45.6
B. 82.5
C. 46.1
D. 39.9
E. 26

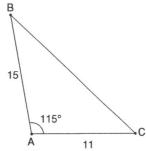

58. The geometric mean for three numbers is 6. If two of the numbers are 3 and 9, what must the third number be?

F. 6
G. 8
H. 2
J. 54
K. 27

59. Write $\log_2 x + 3\log_2 y - \log_2 z^4$ as a single logarithm.

A. $\dfrac{\log_2 x + 4\log_2 z}{\log_2 y^3}$

B. $\dfrac{\log_2 x + 3\log_2 y^2}{4\log_2 z}$

C. $\log_2\left(\dfrac{x + y^3}{z^4}\right)$

D. $\log_2\left(\dfrac{xy^3}{z^4}\right)$

E. $\log_2\left(x + y^3 - z^4\right)$

60. What is the 10th term in the sequence {3, 4, 7, 11, 18, …}?

F. 123
G. 33
H. 4374
J. 199
K. 54

END OF TEST

Answers to Math Practice Test 1

ANSWER KEY																	
#	Key	Your Answer	#	Key	Your Answer	#	Key	Your Answer	#	Key	Your Answer	#	Key	Your Answer	#	Key	Your Answer
1	D		11	G		21	A		31	C		41	B		51	A	
2	H		12	A		22	H		32	G		42	G		52	J	
3	C		13	F		23	C		33	D		43	B		53	A	
4	G		14	H		24	G		34	H		44	K		54	F	
5	A		15	B		25	E		35	A		45	B		55	B	
6	H		16	G		26	G		36	J		46	H		56	J	
7	B		17	D		27	B		37	C		47	A		57	C	
8	H		18	J		28	H		38	F		48	H		58	F	
9	D		19	E		29	A		39	E		49	C		59	B	
10	I		20	G		30	G		40	G		50	J		60	G	

ANSWERS – TEST 1

Each problem number is followed with: **Correct answer/ Topic(s)/ Level of difficulty (1-3)**.

Legends: **N** = Numerical, **A** = Algebra, **F** = Functions, **G** = Geometry, **S** = Statistics and Probability, **IES** = Integrating Essential Skills, **M** = Modeling, **1** = Easy, **2** = Medium, **3** = Difficult

---

1. D./ S–IES/ 2

Let n be the grade for the 5th assignment. The average is,

$$\frac{79 + 84 + 92 + 79 + n}{5} = 85$$

$$\frac{334 + n}{5} = 85$$

$$334 + n = 425$$

$$n = 91$$

Arranging the five scores from least to greatest you have 79, 79, 84, 91, 92.

So, the median score is an 84.

2. H./ A/ 2

Using the one-to-one property for exponential equations you have,

$$x^2 - 2x = 3$$
$$x^2 - 2x - 3 = 0$$
$$(x + 1)(x - 3) = 0$$
$$x + 1 = 0 \text{ or } x - 3 = 0$$
$$x = -1 \text{ or } x = 3$$

3. C./ IES–M/ 3

Let the length and width of the rectangular plot be l and w respectively. Then,

$2l + 2w = 1000$
Solving for l,
$l = 500 - w$.

The area, A of the rectangular plot is $A = lw$.

Substituting the perimeter into the area you can write the area in terms of the width,

$$A(w) = (500 - w)w$$
$$A(w) = 500w - w^2$$

The maximum for the graph of A will occur at its vertex. Using $w = -\dfrac{b}{2a}$, where $a = -1 \text{ and } b = 500$, you have:

$$w = -\frac{500}{-2}$$
$$w = 250$$

Then,

$$A(250) = 500(250) - 250^2$$
$$= 62,500$$

So, the area is 62,500 square feet.

4. G./ G–IES/ 2

The legs for a $45° - 45° - 90°$ triangle are equal in measure so, the radius is 10 inches. The volume of a right circular cone is $V = \dfrac{\pi r^2 h}{3}$. Substituting you get,

$$V = \frac{\pi (10)^2 (10)}{3}$$

$$V = \frac{1000}{3}\pi$$

5. A./ A/ 2

Substituting $t = 53$ into the equation for the time it takes the reaction to occur and solving for d you get,

$$53 = 7\sqrt{d - 10}$$

$$\frac{53}{7} = \sqrt{d - 10}$$

$$\left(\frac{53}{7}\right)^2 = d - 10$$

$$d = \left(\frac{53}{7}\right)^2 + 10 = 67.327$$

$$d \approx 67$$

6. H./ N/ 2

Substituting the given values for a and b into the expression and simplifying you have,

$$\frac{\left(\frac{2}{5}\right)+1}{\frac{1}{3}}=\frac{\frac{7}{5}}{\frac{1}{3}}=\frac{7}{5}\times\frac{3}{1}=\frac{21}{5}$$

7. B./ G–IES/ 2

Since segment OD divides $\angle BOC$ into two parts you have,

$$\angle BOD+\angle DOC=\angle BOC$$

Substituting in the given values you get,

$$\angle BOD+(d+13°)=125°$$
$$\angle BOD=125°-(d+13°)$$
$$\angle BOD=112°-d$$

8. H./ IES–M/1

The cost for the repair is the fixed cost plus the cost for each hour the car is worked on. Let h be the number of hours the car is worked on. Then,

$125 + 75h = 535.50$.

Solving for h you get,

$$125+75h=535.50$$
$$75h=410.50$$
$$h=5.47\bar{3} \text{ or } 5.5 \text{ hours}$$

9. D./ A/ 3

Recall the equation for an arithmetic sequence is $a_n=a_1+d(n-1)$ where a_1 is the first term in the sequence, a_n is the nth term, d is the common difference, and n is a counting number that indicates a particular term in the sequence. Substituting in the given terms and solving for d you get,

$$24=15+d(4-1)$$
$$24=15+3d$$
$$9=3d$$
$$d=3$$

So, $a_n=15+3(n-1)$.

Then,

$$a_{45}=15+3(45-1)$$
$$a_{45}=15+132$$
$$a_{45}=147$$

10. I./ S−IES/ 2

The probability that there will not be a delay for your flight is 100% − 12% = 88% or 0.88.

One flight being delayed due to a mechanical issue is independent of any other flight so, the probabilities that the flights will not be delayed will be multiplied to determine the probability that there will not be a delay for the round trip. Then,

$$0.88\times0.88=0.7744\approx0.77 \text{ or } 77\%.$$

11. G./ F/ 2

The composition $f(g(x))$ can be simplified to,

$$f(g(x))=f(x^2-3)=3(x^2-3)+5$$

Substituting $x=4$ you get,

$$f(g(4))=3(4^2-3)+5$$
$$=3(13)+5$$
$$=44$$

12. A./ G/ 3

Triangle BCD is a $30°-60°-90°$ triangle since $\angle BCD$ is a right angle and $\angle BDC=60°$. The lengths of the ratio of the sides is $x-x\sqrt{3}-2x$, where x is the side opposite 30°, $x\sqrt{3}$ is the side opposite 60°, and $2x$ is the side opposite 90°. So, BD = 12 = 2x, then $x=6$.

Now, the length and the width of the rectangle are BC = $6\sqrt{3}$, and CD = 6.

The area is,

$$A=lw$$
$$=6\sqrt{3}\times6$$
$$=36\sqrt{3}$$

13. F./ A–M/ 3

The change value for d is constant between each successive second, which suggests the data in the table is linear. Choosing the first and second points the slope is,

$$m=\frac{9-5}{2-1}=4$$

Using the point–slope formula, $d - d_1 = m(t - t_1)$ with $(t_1, d_1) = (3, 13)$ you can write d as,

$$d - 13 = 4(t - 3)$$
$$d - 13 = 4t - 12$$
$$d = 4t + 1$$

14. H./ G–IES/ 2

Subtract the area of the circle from the area of the square to find the area, A, of the region. The circle has a radius of one–half the length of the side of the square then,

$$A = 8^2 - \pi(4)^2$$
$$= 64 - 16\pi$$

15. B./ A/ 3

Completing the square, you have,

$$y = x^2 + 8x - 5$$
$$y = x^2 + 8x + \left(\frac{8}{2}\right)^2 - 5 - \left(\frac{8}{2}\right)^2$$
$$y = \left(x^2 + 8x + 16\right) - 5 - 16$$
$$y = \left(x^2 + 8x + 16\right) - 21$$
$$y = (x + 4)^2 - 21$$

16. G./ IES-M/ 2

3% of the people walked to work. Since 45 people walked to work, the number of people in the survey can be determined by dividing 45 by 3% then, $\frac{45}{0.03} = 1500$. So, there are 1500 people in the survey.

65 of 1500 people drove a car to work then, $0.65 \times 1500 = 975$ people drove a car to work.

17. D./ A/ 1

Convert the equation from standard form to slope intercept form, $y = mx + b$ to determine the slope m.

$$4x + 5y = -10$$
$$5y = -4x - 10$$
$$y = -\frac{4}{5}x - 2$$

So, $m = -\frac{4}{5}$.

18. J./ N/ 3

Simplifying the denominator, you get,

$$\frac{4}{\sqrt{-2}} = \frac{4}{\sqrt{-1 \cdot 2}} = \frac{4}{\sqrt{-1}\sqrt{2}} = \frac{4}{i\sqrt{2}}.$$

Rationalizing you have,

$$\frac{4}{i\sqrt{2}} \cdot \frac{i\sqrt{2}}{i\sqrt{2}} = \frac{4\sqrt{2}i}{2i^2} = \frac{4\sqrt{2}i}{2(-1)} = -2\sqrt{2}i.$$

19. E./ G–IES/ 2

The distance from A to B is $23 - 5 = 18$. $\frac{2}{3}$ of 18 is 12 so, C is 12 units from A to B. Since A is at 5, C is at $5 + 12 = 17$.

20. G./ G/ 2

Substitute the point $(6, -5)$ into the left–hand side of the equation of the circle and compare it value to the right–side to get,

$$(6)^2 + (-5)^2 = 48$$
$$36 + 25 = 48$$
$$61 > 48$$

Since $61 > 48$, the point lies outside of the circle.

21. A./ A–IES/ 2

A polynomial is continuous which means there will be function values, $f(x)$, for all real numbers x. Since $f(x)$ changes from negative to positive in value between $x = -5$ and -2, there must be some x value between -5 and -2 where $f(x) = 0$. Similarly, since $f(x)$ changes from positive e to negative in value between $x = -2$ and 1, there must be some x value between -2 and 1 where $f(x) = 0$. $x = -3$ and -1 satisfies both conditions.

22. H./ N/ 1

Convert $\frac{3}{5}$ and 32% to numerical values before multiplying the 3 numbers together.

$\frac{3}{5} = 0.6$ and 32% = 0.32 then.

$0.6 \times 0.32 \times 115 = 22.08$.

23. C./ N/ 3

The components for vectors u, v, and w must have a sum of -13 and 25 respectively. Let the components for $w = \langle w_1, w_2 \rangle$ Then,

$\langle 1,3 \rangle - 2 \langle 5,8 \rangle + \langle w_1, w_2 \rangle = \langle -13, 25 \rangle$. So,

$1 - 10 + w_1 = -13$ and $3 - 16 + w_2 = 25$

$-9 + w_1 = -13$ and $-13 + w_2 = 25$

$w_1 = -4$ and $w_2 = 38$

24. G./ G–IES/2

The volume of the cube that has an edge of 6 cm is $(6)^3 = 216$ cm³.

The 2ⁿᵈ cube's edge is 3 times longer than the 1ˢᵗ cube so its edge is $6 \times 3 = 18$ cm long. The volume of the 2ⁿᵈ cube is $(18)^3 = 5832$ cm³.

Dividing the volume of the 2ⁿᵈ cube by the first you have $\dfrac{5832}{216} = 27$ thus, the 2ⁿᵈ cube is 27 times the volume of the 1st cube.

25. E./ A/ 3

Using the sum of cubes formula, $a^3 + b^3 = (a+b)(a^2 - ab + b^2)$ with $a = 2x$ and $b = 25$ you have,

$(2x)^3 + (5)^3 = (2x+5)\left((2x)^2 - 2x \cdot 5 + (5)^2\right)$

$= (2x+5)(4x^2 - 10x + 25)$

So, $2x+5$ and $4x^2 - 10x + 25$ are the two factors to choose from.

26. G./ S/ 2

There are $15 + 10 + 22 = 47$ coins in the container. If a coin is not a penny, it must be a nickel or a dime. There are $10 + 22 = 32$ coins that are not pennies in the container. The probability is,

$P(\text{not a penny}) = \dfrac{32}{47} = 0.68$.

27. B./ IES–M/ 1

Let A be the area of the wall. Marci has painted $\dfrac{3}{5}$ of the area which equals 594 square feet. Writing the equation for A and solving you have,

$\dfrac{3}{5} \times A = 594$

$A = 594 \times \dfrac{5}{3}$

$A = 990$ square feet

28. H./ A/ 3

For the shaded region, the graph of the parabola lies above the line, so the y values for the parabola will be greater than the y values for the line. Since $y = -x^2 + 4x + 3$ and $y = x - 4$ you get,

$-x^2 + 4x + 3 \geq x - 4$

$-x^2 + 3x + 7 \geq 0$

29. A./ IES–M/ 1

You spend $\$50 - \$31.75 = \$18.25$ for both menu items. Only the combination of the fish and chicken cost $\$18.25$ since $\$9.50 + \$8.75 = \$18.25$.

30. G. – IES/ 3

Let the volume be represented by V, the area of the base by A, and the height, h for the cone. Since the volume varies jointly with the area of the base and the height, $V = kAh$, where k is the constant of variation. Substituting the given values for the volume, area of the base, and height,

$\dfrac{20}{3}\pi = k(4\pi)5$

$\dfrac{20}{3}\pi = 20\pi k$

$k = \dfrac{\frac{20}{3}\pi}{20\pi}$

$k = \dfrac{1}{3}$

31. C./ A/ 3

The slope for l is $m = \dfrac{-4-11}{7-(-5)} = -\dfrac{15}{12} = -\dfrac{5}{4}$. The slope for k is the negative reciprocal since it is perpendicular to l so the slope for k is $m = -\left(-\dfrac{4}{5}\right) = \dfrac{4}{5}$.

32. G./ IES–M/ 2

The distances form a right triangle with the legs being 25 miles and 35 miles. The hypotenuse, c, is the distance of the skyscraper from the airport in miles. Then,

$$c^2 = 125^2 + 35^2$$
$$c^2 = 15,625 + 1225$$
$$c^2 = 16,850$$
$$c = 129.808$$
$$c \approx 130$$

33. D./ IES/ 2

First, Zack only pays 80% of the list price of the laptop computer that is on sale so,

$$0.80 \times 425 = 340.$$

Next, with the coupon Zack pays 85% of the sales price then,

$$0.85 \times 340 = 289.$$

So, Zack pays $289 for the laptop computer.

34. H./ G/ 2

In square feet, the area of the base is $12 \times 7 = 84$. You can use the conversion factor of 1 ft.^{2} = 144 in.^{2} to get,

$$84 \ \cancel{\text{ft.}^2} \times \frac{144 \text{ in.}^2}{1 \cancel{\text{ft.}^2}} = 12,096.$$

So, the area of the base in square inches is 12,096.

35. A/ N/ 3

Solving as a system of equations by substitution you have,

$$a + b = 23$$
$$a = 23 - b$$

Substituting into the second equation you get,

$$2ab = 240$$
$$2(23 - b)b = 240$$
$$46b - 2b^2 = 240$$
$$b^2 - 23b - 120 = 0$$
$$(b - 8)(b - 15) = 0$$
$$b = 8 \text{ or } b = 15$$

So, $a = 15$ or $a = 8$ respectively. Since $a > b$, $a = 15$ and $b = 8$. Then,

$$b - a = 8 - 15 = -7.$$

36. J./ G/ 3

The coordinates of the midpoint are the averages of the coordinates of the endpoints. Since you are given

one of the endpoints, $F(x_1, y_1)$ and the midpoint, H (x_m, y_m), you can find the other endpoint, G (x_2, y_2) as follows;

$$(x_m, y_m) = \left(\frac{x_1 + x_2}{2}, \frac{y_1 + y_2}{2} \right). \text{ Then,}$$

$$9 = \frac{3 + x_2}{2} \text{ and } 12 = \frac{5 + y_2}{2}$$
$$18 = 3 + x_2 \text{ and } 24 = 5 + y_2$$
$$x_2 = 15 \text{ and } y_2 = 19$$

37. C./ S/ 2

The mean or average for the set is $\frac{7 + 9 + 1 + 14 + 2 + 16 + 7}{7} = \frac{56}{7} = 8$. The mode is the number that occurs most often in the set so, the mode is 7. The sum of the mean and mode is $8 + 7 = 15$.

38. F./ IES−M/ 1

To find how many gallons of gas the gas tank can hold, divide the cost to fill the tank by the cost per gallon of gas. So, there are $\frac{36.75}{2.45} = 15$ gallons of gas in the gas tank when it is filled. Next, to determine how far Albert can travel in the car before running out of gas, multiply the number of gallons in the gas tank by the miles per gallon the car averages to get, $15 \times 25 = 375$ miles.

39. E./ N/ 1

Convert $\frac{79}{50}$ and 148% to numerical values to make it easier to compare.

$\frac{79}{50} = 1.58$ and $148\% = 1.48$. So, in ascending order the numbers are,

$$148\%, \frac{79}{50}, 1.67.$$

40. G./ G/ 3

For a right triangle, $\sin\theta = \frac{\text{opposite side}}{\text{hypotenuse}}$. Substituting the value for $\sin A$ and the hypotenuse you have,

$$\frac{3}{4} = \frac{\text{opposite side}}{10}$$

$$\text{opposite side} = \frac{3}{4} \times 10$$

$$= \frac{30}{4} = 7.5.$$

41. B./ F/ 2

For a function in the form $y = af(x-h)+k$, h represents a horizontal translation to the right h units if $h > 0$ and to the left if $h < 0$. Formatting $y = (x+4)^3$ you have,

$y = (x+4)^3 = (x-(-4))^3$ so, $h = -4$. Thus, the parent function $y = x^3$ is a horizontal translation to the left 4 units.

42. G./ A/ 3

Let x represent the number. Then $(x+3)^2 = 16x$. Solving for x,

$$(x+3)^2 = 16x$$
$$x^2 + 6x + 9 = 16x$$
$$x^2 - 10x + 9 = 0$$
$$(x-1)(x-9) = 0$$
$$x = 1 \text{ or } x = 9$$

So, $x = 10$ is the only correct choice from the answer selections.

43. B./ G–IES/ 2

Let w represent the width in feet then, the length, l, is $2w$, and the height, l is w. Since the volume, V, of the metal container is $V = lwh$ you have,

$$432 = 2w \cdot w \cdot w$$
$$432 = 2w^3$$
$$216 = w^3$$
$$w = 6$$

So, the length is $2 \times 6 = 12$ feet.

44. K./ G/ 2

The period for the graph of $y = a\tan(bx)$ is per. $= \dfrac{\pi}{|b|}$.

Since $b = 2$ for, $y = 3\tan(2x)$ the period is $\dfrac{\pi}{|2|} = \dfrac{\pi}{2}$.

45. B./ F/ 3

The sequence of numbers is arithmetic. The sum, S, of an arithmetic sequence with n terms is $S = \dfrac{n}{2}(a_1 + a_n)$ where a_1 and a_n are the first and last terms in the sequence respectively. Then,

$$S = \frac{1000}{2}(1+1000)$$
$$= 500(1001)$$
$$= 500,500$$

46. H./ S–M/ 2

Converting the stem–leaf scores to standard numbers, the set of scores is {55, 57, 61, 63, 64, 69, 71, 71, 83}.

The mode is 71 and the mean or average is,

$$\bar{x} = \frac{55+57+61+63+64+69+71+71+83}{9}$$
$$= \frac{594}{9}$$
$$= 66$$

The sum of the mean and mode is $71 + 66 = 137$.

47. A./ IES–M/2

Let c be the number of children and a be the number of adults that attend the game. Setting up a system of 2 equations you have,

$$1.50c + 3.750a = 3562.50$$
$$c + a = 1250$$

Solving the 2nd equation for c and substituting its value into the 1st equation you get,

$$c = 1250 - a$$
$$1.50(1250-a)+3.75a = 3562.50$$
$$1875 - 1.50a + 3.75a = 3562.50$$
$$2.25a = 1687.50$$
$$a = 750$$

So, there are 750 adults that attend the movie.

48. H./ G/ 2

Since l and m are parallel, the alternate interior angles formed by transversal n are equal in measure. Thus, $x = 50°$. Angles y and $50°$ form a linear pair so, $y = 180° - 50° = 130°$.

So, $x + y = 50° + 130° = 180°$.

49. C./ G/ 3

Since the amplitude for $3\cos x$ is 3, the range is $-3 \le y \le 3$. The range for $\sin 2x$ is $-1 \le y \le 1$. Finding the sums of the minimum and maximum values for the two functions determines the range for $y = 3\cos x + \sin 2x$. Now, $-3 + -1 -4$, and $3 + 1 = 4$. So, the range is $-4 \leq y \leq 4$.

50. J./ S–IES/ 3

The Venn diagram below shows the relationships of a person that likes candy bars, spinach, or both.

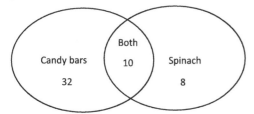

Since 42 out of 50 people surveyed only like candy bars, 8 only like spinach. Similarly, 18 out of 50 people only like spinach, so 32 people only like candy bars. Thus, of the 50 people surveyed, 10 must like both. The probability that a person chosen likes both candy bars and spinach out of the 50 people surveyed is $\dfrac{10}{50} = 0.2$.

51. A./ F/ 3

For a matrix in the form $\begin{bmatrix} a & b \\ c & d \end{bmatrix}$, the value of the determinant is $ad - bc$. So,

$$5 \cdot 3 - a \cdot a = 2a$$
$$15 - a^2 = 2a$$
$$a^2 + 2a - 15 = 0$$
$$(a+5)(a-2) = 0$$
$$a = -5 \text{ or } a = 2$$

Since a must be negative, $a = -5$.

52. J./ F/ 2

The range for the graph is the y values for all points on the graph of the function. The open circles at $x = 1$ exclude the points on the graph and the closed points at $x = -3$ and 6 include the points on the graph. So, the range includes $-4 \leq y < 1$ or $2 < y \leq 6$.

53. A./ A–MDL/ 2

Let m be the number of miles Samantha drives the car each day. The expression that represents the cost in dollars Samantha spends on driving the car each day is $35 + 0.15m$. Her budget is \$85. Setting the cost in dollars to 85 you have,

$$35 + 0.15m = 85$$
$$0.15m = 50$$
$$m = 333.\overline{3}$$

So, Samantha can drive approximately 333 miles each day on her budget.

54. F./ N–IES/ 4

Solving for y and z you have,

$$x \cdot yz = \frac{1}{yz} \cdot yz \qquad x \cdot yz = \frac{1}{yz} \cdot yz$$
$$xyz = 1 \qquad\qquad xyz = 1$$
$$\frac{xyz}{xz} = \frac{1}{xz} \qquad\qquad \frac{xyz}{xy} = \frac{1}{xy}$$
$$y = \frac{1}{xz} \qquad\qquad z = \frac{1}{xy}$$

Adding the expression for y and z you get,

$$y + z$$
$$= \frac{1}{xz} + \frac{1}{xy}$$
$$= \frac{y+z}{xyz}$$

55. B/ N/ 2

$$\frac{7.2 \times 10^{-3}}{1.8 \times 10^{-8}}$$
$$= \frac{7.2}{1.8} \times \frac{10^{-3}}{10^{-8}}$$
$$= 4.0 \times 10^{-3-(-8)}$$
$$= 4.0 \times 10^{5}$$

56. J./ F–M/ 2

You can use the "rule of 72" to since you are only approximating the time to double the investment. Dividing 72 by the numerical value of the interest rate you have, $\dfrac{72}{8} = 9$. So, it will take approximately 9 years to double the investment.

57. C./ A/ 2

The absolute value inequality for less than can be written as a compound inequality or broken into two separate inequalities. As a compound statement you have, $-15 < 3x - 5 < 15$ which can be separated to

$-15 < 3x - 5$ and $3x - 5 < 15$ where $-15 < 3x - 5$ can be written as $3x - 5 > -15$.

58. F./ A−IES/ 3

Setting the ratios of gallons of milk produced daily to glasses of milk you have,

$\dfrac{992}{7\frac{3}{4}} = \dfrac{1550}{g}$ where g is the number of glasses of milk.

Solving for g,

$$\dfrac{992}{7\frac{3}{4}} = \dfrac{1550}{g}$$

$$992g = 1550 \times 7\frac{3}{4}$$

$$992g = 11,625$$

$$g = 11.719$$

So, there are about 12 gallons of milk needed to produce 1550 glasses of milk.

59. B./ A−IES/ 2

The perimeter is the sum of the sides of the triangle. Let x be the length of the base in inches then,

$$x + 3x + 3x = 63$$

$$8x = 63$$

$$x = 9$$

The area, A, in square inches is the product of one−half the base and the height.

$$A = \dfrac{1}{2}(9)12$$

$$A = 54$$

60. G./ N/ 3

$$x^{\frac{1}{2}}\left(x^{\frac{3}{4}}\right)^{\frac{1}{2}} = x^{\frac{1}{2}}\left(x^{\frac{3}{4}\cdot\frac{1}{2}}\right) = x^{\frac{1}{2}}\left(x^{\frac{3}{8}}\right) = x^{\frac{1}{2}+\frac{3}{8}} = x^{\frac{7}{8}}.$$

Using $x^{\frac{m}{n}} = \sqrt[n]{x^m}$, have $x^{\frac{7}{8}} = \sqrt[8]{x^7}$.

This page is intentionally left blank

Answers to Math Practice Test 2

ANSWER KEY						

#	Key	Your Answer	#	Key	Your Answer	#	Key	Your Answer	#	Key	Your Answer	#	Key	Your Answer	#	Key	Your Answer
1	E		11	B		21	C		31	C		41	A		51	C	
2	G		12	G		22	H		32	H		42	H		52	J	
3	B		13	B		23	C		33	A		43	A		53	B	
4	F		14	H		24	F		34	H		44	K		54	H	
5	C		15	B		25	B		35	B		45	E		55	C	
6	H		16	K		26	H		36	K		46	G		56	G	
7	E		17	B		27	A		37	D		47	B		57	A	
8	J		18	G		28	F		38	F		48	H		58	G	
9	E		19	C		29	C		39	B		49	C		59	C	
10	K		20	F		30	J		40	H		50	K		60	K	

ANSWERS – TEST 2

Each problem number is followed with: **Correct answer/ Topic(s)/ Level of difficulty (1-3)**.

Legends: **N** = Numerical, **A** = Algebra, **F** = Functions, **G** = Geometry, **S** = Statistics and Probability, **IES** = Integrating Essential Skills, **M** = Modeling, **1** = Easy, **2** = Medium, **3** = Difficult

---

1. **E./ IES & MDL/ 2**

   The cost for the repair is the fixed cost plus the cost for each hour the car is worked on. Let h be the number of hours the air conditioner is worked on then,

   $55 + 27.50h = 327.50$.

   Solving for h you get,

   $$55 + 27.50h = 327.50$$
   $$27.50h = 272.50$$
   $$h = 9.\overline{90} \text{ or } 10 \text{ hours}$$

2. **G./ F/ 1**

   Substituting $x = -2$ into the function you get,

   $$f(-2) = (4-(-2))^2 + 5$$
   $$= (4+2)^2 + 5$$
   $$= 6^2 + 5$$
   $$= 41$$

3. **B./ F/ 2**

   The graph of the function in the form $f(x) = ax^2 + c$ is a parabola that opens up if $a > 0$ and opens down if $a < 0$. Additionally, c is the y-intercept. Since the graph opens down, $a < 0$, and since the y-intercept is 3.5, $c > 0$.

4. **F./ IES–MDL/ 2**

   Jeni's hourly wage beginning in month 7 increases by 3% so, her new hourly wage is $12.50 \times 1.03 = 12.875$ or \$12.88. Let h be the number of hours she works in the 7th month. Her wages are $12.88h$. Since she makes \$1850 in the 7th month you have,

   $$12.88h = 1850$$
   $$h = 143.634 \text{ or } 144 \text{ hours.}$$

5. **C. /N/ 2**

   Substituting p and q and solving for r,

   $$120 = 8r^2 - 8$$
   $$128 = 8r^2$$
   $$16 = r^2$$
   $$\pm 4 = r$$

   So, $r = 4$ only since r must be greater than 0.

6. **H./ IES & MDL/ 2**

   Since the weight and cost per pound are directly proportional to each other, the ratio of the weight to the cost per pound for any given watermelon will be the same. So set up a proportion and then cross multiply and divide.

   $$\frac{25}{0.38} = \frac{32}{c}$$
   $$25c = 12.16$$
   $$c = 0.4864 \text{ or } \$0.49$$

7. **E./ F/ 1**

   Rotating the graph around the origin produces the original graph of the function. The graph of a function that has origin symmetry is a combination of both types of reflections. (B looks correct, but that is not the domain, it is the range.)

8. **J./ N/ 3**

   Let n be the smaller integer. Then, $n + 1$ is the larger, consecutive (next) integer. Then,

   $4n + [(n+1) - 3] = 523$. Solving for n,

   $$4n + [(n+1) - 3] = 523$$
   $$5n - 2 = 523$$
   $$5n = 525$$
   $$n = 105$$

   So, the consecutive integers are 105 and 106.

9. E./ A/ 2

Simplifying by distributing the -x and collecting like terms, you have:

$$\left(4x^3+3xy-5\right)-x\left(2x^2-7y+6\right)$$
$$=4x^3+3xy-5-2x^3+7xy-6x$$
$$=\left(4x^3-2x^3\right)+\left(3xy+7xy\right)-6x-5$$
$$=2x^3+10xy-6x-5$$

10. K./ A–MDL/ 3

Notice the rate at which the number of gallons of water poured into the pool per hour is constant,

$$\frac{17.5-7}{5-2}=\frac{45.5-17.5}{13-5}=\frac{77-45.5}{22-13}=3.5 \text{ gallons per}$$
hour.

Let t be time in hours then, $4500 + 3.5t$ represents the number of gallons of water in the tank at time t and $10{,}000 = 4500 + 3.5t$ is equation that could be used to find the time it takes to fill the pool.

11. B./ N/ 2

Substituting x and y into the expression you get,

$$\frac{x}{y}=\frac{a^{b-c}}{a^{3b}}$$

Using the rules for exponents to simplify,

$$\frac{x}{y}=\frac{a^{3b}}{a^{b-c}}=a^{3b-(b-c)}=a^{2b+c}$$

12. G./ S/ 3

You know 3 of the numbers must be 42, 51, and 51 since they are the median and the mode for the set. Let x_4,x_5,x_6,x_7 be the other 4 numbers in the set. Using the mean of the set you get,

$$\frac{42+51+51+x_4+x_5+x_6+x_7}{7}=45$$
$$\frac{144+x_4+x_5+x_6+x_7}{7}=45$$
$$144+x_4+x_5+x_6+x_7=315$$
$$x_4+x_5+x_6+x_7=171$$

So, the sum of the other 4 numbers is 171.

13. B./ G/ 2

The sum of an exterior angle for a triangle is the sum of its two remote interior angles. Angle BAE is an exterior angle for the triangle and angles B and C are its remote interior angles.

The sum of an exterior angle for a triangle is the sum of its two remote interior angles. Angles B and C are the two remote interior angles whose sum exterior angle BAE. So,

$$\angle BAE = \angle B + \angle C$$
$$142 = 85 + \angle C$$
$$\angle C = 57$$

14. H./ IES–MDL/ 3

Convert the dimensions of the garden to feet before finding the area so you can compare like units with the fish emulsion. Since there are 3 feet in a yard, the length of the garden is $15\times3=45$ feet, and width is $8\times3=24$ fee. So, the area of the garden is $45\times24=1080$ ft.^{2} .

Each bottle of fish emulsion covers 360 ft.^{2}, so you will need $\dfrac{1080}{360}=3$ bottles of fish emulsion to cover the garden one time, and $3\times3=9$ bottles to cover the garden 3 times.

15. B./ S/ 2

Let n be the number of dimes that need to be added, then the number of dimes that will be in the piggy bank is $28 + n$, and the number of coins will be $55 + n$. The probability of randomly selecting a dime is,

$$\frac{28+n}{55+n}=\frac{3}{4}$$

Cross multiplying and solving for n,

$$\frac{27+n}{55+n}=\frac{3}{4}$$
$$4(27+n)=3(55+n)$$
$$108+4n=165+3n$$
$$n=57$$

So, 57 dimes need to be added.

16. K./ N/ 2

An absolute value expression measures the distance of some value from the origin. The distance can be either to the right, measured as a positive number, or to the left, measured as a negative number of the origin. Using -8 and 8 as the two distances from the origin you have:

Solving for b:

$$a - 2b = 8 \qquad \text{OR} \qquad a - 2b = -8$$
$$-2b = -a + 8 \qquad\qquad -2b = -a - 8$$
$$b = \frac{a}{2} - 4 \qquad\qquad \boldsymbol{b = \frac{a}{2} + 4}$$

Solving for a:

$$a - 2b = 8 \qquad \text{OR} \qquad a - 2b = -8$$
$$a = 2b + 8 \qquad\qquad a = 2b - 8$$

The only solution that matches the answers is the bolded one.

17. B./ F/ 2

Undoing the composition for $f(g(x))$ to determine the function values for f and g, you get $f(x) = x^2 + 5$ and $g(x) = 4 - x$. Composing f and g to check our answer we get, $f(g(x)) = f(4 - x) = (4 - x)^2 + 5$.

18. G./ F/ 2

Jana travels $\frac{2}{3}$ of 9 miles or 6 miles before she realizes she forgot her assignment. She travels an additional 6 to get back home to pick up her assignment. Finally, she travels 9 miles to get to school for a total of $6 + 6 + 9 = 21$ miles travelled.

19. C./ A/ 3

Simplify $(2x - 1)^2 - 3x + 5$ to find an equivalent expression.

$$(2x - 1)^2 - 3x + 5 = 4x^2 - 4x + 1 - 3x + 5$$
$$= 4x^2 - 7x + 6$$

20. F./ S/ 3

Let S_1 be the sum of the 5 numbers, and $\bar{x}$ be the original mean. Then, $S_1 = 5 \cdot \bar{x}$.

Increase the mean by $\frac{1}{3}$ then the new mean is $\frac{4}{3} \cdot \bar{x}$ so, the new sum, $S_2 = \frac{20}{3} \cdot \bar{x}$.

The differnce in the new sum and original is the how much the sum of the orignal 5 numbers must increase. Now,

$$S_2 - S_1 = \frac{20}{3} \cdot \bar{x} - \frac{\bar{x}}{5} = \frac{5}{3}\bar{x}.$$

So the original sum must increase by $\frac{5}{3}$ of the original mean whenever the original mean increases by $\frac{1}{3}$.

21. C./ A/ 2

Since the equation is a linear function, you can find the x and y-intercepts to determine the correct graph.

Setting $x = 0$, the y-intercept is,

$$2(0) - 3y = -12$$
$$-3y = -12$$
$$y = 4$$

Setting $y = 0$, the x-intercept is,

$$2x - 3(0) = -12$$
$$2x = -12$$
$$x = -6$$

So, the correct graph is answer choice B.

22. H./ IES–MDL/ 2

Because of the sale of 15% off, you pay 85% for the cell phone or $0.85 \times 475 = \$403.75$. Taking an additional 5% off the sales price as an incentive, means you only pay 95% of the sales price or $0.95 \times 403.75 = \$383.56$. Finally, adding the tax rate of 8% to the final price of the cell phone you pay $1.08 \times 383.56 = \$414.25$.

23. C./ F / 3

The common ratio, r, for geometric sequence is the ratio of a term to it preceding term. So, $r = \frac{\frac{3}{4}}{2} = \frac{3}{4} \times \frac{1}{2} = \frac{3}{8}$. The nth term, a_n, in a geometric sequence is $a_n = a_1 \cdot r^{n-1}$, where a_1 is the 1st term in the sequence. So, the 10th term is,

$$a_{10} = 2 \cdot \left(\frac{3}{8}\right)^{10-1} = 2 \cdot \left(\frac{3}{8}\right)^9.$$

24. F./ G–MDL/ 3

You can use the law of cosines to find the length of the side opposite the given angle since you are given an angle and its 2 included sides, or SAS, for the triangle. The formula for the law of cosines is, $c^2 = a^2 + b^2 - 2ab \cos C$.

Let $C = 25°$, $a = 85$, and $b = 73$, and $c = EF$ then,

$c^2 = 85^2 + 73^2 - 2 \cdot 85 \cdot 73 \cos 25°$

$c^2 = 1306.72$

$c = 36.14$ or 36 feet.

25. B./ N/ 1

Convert 152% and $\dfrac{8}{5}$ to standard numbers before comparing. $152\% = 1.52$ and $\dfrac{8}{5} = 1.6$ so, in descending (decreasing) order the arrangement is $\dfrac{8}{5}$, 152%, 1.48.

26. H./ F/ 2

In slope intercept form $3x + 4y = -5$ is

$3x + 4y = -5$

$4y = -5 - 3x$

$y = -\dfrac{3}{4}x - \dfrac{5}{4}$

So, the slope of the line is $m = -\dfrac{3}{4}$. The slope of the perpendicular line has a slope that is the negative or opposite reciprocal so, $m = \dfrac{4}{3}$ for the perpendicular line.

27. A./ A/ 3

Using the formula for the sum of 2 cubes, $a^3 + b^3 = (a + b)(a^2 - ab + b^2)$ where $a = 3x$ and $b = 4$ you have,

$27x^3 + 64$

$= (3x + 4)\left((3x)^2 - 3x \cdot 4 + 4^2\right)$

$= (3x + 4)(9x^2 - 12x + 16)$

28. F./ IES–MDL/ 2

Let m be the number of tickets people under 62 years of age purchased and n be the number of tickets people 62 years or older purchased. The sum m and n is 60,000, so $m + n = 60,000$.

The revenue generated by people 62 and under is $18m$ and for people 62 and over is $15n$. Total revenue generated is $1,250,000 so $18m + 15n = 1,250,000$.

29. C./ N/ 2

$\dfrac{a}{b} = \dfrac{3}{5}$ then $a = \dfrac{3b}{5}$ and $\dfrac{c}{d} = \dfrac{4}{6}$ then $c = \dfrac{2d}{3}$. So,

$\dfrac{a}{c} = \dfrac{\frac{3b}{5}}{\frac{2d}{3}} = \dfrac{3b}{5} \times \dfrac{3}{2d} = \dfrac{9b}{10d}$.

30. J./ G/ 2

Using the trigonometric identity $\cos^2 x + \sin^2 x = 1$,

$\dfrac{\cos^2 x}{\sin x} = \dfrac{1 - \sin^2 x}{\sin x} = \dfrac{1}{\sin x} - \dfrac{\sin^2 x}{\sin x} = \csc x - \sin x$.

31. C./ IES–MDL/ 3

Let x be the speed of the slower car, then $x + 4$ is the speed of the faster car. The distance the slower car travel in 3 hours is $3x$ and the faster cars distance is $3(x + 4)$. Since one car travels due north and the other due south, they are traveling along a vertical line, so the total distance travelled is the sum of their distances travelled. Then,

$3x + 3(x + 4) = 240$

$6x + 12 = 240$

$6x = 228$

$x = 38$

So, the slower car's speed is 38 miles per hour.

32. H./ N/ 2

Let the positive number be n. Then,

$4n + n^2 = 96$

$n^2 + 4n - 96 = 0$

$(n + 12)(n - 8) = 0$

$n = -12$ or $n = 8$

Since $n > 0$, only 8 is a solution.

33. A./ G /3

The measure of an exterior angle of a circle is one-half the difference of its two intercepted arcs.

Arc $\overset{\frown}{AFE} = \dfrac{1}{3} \times 360° = 120°$. Now,

$$22° = \frac{1}{2}\left(120° - \overset{\frown}{BGD}\right)$$

$$44° = 120° - \overset{\frown}{BGD}$$

$$-76° = -\overset{\frown}{BGD}$$

$$\overset{\frown}{BGD} = 76°$$

34. H./ N/ 2

$$|2x - 8| = 17$$

$$2x - 8 = -17 \text{ or } 2x - 8 = 17$$

$$2x = -9 \text{ or } 2x = 25$$

$$x = -\frac{9}{2} \text{ or } x = \frac{25}{2}.$$

The sum of the solutions is $-\dfrac{9}{2} + \dfrac{25}{2} = \dfrac{16}{2} = 8$.

35. B./ N/ 3

Multiplying the numerator and denominator by the complex conjugate of $1 + i$.

$$\frac{4}{1+i} \cdot \frac{1-i}{1-i} = \frac{4-4i}{1-i^2} = \frac{4-4i}{1-(-1)} = \frac{4-4i}{2} = 2-2i.$$

36. K./ F/ 2

Write $10x - 2y = 16$ in slope-intercept form.

$$10x - 2y = 16$$

$$-2y = -10x + 16$$

$$y = 5x - 8$$

So, the slope is 5.

The slope of $y = 5x + 3$ is also 5 so, the lines are parallel. The lines do not intersect since they have different y-intercepts.

37. D./ IES–MDL/ 3

You fill $\dfrac{1}{15}$ of the bathtub each minute. With the plug out, you drain $\dfrac{1}{20}$ of the bathtub each minute.

When the drain is not plugged, you fill $\dfrac{1}{15} - \dfrac{1}{20} = \dfrac{4}{60} - \dfrac{3}{60} = \dfrac{1}{60}$ of the bathtub each minute

for a total of $\dfrac{8}{60}$ or $\dfrac{2}{15}$ for the first 8 minutes. You

still need to fill $\dfrac{13}{15}$ of the bathtub. Filling $\dfrac{1}{15}$ of the bathtub each minute, it takes 13 minutes to completely fill the bathtub after the drain is plugged. So, it takes $8 + 13 = 21$ minutes to fill the bathtub.

38. F./ F/ 2

By the definition of a logarithm, $M = a^b \Leftrightarrow b = \log_a M$ and $N = a^c \Leftrightarrow c = \log_a N$

Using the product rule for logs, $\log_a(MN) = \log_a M + \log_a N$ so,

$$\log_a(MN) = \log_a M + \log_a N = b + c.$$

39. B./ G/ 2

The center of the circle is the intersection of the horizontal line thru the point of tangency $(0, -4)$ and the vertical line thru the point of tangency at $(4, 0)$. So, the center, (h, k) is $(4, -4)$. The radius can be found by counting vertically or horizontally the distance from the center of the circle to either point of tangency. So, $r = 4$. (Common error: the x and y axes go by 2's)

Substituting the center and radius into the standard form for a circle $(x - h)^2 + (y - k)^2 = r^2$,

$$(x - 4)^2 + (y - (-4))^2 = 4^2$$

$$(x - 4)^2 + (y + 4)^2 = 16$$

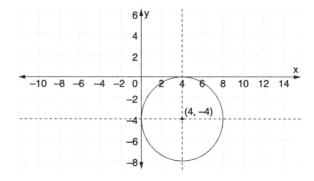

40. H,/ N/ 3

In exponential form, $\sqrt[4]{5^3} = 5^{\frac{3}{4}}$ and $\sqrt{5} = 5^{\frac{1}{2}}$. Adding the exponents when multiply terms with common bases,

$$\sqrt[4]{5^3} \cdot \sqrt{5} = 5^{\frac{3}{4}} \cdot 5^{\frac{1}{2}} = 5^{\frac{3}{4}+\frac{1}{2}} = 5^{\frac{5}{4}}.$$

41. A./ S–MDL/ 3

Since 18% prefer action and 32% prefer comedy, the ratio 18:32 can be simplified to 9:16.

42. H./ IES/ 3

You need to subtract the volume of the right circular cylinder created from boring a hole in the center of the metal pipe from the volume of the right circular cylinder that is the metal pipe. The volume, V_m of the metal pipe is $V_m = \pi(2)^2 \cdot 6 = 24\pi$ cubic feet, and the volume, V_b, of the hole in the metal pipe is $V_b = \pi(0.5)^2 \cdot 6 = 1.5\pi$ cubic feet. So,

$V_m - V_b = 24\pi - 1.5\pi = 70.69$ or 71 cubic feet.

43. A./ G/ 2

For the graph of the function in the form $y = a\cos(bx)$, the period is $\dfrac{2\pi}{|b|}$.

For $y = 4\cos\left(\dfrac{x}{2}\right)$, $b = \dfrac{1}{2}$. So, the period is

$\dfrac{2\pi}{\left|\dfrac{1}{2}\right|} = 2\pi \cdot \dfrac{2}{1} = 4\pi.$

44. K./ F/ 3

Set $y = 0$ and solve for x to find any x-intercepts for the function. Remember to simplify the function before setting the numerator equal to 0.

$0 = \dfrac{2x}{x^3 - 4x}$

$0 = \dfrac{2\cancel{x}}{\cancel{x}(x+2)(x-2)}$

$0 = \dfrac{2}{(x+2)(x-2)}$

Since $0 \neq 2$ no solution exists.

45. E./ A/ 3

Substitute $p = -7$ to find n.

$(-7)^2 + n(-7) - 28 = 0$

$49 - 7n - 28 = 0$

$-7n = -21$

$n = 3$

Now, factor the quadratic equation with $n = 3$ to find the other root.

$p^2 + 3p - 28 = 0$

$(p+7)(p-4) = 0$

$p + 7 = 0$ or $p - 4 = 0$

$p = -7$ or $p = 4$

So, the other root is 4.

46. G./ F/ 3

Switch the x and y values for function h, then solve for y to find the inverse function.

For $y = \sqrt{x-5}$ the inverse is $x = \sqrt{y-5}$.

Solve for y, the inverse function is,

$x = \sqrt{y-5}$

$x^2 = \sqrt{y-5}^2$

$x^2 = y - 5$

$y = x^2 + 5.$

The graph of the inverse function is a parabola that opens upward and has a minimum value of y = 5 so, the range is $y \geq 5$ or $[5,\infty)$ in interval notation.

47. B./ A/ 3

Using the points (–2, 0) and (0, –2), the solid line has a slope of $m = \dfrac{-2-0}{0-(-2)} = -1$ and a y-intercept of $b = -2$. Since the graph is also shaded below the solid line, the inequality less than or equal to is used and $y \leq -x - 2$. Using the points (–8, 0) and (0, 4), the dashed line has a slope of $m = \dfrac{4-0}{0-(-8)} = \dfrac{1}{2}$ and a y-intercept of $b = 4$. Since the graph is shaded below the dashed line, the strict inequality less than is used and $y < \dfrac{1}{2}x + 4$.

48. H./ IES–MDL/ 3

For 7 stereo systems at $25, Miles receives $25·7 =$125. He also gets 5% of the total of $2520, or $25 \times 7 + 0.05 \times 2520 = 301$ dollars for selling 7 stereo systems.

49. C./ A/ 2

Combining the products of the corresponding entries in the rows of first matrix with the entries in the 2nd matrix produce the 2 expressions on the left-hand side of the given system. For answer choice C you have,

$$\begin{bmatrix} 3 & 1 \\ 5 & -2 \end{bmatrix}\begin{bmatrix} x \\ y \end{bmatrix} = \begin{bmatrix} 3x + y \\ 5x - 2y \end{bmatrix}$$

The solution for both equations in the given system is written in matrix form as $\begin{bmatrix} 9 \\ 4 \end{bmatrix}$. So, the given system written in matrix form is $\begin{bmatrix} 3 & 1 \\ 5 & -2 \end{bmatrix}\begin{bmatrix} x \\ y \end{bmatrix} = \begin{bmatrix} 9 \\ 4 \end{bmatrix}$.

50. K./ G/ 2

$\angle ABC = \dfrac{1}{3}\angle DBC$ and $\angle ABC = \angle ABD + \angle DBC$. Substituting you get,

$$82° = \frac{1}{3}\angle DBC + \angle DBC$$

$$82° = \frac{4}{3}\angle DBC$$

$$\angle DBC = \frac{3}{4}\times 82°$$

$$\angle DBC = 61.5°$$

51. C./ G/ 3

Simplifying the expression using the trigonometric identities $1 + \tan^2 x = sec^2 x$ and $\cos^2 x + \sin^2 x = 1$ you get,

$$\frac{2\sec^2 x - 2\tan^2 x}{5\cos^2 x + 5\sin^2 x} = \frac{2(\sec^2 x - \tan^2 x)}{5(\cos^2 x + \sin^2 x)} = \frac{2(1)}{5(1)} = \frac{2}{5}.$$

Note that,

$$1 + \tan^2 x = sec^2 x$$
$$1 = sec^2 x - \tan^2 x$$

52. J./ IES/ 2

Graphing the function, you can see that the temperature, T increases in terms of weeks, w, but at a decreasing rate since the increase from one week to the next is decreasing.

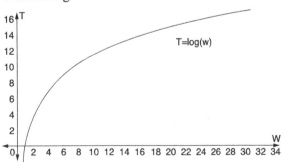

53. B./ G/ 2

Shifting A horizontally to the left 7 units takes A to $(3 - 7, 5) = (-4, 5)$.

Next reflecting the point $(-4, 5)$ across the y-axis changes the sign of the y-coordinate so, $(-4, 5)$ is reflected to $(-4, -5)$.

54. H./ S/ 3

Of the 42% of the men in the group 35% are given a placebo, so there is 35% of 42% or $0.35 \times 0.42 = 0.14$ or 0.15 probability of choosing a man that was given a placebo.

55. C./ G/ 2

Since $180° = \pi$ radians, use the conversion factor $1 = \dfrac{180°}{\pi \text{ radians}}$ to change θ to degrees.

$$\frac{21\pi \text{ radians}}{4} \times \frac{180°}{\pi \text{ radians}} = 945°.$$

To determine a coterminal angle for $945°$, subtract as many rotations as possible from $945°$.

$945° - 2\times 360° = 945° - 720° = 225°$. So, $225°$ is coterminal to $945°$.

56. G./ S/ 3

Converting the stem–leaf assignment scores to standard numbers, the set of scores is {52, x, 68, 73, 79, 79, 81, 85, 85, 85, 88, 92, 94, 98} where x is the unknown assignment score in the 60's.

The average, $\bar{x}$, is,

$$\bar{x} = \frac{52 + x + 68 + 73 + 79 + 79 + 81 + 85 + 85 + 85 + 88 + 92 + 94 + 98}{14}$$

$$80 = \frac{x + 1059}{14}$$

$$1120 = x + 1069$$

$$x = 61$$

So, there must be an assignment score of 61 for your average to be an 80, then $n = 1$.

57. A./ IES–MDL/ 3

Let x be the number of quarts that contain the 4% orange oil mixture, then the 4% mixture contains $0.04x$ quarts of orange oil. The 12% mixture contains $0.12\times 3 = 0.36$ quarts of orange oil. The 8% mixture contains $0.08(x + 3)$ quarts of orange oil.

The sum of the 4% mixture and 12% mixture produces the 8% mixture so,

$0.04x + 0.36 = 0.08(x + 3)$

$4x + 36 = 8(x + 3)$

$4x + 36 = 8x + 24$

$-4x = -12$

$x = 3$

3 quarts of the mixture containing 4% orange oil needs to be mixed.

58. G./ IES/ 3

We are looking for the side across from angle G, or side EF. Since $\triangle ABC \sim \triangle EFG$, the ratio of the corresponding sides of the 2 triangles are equal. Then,

$\dfrac{5}{g} = \dfrac{12}{8}$

$12g = 40$

$g = \dfrac{40}{12} = \dfrac{10}{3}$

59. C./ IES/ 3

Noah can plant $\dfrac{12}{1.5} = 8$ tomato plants an hour. Working together, Sophia and Noah can plant $16 + 8 = 24$ tomato plants per hour. Together it will take them $\dfrac{84}{24} = 3.5$ hours to plant 84 tomato plants.

60. K./ IES/ 3

Since CF is 3 parts of CE and FE is 1 part of CF so, CF is three-fourths of CE and FE is one-fourth of CE. This correlates to option J, CF = ¾CE

This page is intentionally left blank

Answers to Math Practice Test 3

			ANSWER KEY														
#	Key	Your Answer	#	Key	Your Answer	#	Key	Your Answer	#	Key	Your Answer	#	Key	Your Answer	#	Key	Your Answer
1	B		11	D		21	B		31	B		41	B		51	E	
2	J		12	J		22	G		32	G		42	G		52	H	
3	C		13	A		23	C		33	B		43	B		53	C	
4	H		14	G		24	G		34	G		44	F		54	F	
5	A		15	C		25	D		35	E		45	C		55	C	
6	F		16	F		26	K		36	F		46	G		56	J	
7	C		17	B		27	A		37	C		47	D		57	C	
8	H		18	H		28	H		38	H		48	G		58	F	
9	B		19	D		29	E		39	E		49	C		59	B	
10	K		20	G		30	F		40	J		50	H		60	G	

ANSWERS – TEST 3

Each problem number is followed with: **Correct answer/ Topic(s)/ Level of difficulty (1-3)**.

Legends: **N** = Numerical, **A** = Algebra, **F** = Functions, **G** = Geometry, **S** = Statistics and Probability, **IES** = Integrating Essential Skills, **M** = Modeling, **1** = Easy, **2** = Medium, **3** = Difficult

---

1. B./ A/ 1

Distributing and combining like terms you get,

$a^3 - 2ab + 5b - 2a^3 + 7ab - 2b^2 - 3b$
$= a^3 - 2a^3 - 2ab + 7ab - 2b^2 - 3b + 5b.$
$= -a^3 + 5ab - 2b^2 + 2b.$

Forgetting to distribute the negative values for a and b leads to combining terms that have the incorrect signs, leading to the other answer choices.

2. J./ A/ 2

In vertex form the equation of a parabola is $y = a(x-h)^2 + k$ where (h, k) is the vertex. Substituting you get,

$y = a(x+2)^2 + 4$.

Substitute (1,22) to find the value for a.

$22 = a(1+2)^2 + 4$
$22 = 9a + 4$
$9a = 18$
$a = 2$

So, $y = 2(x+2)^2 + 4$.

3. C./ IES/ 1

Since Marci counted 5 road signs in 2 minutes, she counts 2.5 road signs each minute. In 24 minutes, she counts $24 \times 1.5 = 36$ road signs. Choice A is a product of 2 minutes and 24 minutes. Choice B is the product of 5 road signs and 24 minutes. Neither choice considers the ratio of road signs counted per minute.

4. H./ G/ 2

$\angle ABC = \angle ADB + \angle CBD$. Let $\angle ABD = x$, then $\angle CBD = 3x - 11$ then,
$137 = x + (3x - 11)$
$137 = 4x - 11$
$4x = 148$
$x = 37$

So, $\angle CBD = 3 \times 48 - 11 = 100°$.

Remember, the drawings are stated to not be to scale, so don't assume choice J is correct just because $\angle CBD$ appears to be a right angle. Choice G is the measure of $\angle ABD$.

5. A./ N/ 3

Substituting the values for x and y,

$\dfrac{3 + \dfrac{1}{6}}{\dfrac{1}{3}} = \dfrac{\dfrac{19}{6}}{\dfrac{1}{3}} = \dfrac{19}{6} \times \dfrac{3}{1} = \dfrac{19}{2}$. Choice B does not consider

that you need to multiply the numerator by the reciprocal of the denominator. Choice C substitutes the $x = 6$ and $y = 3$ into the expression and multiplies the numerator and does not consider that you need to multiply the numerator by the reciprocal of the denominator.

6. F./ A/ 3

The slope of the line containing (5, 10) is,

$m = \dfrac{10-4}{5-3} = 3$

So, the slope of the perpendicular line containing (3, 4) is $m = -\dfrac{1}{3}$ and has an equation $y = -\dfrac{1}{3}x + 5$.

The equality holds when substituting (6, 3) into the equation of the line,

$3 = -\dfrac{1}{3}(6) + 5$
$3 = -2 + 5$
$3 = 3$

Choices H, I, and J are points on the line containing (5, 10).

7. C./ F/ 2

$f(3) = 3(3)^2 - 18 = 27 - 18 = 9$ and
$g(3) = 4(3) - 2(5 - 3) = 12 - 4 = 8$. Then,
$2f(3) - g(3) = 2(9) - 8 = 18 - 8 = 10$.

Choice A adds $g(3)$ to $2f(3)$ to arrive at 26, and choice D evaluates $2f(3)$ as $f(6)$ in order to get 82.

8. H./ G/ 2

Let D be the midpoint of $\overline{AC}$ and E be the midpoint of $\overline{BC}$, then $\overline{CD} = 12$ and $\overline{CE} = 9$ for right triangle $\triangle DEC$ shown below. Hypotenuse $\overline{DE}$ is the line segment joining midpoints D and E then,

$$\overline{DE}^2 = 9^2 + 12^2$$
$$\overline{DE}^2 = 225$$
$$\overline{DE} = 15$$

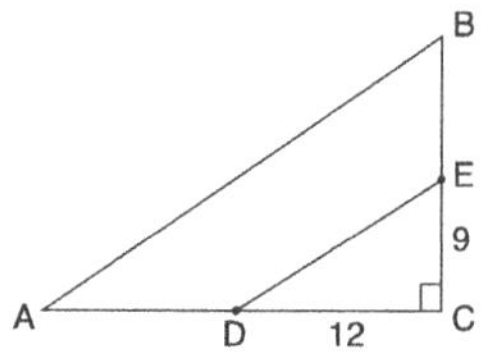

Choice I is the length of $\overline{AB}$.
Choice J is taking the average of sides $\overline{AC}$ and $\overline{BC}$.

9. B./ F/ 2

Using the formula for a geometric sequence, $a_n = a_1 r^{n-1}$ where $a_3 = 48$ and $a_1 = 3$ you get,

$$48 = 3r^{3-1}$$
$$48 = 3r^2$$
$$16 = r^2$$
$$r = 4$$

So, any term in the sequence can be found by using $a_n = 3(4)^{n-1}$. When $n = 10$, the 10th term is,

$$a_{10} = 3(4)^{10-1}$$
$$= 3(4)^9$$
$$= 786,432$$

Choice C is the 11th term in the sequence that was found using $3(4)^{10}$. Choices D and E are the 10th and 11th terms in the arithmetic sequence with the given terms.

10. K./ A/ 2

$16x^2 - 49$ is a difference of two perfect squares that can be factored using $a^2 - b^2 = (a-b)(a+b)$ where $a = 4x$ and $b = 7$ so,
$16x^2 - 49 = (4x-7)(4x+7)$.

11. D./ IES/ 1

The volume of the shed is a product of 3 lengths given in feet. Since 1 foot is $\frac{1}{3}$ of a yard, the volume in cubic feet can be multiplied by $\frac{1}{3} \times \frac{1}{3} \times \frac{1}{3} = \frac{1}{27}$ to convert the

volume to cubic yards. So, in cubic yards, the volume is $\frac{1}{27} \times 1080 = 360$. Choice A only uses the conversion factor of $\frac{1}{3}$ to convert to cubic yards. Choice D converts 1080 cubic yards to cubic feet by multiplying 1080 by 27.

12. J./ F/ 1

Converting an exponential expression to radical form using $x^{\frac{m}{n}} = \sqrt[n]{x^m}$ you get,

$2x^{\frac{5}{3}} = 2 \cdot \sqrt[3]{x^5}$ where $m = 5$ and $n = 3$. Choice J uses $m = 3$ and $n = 5$. The other choices incorrectly use the exponent laws.

13. A./ M/ 2

Let n be the number of appliances Julian sales for the given week. His gross salary for the week is his base salary plus the money he generates for selling n appliances. Then,

$$1250 = 350 + 25n$$
$$900 = 25n$$
$$n = 36$$

So, Julian sold a total of 36 appliances. Choice B only takes his gross salary and divides it by the money he receives for well an appliance.

14. G./ S/ 2

Since $\frac{4}{5}$ of the students in the survey do not like spinach, $\frac{1}{5}$ do. Also, since a student chosen at random can be chosen again, the probability that the 2nd student chosen at random is also $\frac{1}{5}$.
The events of choosing a student at random that likes spinach are independent of each other so, the multiplication property can be used to get a probability of $\frac{1}{5} \times \frac{1}{5} = \frac{1}{25}$ that both students chosen will like spinach.
Choice F is the probability that both students chosen do not like spinach, and choice C adds the H probabilities that both students like spinach.

15. C./ A/ 1

The coordinates of the points for the x and y-intercepts respectively are $(4, 0)$ and $(0, -9)$. Finding the slope using the 2 points, $m = \frac{-9-0}{0-4} = \frac{-9}{-4} = \frac{9}{4}$. Choice C is the difference in the y-coordinate divided by the difference in the x-coordinates. Choice B neglects a negative divided by a negative is a positive number.

16. F./ IES/ 2

As seen in the table, the oil is decreasing over the 5-minute interval. Since the difference in the temperatures from one minute to the next is getting larger, we say the rate of change in the difference in the temperatures is increasing so, choices G and H can be eliminated. There is no direct variation in the temperature in terms of time, and the temperature and time are not inversely proportional with each other so, choices J and I can be eliminated, leaving F as the correct choice.

17. B./ F/ 2

Let the component of $w = \langle w_1, w_2 \rangle$. Then,

$$u - v + w = \langle 9, 15 \rangle$$
$$\langle 5, 11 \rangle - \langle -8, 16 \rangle + \langle w_1, w_2 \rangle = \langle 9, 15 \rangle$$
$$\langle 5 - (-8) + w_1, 11 - 16 + w_2 \rangle = \langle 9, 15 \rangle$$

Combining the corresponding components for the vectors you have,

$$5 - (-8) + w_1 = 9 \quad \text{and} \quad 11 - 16 + w_2 = 15$$
$$13 + w_1 = 9 \qquad\qquad -5 + w_2 = 15$$
$$w_1 = -4 \qquad\qquad w_2 = 20$$

18. H./ G/ 2

The radius of the circle is 11. The horizontal line that intersects the center of the circle is on a diameter of the circle so, counting 11 units horizontally (along the x-axis) to the left and right of the center, two points on the circle and the line are, $(4 + 11, -5) = (15, -5)$ and $(4 - 11, -5) = (-7, -5)$. Choices I and J are points on the vertical line that passes through the center of the circle.

19. D./ A/ 3

Completing the square, you get,

$$x^2 + 16x + \left(\frac{16}{2}\right)^2 - \left(\frac{16}{2}\right)^2$$
$$= \left(x^2 + 16x + 64\right) - 64$$
$$= \left(x + 8\right)^2 - 64$$

20. G./ A/ 2

Solve for x.

$$z = yx^2 - y$$
$$z + y = yx^2$$
$$\frac{z + y}{y} = x^2$$
$$x = \sqrt{\frac{z + y}{y}}$$

21. B./ G/ 2

Find the radius to the circle using the given area,

$$9\pi = \pi r^2$$
$$9 = r^2$$
$$r = 3 \text{ inches}$$

So, the diameter is 6 inches. The diameter is also the hypotenuse of a right triangle which has both legs as the sides of the square in the figure. Using the Pythagorean Theorem to find the length of a side of the square you get,

$$s^2 + s^2 = 6^2$$
$$2s^2 = 36$$
$$s^2 = 18$$
$$s = \sqrt{18} = 3\sqrt{2}$$

So, the length of a side of the square is $3\sqrt{2}$ inches.

22. G./ N/ 1

Convert $\frac{4}{7}$ and 41% to standard numbers, then multiply the 3 values. $\frac{4}{7} \approx 0.571\, 41\% = 0.41$ then, $0.571 \times 0.41 \times 249 = 58.29$. Choice F considers that 0.571 or 0.41 was calculated using 0.0571 or 0.041. Choice I is the sum of the 3 numbers.

23. C./ F/ 2

The relationship between the weight Johnathan gained and the increase in calories is linear. The difference between any 2 values of weight gained divided by the difference between any 2-corresponding increase in calories is 0.002. For example, $\frac{0.8 - 0.4}{400 - 200} = 0.002$.

24. G./ F/ 1

The inverse of a function interchanges the domain and range values. The inverse of $f(x) = y$ is $g(y) = x$. So, $g(7) = 3$ since it is given that $f(3) = 7$. Performing the composition you have, $f(g(7)) = f(3) = 7$. Choice F is the product of $f(7)$ and $g(7)$ and choice H is the product of $f(3)$ and $g(7)$. Choice I appears to be a misinterpretation of the inverse as the reciprocal of the composition.

25. D./ S/ 2

Ordering the values in the set you have, $\{x, x, 2x, 3x, 5x, 6x, 7x, 10x\}$. The mode is the value that occurs most often, x. Since there are an even number of values in the set, the median is the average of the 2 most "middle" values, $3x$ and $5x$. So, the median is $4x$. The sum of the median and mode is $x + 4x = 5x$.

Choice A uses $5x$ as the median and choice C uses $3x$ as the median when finding the sum of the mode and median.

26. K./ F/ 2

The transformations for a function in the form $y = af(x - h) + k$, a stretches, compresses, or reflects the graph $y = f(x)$, h is a horizontal translation, and k is a vertical translation. Since the parent function is 3 units to the left, $h = -3$, and 5 units down means $k = -5$. Choice F can be eliminated since $a = 5$ represents a vertical stretch. Choices H and I can be eliminated since $h = 3$ represents a horizontal translation to the right 3 units.

27. A./ G/ 1

The center of the circle is $(-2, 6)$. The length of the radius can be found by counting from the center vertically or horizontally to a point on the circle so, $r = 4$. In the form $(x - h)^2 + (y - k)^2 = r^2$, the equation of the circle is $\left(x - (-2)\right)^2 + (y - 6)^2 = 4^2$ or $(x + 2)^2 + (y - 6)^2 = 16$. Choices B and C can be eliminated since $h = 2$. Choices D and E can be eliminated since the radius is not squared.

28. H./ IES/ 3

Let x be the number of ounces of frozen peas, then the total cost of peas is $0.03x$. The total cost of frozen carrots is $0.06 \times 14 = 0.84$. The total cost for the mixture of peas and carrots is $0.05(x + 14)$. Adding the frozen peas and carrots to get the mixture you have,

$$0.03x + 0.84 = 0.05(x + 14)$$
$$3x + 84 = 5(x + 14)$$
$$3x + 84 = 5x + 70$$
$$-2x = -14$$
$$x = 7$$

7 ounces of frozen peas need to be added.

29. E./ N/ 2

$\sqrt{-2} = \sqrt{-1 \cdot 2} = \sqrt{-1} \cdot \sqrt{2} = i\sqrt{2}$. Since $\left(4 + \sqrt{2}\right)$ and $(4 - \sqrt{2})$ are conjugates, you can multiply the 2 binomials by multiplying the first two terms and the last two terms, since the middle two terms will cancel out.

$$\left(4 + \sqrt{-2}\right)\left(4 - \sqrt{-2}\right)$$
$$= \left(4 + i\sqrt{2}\right)\left(4 - i\sqrt{2}\right)$$
$$= 4 \cdot 4 - i^2 \cdot 2$$
$$= 16 - (-1) \cdot 2$$
$$= 16 + 2$$
$$= 18$$

Choices A and B appear to take the product of $\sqrt{2}$ and $\sqrt{2}$ to get 4 for the imaginary part of the answer, and choice C seems to neglect $i^2 = -1$ when simplifying the 3rd step in the correct solution to get $16 - 2 = 14$.

30. F./ S/ 2

The absolute value inequality tells you that $3x - 7$ is greater than -11 and less than 11 so, placing $3x - 7$ between these values and solving the inequalities simultaneously,

$$|3x - 7| < 11$$
$$-11 < 3x - 7 < 11$$
$$-4 < 3x < 18$$
$$-\frac{4}{3} < x < 6$$

G can be eliminated since there is no value of x that can be greater than 6 and less than $-\frac{4}{3}$. Choices H and I can also be eliminated because their solutions pertain to an absolute value inequality $|3x - 7| > 11$ which is a disjunction.

31. B./ G/ 1

The measure of an inscribed angle is one-half the measure of the arc it inscribes in a circle. In the diagram, $\angle ACE$ inscribes $\overset{\frown}{ADE}$ then,

$$\angle ACE = \frac{1}{2}\overset{\frown}{ADE}$$
$$82 = \frac{1}{2}\overset{\frown}{ADE}$$
$$\overset{\frown}{ADE} = 164°$$

32. G./ G/ 2

When the pool is one-quarter full, there is 2500 gallons of water in it so, you need to pour 7500 gallons of water to fill it. Your water hose pours $20m$ gallons of water in m minutes, and your friends hose pours $30(m - 10)$ gallons of water. Pouring together,

$$20m + 30(m - 10) = 7500$$
$$20m + 30m - 300 = 7500$$
$$50m = 7800$$
$$m = 156$$

It takes 156 minutes to fill the pool.

33. B./ F/ 2

By the definition of a logarithm $\log_a x = y \Leftrightarrow x = a^y$ so, $M = a^b \Leftrightarrow \log_a M = b$ and $N = a^c \Leftrightarrow \log_a N = c$.

Expanding $\log_a\left(\dfrac{M^2}{N}\right) = \log_a M^2 - \log_a N = 2\log_a M - \log_a N$. Substituting, you have, $2\log_a M - \log_a N = 2b - c$.

34. G./ F/ 3

H can be eliminated since $(-1, -2)$ is not a point on the graph of $y = 6x - 5$. Choice I can be eliminated since the graph of the parabola $y = (x+1)^2 - 2$ cannot be perpendicular to the line $y = 6x - 5$. Graphing the 2 functions, you can see they intersect so, J can be eliminated. Also, the graphs show the functions intersect at only one point $(2, 7)$ so, they are tangent at that point. (Tangent means to touch once.)

35. E./ G/ 3

Combining the terms,
$$\frac{\sin x}{\cos x} + \frac{\cos x}{\sin x} = \frac{\sin x \sin x + \cos x \cos x}{\cos x \sin x}$$
$$= \frac{\sin^2 x + \cos^2 x}{\sin x \cos x} = \frac{1}{\sin x \cos x}.$$ (Remember the trigonometric identity $\sin^2 x + \cos^2 x = 1$.)

36. F./ S/ 1

The frequency table tells you there are 163 people that spend from 2 to 6 days at the hotel. 27 people spend more than 4 days (5 or 6 days) at the hotel so, the probability is $\dfrac{27}{163} = 0.17$. Choice G includes 4 nights spent when determining the probability, and choice H is the probability of less than 4 days.

37. C./ N/ 3

The sum, S_n, of an arithmetic sequence with n terms is $S_n = \dfrac{n}{2}(a_1 + a_n)$ where a_1 and a_n are the first and last terms respectively. Substituting and solving for n you get,

$$264 = \frac{n}{2}(9 + 39)$$
$$264 = 24n$$
$$n = 11$$

There are 11 terms. Choice A is the average of the two terms.

38. H./ N/ 2

Let x be the 2nd number, then $4 + x$ is the 1st number, and $2 + x$ is the 3rd number. The sum is,

$$(4 + x) + x + (2 + x) = 348$$
$$6 + 3x = 348$$
$$3x = 342$$
$$x = 114$$

So, the 1st number is 118, the 2nd is 114, and the third is 116. The sum of the numbers for choice G is 348 but the numbers do not meet the given conditions. Choices F, I, and J can be eliminated since their sum is not 348.

39. E./ G/ 1

The period can be determined for a sine wave by counting the horizontal distance from 1 high point to the next high point (maximum to maximum) on the graph. The horizontal distance from $(-3\pi, 5)$ to $(\pi, 5)$ is 4π units. To find the value for b use the formula for the period $period = \dfrac{2\pi}{|b|}$. Then,

$$4\pi = \frac{2\pi}{|b|}$$
$$4\pi|b| = 2\pi$$
$$b = \frac{1}{2}$$

Choice B is the period of the graph, and choice C is the period for $y = \sin(x)$ so, b would be 1. Choice E can be eliminated since a negative value for b reflects the graph across the y-axis.

40. J./ M/ 3

Let x be the length and y be the width of the rectangular pen. Using only one length for the length since the stone wall is used for the other length, the perimeter is

$200 = 2x + y$ then $y = 200 - 2x$. The area of the pen is,

$A = lw$

$A = x(200 - 2x)$

$A = -2x^2 + 200x$

The graph of the area function is a parabola that opens downward. Its vertex is the maximum point that gives the maximum area, Using $x = -\dfrac{b}{2a}$ where $a = -2$ and $b = 200$,

$x = -\dfrac{200}{2(-2)} = 50$ produces as maximum area of,

$A = -2(50) + 200(50)$

$\quad = -100 + 10,000$

$\quad = 9900$

The maximum area is 9900 square feet occurs when the width is 50 feet and the length is 100 feet.

41. B./ N/ 3

To rationalize the expression, multiply the numerator and denominator by the conjugate of $3 + \sqrt{5}$ and simplify.

$\dfrac{2}{3+\sqrt{5}} \cdot \dfrac{3-\sqrt{5}}{3-\sqrt{5}} = \dfrac{2\left(3-\sqrt{5}\right)}{9-5} = \dfrac{2\left(3-\sqrt{5}\right)}{4} = \dfrac{\left(3-\sqrt{5}\right)}{2}$

or $\dfrac{3}{2} - \dfrac{\sqrt{5}}{2}$. Choice C is incorrect since the numerator in the conjugate appears to be $3 + \sqrt{5}$. Choices D and E are incorrect since it appears the denominator in the conjugate appears to be $3 + \sqrt{5}$ and was incorrectly multiplied to $3 + \sqrt{5}$.

42. G./ G/ 2

A right triangle can be formed with sides 3 and 13 as shown in the figure below. Angle θ is the smallest angle formed the line and the x-axis. Using the trigonometric ratio for tangent, you get,

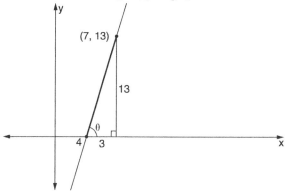

$\tan\theta = \dfrac{13}{3}$

$\theta = \tan^{-1}\left(\dfrac{13}{3}\right)$

$\theta = 77°$

Choice F is the largest angle that is formed by the line and the x-axis. It forms a linear pair with θ. Choice H uses the ratio $\dfrac{3}{13}$ when finding θ. Choice G considers the complement of choice G.

43. B./ A/ 2

The values for a and b must be factors of -15 and have a sum of -2.

$-5 \times 3 = -15$ and $-5 + 3 = -2$ so, the values for a and b are -5 and 3. Theirs average is 1. Choice D is the average of -3 and 5. Choice A is the distance between -5 and 3. Choice C is the difference between -5 and 3.

44. F./ A/ 1

The shaded portion of the number line includes x values $-6 < x \leq 1$ or $x \geq 3$. The open circle around -6 indicates that is not shaded and therefore should not be included in the solution set.

45. C./ A/ 3

Rewrite $(x-2)^{-1}$ as $\dfrac{1}{x-2}$ and combine the terms.

$\dfrac{2}{x-1} + (x-2)^{-1}$

$= \dfrac{2}{x-1} + \dfrac{1}{x-2}$

$= \dfrac{2(x-2) + (x-1)}{(x-1)(x-2)}$

$= \dfrac{3x-5}{(x-1)(x-2)}$

Choice A neglects to correctly distribute $2(x - 2)$ in the 2nd step of the correct solution. Choice B has the correct denominator but, combines the numerators of 2 and 1 in the 1st step of the correct solution.

46. G./ F/ 2

Let t be the time, in hours, it takes Nick to catch up with Karen. The distance Karen walks is $3t$, and the distance Nick walks is $15(t - \dfrac{1}{6})$ where 10 minutes is $\dfrac{1}{6}$ of an hour. Nick catches Karen when their distances are equal so.

$$3t = 15\left(t - \frac{1}{6}\right)$$

$$3t = 15t - \frac{5}{2}$$

$$-12t = -\frac{5}{2}$$

$$t = \frac{5}{24} \text{ hours}$$

Converting to minutes, Nick catches up in $\frac{5}{24} \times 60 = 12.5$ minutes.

47. D./ F/ 2

Let's focus on transforming the vertex for the graph of f to the graph of g. Reflecting the graph of f across the x-axis first moves the vertex of the graph to $(3, -4)$. Next shifting the graph transformed graph of f to the left 6 units moves the vertex to $(-3, -4)$. Finally, shifting the transformed graph of f up 6 units takes the vertex to $(-3, 2)$ which is the vertex for the graph of g.

48. G./ F/ 2

The range for the parent function $y = \sqrt{x}$ is $y \geq 0$. Reflecting the parent function across the x-axis, gives you $y = -\sqrt{x}$ which has a range of $y \leq 0$. Shifting $y = -\sqrt{x}$ up 3 units, gives you $y = -\sqrt{x} + 3$ which moves the range of $y \leq 0$ up 3 units to $y \leq 3$.

Choice F has the correct values, but the smaller value must be listed first when using interval notation. Choice H only considers the range for the parent function and choice I only considers the reflection of the parent function when determining the range.

49. C./ G/ 2

It will probably be easier to find the coterminal angle in degrees before converting it to radians. Subtracting 2 complete rotations (1 rotation = $360°$) to $765°$ will produce a coterminal angle. Now,
$765° - 2(360°) = 765° - 720° = 45°$.

Converting to radian using $\dfrac{\pi}{180°}$ you get, $\overset{1}{\cancel{45°}} \times \dfrac{\pi}{\underset{4}{\cancel{180°}}}$
$= \dfrac{\pi}{4}$.

50. H./ G/ 1

The parallelogram could be a square, but the sides must be equal, so choice F must be eliminated. The

diagonals of a rhombus are perpendicular, but the sides are also equal, so choice G is eliminated. A circle is not a quadrilateral, so choice I can be eliminated. The diagonals of a rectangle are perpendicular and opposite sides are congruent as in a parallelogram, so choice H is the correct response.

51. E./ IES/ 1

Joint variation is where on quantity varies directly with the product of 2 other quantities. Choice A is a product of quantities n and s but the constant of variation is $\frac{1}{3}$. Only choice E multiplies the constant of variation of 3 to the product of quantities n and s.

52. H./ N/ 3

Setting the numerators and denominators equal gives you the system of equations,
$$2p - q = 8$$
$$p + 2q = 9$$
Multiply the first equation by 2 and use the elimination method to find p,

$$2(2p - q = 8)$$
$$\underline{p + 2q = 9}$$
$$4p - 2q = 16$$
$$\underline{p + 2q = 9}$$
$$5p = 25$$
$$p = 5$$

Substituting $p = 5$ into the first equation you get,
$$2(5) - q = 8$$
$$10 - q = 8$$
$$q = 2$$

The product of p and q is $5 \times 2 = 10$.

53. C./ N /2

Most scientific calculators will convert an answer for an operation to scientific notation when the value has more than 10 digits. Inputting the product of the two numbers into a calculator you get $1,000,000 \times 3,200,000 = 3.2 \times 10^{12}$ which is choice C. Choice B is correct, but not in scientific notation.

54. F./ G/ 3

Since you are given two sides and an included angle for the triangle, you can use the law of cosines to find the side opposite the included angle, $\overline{BC}$. Now,

172

$$\overline{BC}^2 = 19^2 + 24^2 - 2(19)(24)\cos 32°$$

$$\overline{BC}^2 = 361 + 576 - 773.42$$

$$\overline{BC}^2 = 163.58$$

$$\overline{BC} = 12.8$$

Choice I assumes angle C is a right angle, so the Pythagorean Theorem was used to find $\overline{BC}$. Choice I incorrectly uses the law of sines to find $\overline{BC}$. You need to know either side-side-angle or angle-angle-side to use the law of sines. Choice J assumes $\triangle ABC$ is an isosceles triangle where $\overline{BC} = \overline{AC}$.

55. C./ A/ 2

Before finding the vertical asymptotes, the equation must be simplified.

$$y = \frac{(x+3)(x-4)}{x^2-16} = \frac{(x+3)\cancel{(x-4)}}{(x+4)\cancel{(x-4)}} = \frac{(x+3)}{(x+4)}$$

Setting the denominator equal to zero to find the vertical asymptote you get, $x = -4$.

The horizontal asymptote is found by comparing the coefficients of the highest degreed terms in the numerator and denominator. Any other terms are ignored. Expanding the numerator you have,

$$y = \frac{(x+3)(x-4)}{x^2-16} = \frac{x^2-x-12}{x^2-16}$$

Comparing the highest degreed terms, you get $y = \frac{x^2}{x^2} = 1$. So, $y = 1$ is the horizontal asymptote.

The sum of -4 and 1 is -3. Choice A takes the sum of horizontal asymptotes as -3 and 4 but neglects to find the vertical asymptotes. Choice D is the sum of 3, -4 and -16. Choice E is the sum of -3, 4, and 16.

56. J./ N/ 2

A proper fraction is a number between 0 and 1. Choosing $\frac{1}{4}$ as our proper fraction choice I is the only expression that produces a value greater than 1. Substituting you get,

$$\frac{1}{\frac{1}{4}} = 1 \times \frac{4}{1} = 4$$

Squaring or cubing $\frac{1}{4}$ only makes its value smaller for choices G and H. Taking the square root of $\frac{1}{4}$ makes its value larger, $\sqrt{\frac{1}{4}} = \frac{1}{2}$, but still less than 4.

57. C./ G/ 2

It is probably fastest to use coordinate trigonometry where $\sin\theta = \frac{y}{r}$, $\cos\theta = \frac{x}{r}$ and $r^2 = x^2 + y^2$ to find $\cos\theta$. Since θ is in the 3rd quadrant in the standard (x, y) coordinate plane, $y = -1$ and $r = 2$. Then,

$$2^2 = x^2 + (-1)^2$$

$$4 = x^2 + 1$$

$$x^2 = 3$$

$$x = \pm\sqrt{3}$$

Again, since θ is in the 3rd quadrant, in the standard (x, y) coordinate plane, $x = -\sqrt{3}$ and $\cos\theta = -\frac{\sqrt{3}}{2}$. Choice B considers θ to be in either the 1st or 4th quadrant where the values for x are positive.

58. F./ S/ 1

You only need the mean, $\bar{x}$, and the number of elements, n in set B to find its sum, S. The formula to find the mean is $\bar{x} = \frac{S}{n}$. Now, the mean for set A is,

$$\bar{x} = \frac{7+21+11+9+1+3+11}{7} = \frac{63}{7} = 9.$$ So, the mean for set B is also 9. Then,

$$9 = \frac{S}{13}$$

$$S = 9 \times 13$$

$$S = 117$$

The sum for set B is 117. Choice H uses the mode of 11 when calculating the sum.

59. B./ G/ 2

Since $\triangle ABC \sim \triangle DEF$ you have $\frac{a}{d} = \frac{b}{e} = \frac{c}{f}$. Substituting the given values, you get,

$$\frac{4}{2} = \frac{9}{e}$$

$$4e = 18$$

$$e = \frac{18}{4} \text{ or } \frac{9}{2}$$

Choice C appears to use one of the ratios incorrectly such as $\frac{e}{9}$ instead of $\frac{9}{e}$. Choices D and E also appear to use the ratios incorrectly where $e=\frac{b}{a}$ and $e=\frac{a}{b}$ for choice D and E respectively.

60. G./ A/2

The roots of -3 and 4 mean $x=-3$ and $x=4$. Working backwards from the factoring method for a quadratic expression you get,

$x+3=0$ or $x-4=0$

$(x+3)(x-4)=0$

$x^2-4x+3x-12=0$

$x^2-x-12=0$

So, the expression is x^2-x-12. Choice F uses factors of $(x-3)(x+4)=0$, and choice J uses $(x-3)(x-4)=0$ while incorrectly multiplying -3 and -4 to get -12.

Answers to Math Practice Test 4

ANSWER KEY																			
#	Key	Your Answer	#	Key	Your Answer	#	Key	Your Answer	#	Key	Your Answer	#	Key	Your Answer	#	Key	Your Answer
1	B		11	C		21	A		31	C		41	C		51	D	
2	J		12	G		22	G		32	J		42	J		52	G	
3	D		13	E		23	D		33	B		43	A		53	B	
4	F		14	G		24	H		34	H		44	J		54	G	
5	C		15	C		25	E		35	A		45	B		55	C	
6	G		16	G		26	J		36	J		46	J		56	J	
7	C		17	D		27	C		37	E		47	B		57	A	
8	H		18	F		28	G		38	H		48	F		58	F	
9	B		19	A		29	B		39	B		49	D		59	B	
10	F		20	H		30	G		40	H		50	F		60	H	

ANSWERS – TEST 4

Each problem number is followed with: **Correct answer/ Topic(s)/ Level of difficulty (1-3)**.

Legends: **N** = Numerical, **A** = Algebra, **F** = Functions, **G** = Geometry, **S** = Statistics and Probability, **IES** = Integrating Essential Skills, **M** = Modeling, **1** = Easy, **2** = Medium, **3** = Difficult

---

1. B./ A/ 2

   Distribute $-x$ and $-y$ to get,

   $$(x^3 - 2xy + 4x) - x(3x^2 - 2xy) - y(2x^2 - 7)$$
   $$= x^3 - 2xy + 4x - 3x^3 + 2x^2y - 2x^2y + 7y$$
   $$= (x^3 - 3x^3) - 2xy + 4x + 7y$$
   $$= -2x^3 - 2xy + 4x + 7y$$

   The other answer choices distribute the $-x$ and $-y$ incorrectly.

2. J./ A/ 1

   Put the parallel line in slope-intercept form, $y = mx + b$ where m is the slope to find the slope of the other line.

   $$2x - 3y = 7$$
   $$-3y = -2x + 7$$
   $$y = \frac{-2}{-3}x + \frac{7}{-3}$$
   $$y = \frac{2}{3}x - \frac{7}{3}$$

   So, $m = \frac{2}{3}$ is the slope of the line containing $(4, -7)$. The point is not needed to find the slope. Choice H is slope of the perpendicular line. Choice J is the y-intercept of the parallel line.

3. D./ A/ 1

   The 1st part of the solution set is the shaded region from negative infinity to 3, and the 2nd part is the shaded region from 1 to 6. The inequality in the solution set includes the equal sign whenever the number is filled in. Or is used between each inequality to indicate that a number can be in either of the solutions sets but not both.

4. F./ IES/ 2

   The perimeter of a square with side s, $P = 4s$. So, $s = \frac{P}{4}$. The area of a square is $A = s^2$. Substituting the equation of the perimeter into the area you have,

   $A = \left(\frac{P}{4}\right)^2 = \frac{P^2}{16}$. Choice G fails to square 4 in the substituted area formula. Choices I and J can be eliminated since they use $A = \sqrt{s}$ as the area of a square.

5. C./ A/ 2

   Substitute 19 for $g(x)$ and solving for x,

   $$19 = 2x^2 - 3x + 5$$
   $$0 = 2x^2 - 3x - 14$$
   $$0 = (2x - 7)(x + 2)$$
   $$2x - 7 = 0 \text{ or } x + 2 = 0$$
   $$x = \frac{7}{2} \text{ or } x = -2$$

   $x = -2$ is the chosen value.

6. G./ G/ 1

   The sum of the angles for $\triangle ABC$ is $180°$. Combining the angles, you get,

   $$\angle BAC + 124° + 25° = 180°$$
   $$\angle BAC + 149° = 180°$$
   $$\angle BAC = 31°$$

   $\angle BAC$ and $\angle CAE$ form a linear pair so,

   $$\angle BAC + \angle CAE = 180°$$
   $$31° + \angle CAE = 180°$$
   $$\angle CAE = 149°$$

   Choice F is the measure of the angle at A inside of the triangle.

7. C./ IES/ 2

   You have $\frac{1}{2} \times 18 = 9$ gallons of gasoline when you decide to take a trip. You have $\frac{1}{3} \times 9 = 3$ gallons of gasoline left in the tank when you are at the gas station, so you will need to put $18 - 3 = 15$ gallons of gasoline to fill the car. Choice A appears to only calculate the amount of gasoline you have left in the tank when you are at the gas station.

8. H./ N/ 3

   Substituting m and n into the expression you have,

   $$\frac{\frac{1}{4}}{4+\frac{2}{3}}=\frac{\frac{1}{4}}{\frac{14}{3}}=\frac{1}{4}\times\frac{3}{14}=\frac{3}{56}.$$

   Choice I takes the product of $\frac{1}{14}$ and $\frac{14}{3}$. Choice F multiplies m and n in the denominator of the expression instead of adding. Choice J substitutes $\frac{2}{3}$ into the numerator for n.

9. B./ S/ 2

   Of the graduating class, $0.60\times250=150$ are male. Of the males in the graduating class, $0.82\times150=123$ will attend a four-year college. So, the probability that a person chosen in the graduating class will be male that attends a four-year college is $\frac{123}{250}=0.49.$ Note that 82% of 60% is $0.82\times0.60=0.49.$

10. F./ A /2

    Since f is linear you can write its equation in the slope-intercept form, $y=mx+b$ to find f (10). Recall, a point in function notation $f(x)=y$ has coordinates of $(x,\,f\,(x))$.

    The slope is $m=\dfrac{9-(-6)}{5-2}=5.$ Using the first given point the equation of the line for f is,

    $y-(-6)=5(x-2)$
    $y=5x-10-6$
    $y=5x-16$

    So, f (10) is $y=5(10)-16=50-16=34$. Choice G incorrectly writes the equation of the line for f as $y=5x+16$. Choice H uses a slope of $\frac{1}{5}$ when determining the equation of the line for f.

11. C./ A/ 1

    In the form $y=af(x-h)+k,$ h is a horizontal translation. If $h>0$, the graph of the parent function $y=f(x)$ is translated right h units, and left h units if $h<0$. Choice D considers that $h=-4$.

12. G./ N /1

    In standard form 32% $=0.32$ and $\frac{1}{5}=0.2$. Multiplying the 3 values you have, $0.32\times0.2\times152=9.728$ or 9.73.

Choice A uses 32 for 32% when multiplying the 3 values. Choice I uses 2 for $\frac{1}{5}$ when multiplying the 3 values.

13. E./ A/ 2

    Completely factoring x^5-16x you have,

    $$x^5-16x=x(x^4-16)=x\left(x^2-4\right)\left(x^2+4\right)$$
    $$=x(x-2)(x+2)\left(x^2+4\right).$$

    Every choice is present except $\left(x^2-4\right)$, which are factored further.

14. G./ G/ 1

    The 3 graphs must have a common point of intersection to be a solution for the system. The circle and ellipse intersect at 4 points, so choice I can be eliminated, but the circle, ellipse, and line only intersect at 2 points so choice G is correct.

15. C./ IES/ 2

    The total income generated from the sales is $1.53x$. Since the sales of the 3-ringed binder must be greater than the cost to realize a profit you have, $1.53x>1.15x+475$, so $0.38x-475>0$. Choices A and D are equivalent as well as choices B and E.

16. G./ G/ 2

    From 0 to $\frac{\pi}{2}$ sine increases from 0 to 1 and cosine decreases from 1 to 0. At $\frac{\pi}{4}$ sine and cosine are equal in value, then sine continues to increase while cosine continues to decrease.

17. D./ N/ 3

    Multiplying by the conjugate of the denominator you have, $\dfrac{3+i}{2-i}\times\dfrac{2+i}{2+i}=\dfrac{(3+i)(2+i)}{4-i^2}=\dfrac{6+5i+i^2}{4+1}=$

    $\dfrac{6+5i-1}{5}=\dfrac{5+5i}{5}=1+i.$ Choice A uses $+1$ for i^2.

    Choice E neglects to divide the numerator by 5 when simplifying the answer.

18. F./ S/ 2

    The mode is 51 and the means is,

    $$\frac{42+44+47+51+51+54+60+62+64+65+71+73}{12}=57.$$

    So, the difference is $57-51=6$. Choice J uses the median of 57 as the mode when finding the difference. Choice I calculates the mean as 57 when finding the difference.

19. A./ F/ 2

For the composition $f(g(-3))$ substitute the value for $g(-3)$ into the x value for f. Now, $f(g(-3)) = f(2(-3) + 1) = f(-5) = \sqrt{(-5)^2 + 4} = \sqrt{25 + 4} = \sqrt{29}$. Choice B incorrectly evaluates $f(-3)$ as $f(x) = \sqrt{-3^2 + 4} = \sqrt{-5} = i\sqrt{5}$, then takes the product of $f(-3)$ and $g(-3)$. Choice C is the product of $f(-3)$ and $g(-3)$. Choice E is the sum of $f(-3)$ and $g(-3)$.

20. H./ A/ 1

The slope of $y = 2$ is zero since it is the graph of a horizontal line. The graph of $y = 3$ is also a horizontal line, so its slope is also zero. Choice I is a vertical line passing through the x-axis at 2, and would be perpendicular instead. Choices F, G, and J all have slopes that are not zero, but are defined.

21. A., G, 2

Without having to write the equation of the circle, you can transform the center horizontally or vertically (but not both) to find points on the graph of the circle. Counting to the right 4 units from the center, the point $(3 + 4, 5) = (7, 5)$ is on the circle. Choice C is incorrect since the centered is transformed horizontally right and vertically upwards 4 units. Choice D transforms the center to the left 4 units but also transforms it 4 units downward.

22. G./ G/ 2

Use the trigonometric identity $\cot x = \dfrac{\cos x}{\sin x}$ to simplify the given expression.

$$\dfrac{\sin x \cot x}{\cos^2 x} = \dfrac{\sin x \cdot \dfrac{\cos x}{\sin x}}{\cos^2 x} = \sin x \cdot \dfrac{\cos x}{\sin x} \cdot \dfrac{1}{\cos^2 x} = \dfrac{1}{\cos x} = \sec x.$$ Choice F is the reciprocal function for $\sin x$. Choice F simplifies the expression incorrectly to $\dfrac{\sin x}{\cos x} = \tan x$.

23. D./ S/ 2

Thirty students took only an advanced math course, since 45 of the 75 students that took an advanced math course also took an English course. So, the probability that a student only to an advanced course is $\dfrac{30}{155} = 0.19$. Choice C is the probability that a student took an advanced took course. Choice E is the probability that a student took an English course.

24. H./ A/ 2

Factoring choice H using $(a + b)(a^2 - ab + b^2)$ where $a = x$ and $b = 3$ you have, $(x + 3)(x^2 - x \cdot 3 + 3^2) = (x + 3)(x^2 - 3x + 9)$ so, $x + 3$ is a factor. Choices F and G do not factor. The factors of Choice J are $(2x - 9)(x + 1)$.

25. E./ A/ 2

Since the bacteria is doubling in value, F can be represented by an exponential function, $F = P(a)^h$ where P is the initial amount, h is the time, in hours, it takes for P to grow by a. Substituting $P = \dfrac{1}{10}$, $a = 2$, you get $F = \dfrac{1}{10}(2)^h$.

26. J./ G/ 2

Two chords that intersect in the interior of a circle form 4 angles each having a measure that is the average of the arc it intercepts and the arc that its opposite angle intercepts.

So, $\angle BFC = \dfrac{\overset{\frown}{ADE} + \overset{\frown}{BGC}}{2} = \dfrac{104° + 82°}{2} = 93°$. Choice H one-half of the difference of the two intercepted arcs. Choices F and G only take the measures of the intercepted arcs into account.

Two chords that intersect in the interior of a circle form 4 angles each having a measure that is the average of the arc it intercepts and the arc that its opposite angle intercepts.

27. C./ N/ 1

Using the rules for exponents, simplify the right side of the equation to get, $\left(x^2 \cdot x^3\right)^{-1} \left(x^4\right)^3 = \left(x^5\right)^{-1} \cdot x^{12} = x^{-5} \cdot x^{12} = x^7$. So, $n = 7$. Choice A incorrectly simplifies $\left(x^4\right)^3$ to x^{-5} before combining it to x^{-5}. Choice C incorrectly simplifies $\left(x^2 \cdot x^3\right)^{-1}$ to x^{-6} before combining it to x^{12}.

28. G./ G/ 2

The formula for the nth term in an arithmetic sequence is $a_n = a_1 + d(n - 1)$ where a_1 is the 1st term and d is the common difference in consecutive terms. Substituting $a_1 = 4$ and $a_4 = -5$ where $n = 4$,

$$-5 = 4 + d(4 - 1)$$
$$-5 = 4 + 3d$$
$$3d = -9$$
$$d = -3$$

So, $a_n = 4 - 3(n-1)$, and $a_{10} = 4 - 3(10-1) = 4 - 27 = -23$. Choice F is the 9th term and choice H is the 11 term. Choice I uses a common difference of positive 3 when finding the 10th term and choice J is the 9th term when $d = 3$.

29. B./ N /1

Put the values in standard form to compare them. $\frac{11}{6} = 1.83$ and $173\% = 1.73$. So, in increasing order you have 173%, 1.80, $\frac{11}{6}$. Choice C lists the values in descending order. The other choices incorrectly order the numbers.

30. G./ N/ 2

Solving the inequality, you have,

$$|2x - 6| = 18$$
$$2x - 6 = -18 \text{ or } 2x - 6 = 18$$
$$2x = -12 \quad \text{or} \quad 2x = 24$$
$$x = -6 \quad \text{or} \quad x = 12$$

The difference in the absolute values of the solutions is, $|-6| - |12| = 6 - 12 = -6$ or $|12| - |-6| = 12 - 6 = 6$ so, choice D is correct. Choice F finds the absolute value of the difference in the solutions to get $|-6 - 12| = |-18| = 18|$.

31. C./ N /2

The set is called the Fibonacci sequence where each term is the sum of its 2 preceding terms. So $a_{10} = 21 + 34 = 55$, $a_{11} = 34 + 55 = 89$, and $a_{12} = 55 + 89$. Choice A is the 11th term and choice B is the 13th term in the sequence.

32. J./ IES/2

One pound = 0.454 kilograms so, 103 pounds = 103 × 0.454 = 46.76 kilograms. At \$0.55 per kilograms, 103 pounds costs 46.76 × 0.55 = \$25.71.

33. B./ A/ 2

$y = -\frac{1}{2}x + 3$ is the dashed line since it has a y-intercept of 3, and $y = x - 2$ is the solid line since it has a y-intercept of –2. The solution set is shaded below both lines so less than should replace equal to for $y = -\frac{1}{2}x + 3$ and less than or equal to should replace equal to for $y = x - 2$.

34. H./ N/ 3

Rationalizing you have, $\frac{x}{1-\sqrt{2}} \cdot \frac{1+\sqrt{2}}{1+\sqrt{2}} = \frac{x(1+\sqrt{2})}{1-2} = \frac{x(1+\sqrt{2})}{-1} = -x - x\sqrt{2}$. The denominators for choice F rationalize the denominator as $(1-\sqrt{2})(1+\sqrt{2}) = 1 + 2 = 3$ The denominators for choice G rationalize the denominator as $(1-\sqrt{2})(1+\sqrt{2}) = 1 - 4 = -3$.

35. A./ G/ 1

$\angle ACE$ and $\angle ECB$ form a linear pair so, $\angle ACE + \angle ECB = 180°$. Substituting you have,

$$x - 13 + 3x + 25 = 180$$
$$4x + 12 = 180$$
$$4x = 168$$
$$x = 42$$

So, $\angle ACE = 42 - 13 = 29°$ and $\angle ECB = 3 \cdot 42 + 25 = 151°$. Choice B is the value for x. Choice D is the measure of the larger angle.

36. J./ A/ 2

Since $x = 2$ is an x-intercept $y = 0$. Substitute to get,

$$0 = 2^2 + b \cdot 2 - 12$$
$$0 = 4 + 2b - 12$$
$$2b = 8$$
$$b = 4$$

Choice G is the other x-intercept for the graph of the function. Choice J mistakenly set $2b = -12$ for the solution shown above.

37. E./ F/ 2

You can substitute $x = 0$ to get, $g(0) = f(0 + 4) - 1 = f(4) + 1 = -5 - 1 = -6$. Also, transforming $(4, -5)$ for the graph of f 4 units to the left and 1 unit down you get the point to the graph of g at $(0, -6)$.

38. H./ G/ 2

The period for $y = a\cos(bx) + k$ is $\frac{2\pi}{|b|}$, where $b = \frac{1}{4}$ so, the period for the graph is,

$$\frac{2\pi}{\left|\frac{1}{4}\right|} = 2\pi \cdot \frac{4}{1} = 8\pi.$$

G only considers the fundamental period for cosine (when $b = 1$). Choice J uses $b = 4$ when determining the period.

39. B./ G/ 3

The measure of the 3rd and in the triangle is $180° - 40° - 22° = 118°$. Using the law of sines to find the side opposite 40 degrees you get,

$$\frac{x}{\sin 40°} = \frac{7}{\sin 22°}$$

$$x = \frac{7}{\sin 22°} \times \sin 40°$$

$$x = 12.01$$

So, the perimeter is $7 + 15 + 12.01 = 34.01$.

Choice A uses the Pythagorean theorem to find the 3rd side by assuming the angle opposite the side length of 15 is a right angle. Choice B uses the cosine function instead of the sine function when calculating the 3rd side using the law of sines. Choice D incorrectly uses the law of sines by setting the ratio as $\frac{x}{\sin 22°} = \frac{7}{\sin 40°}$.

40. H./ F/ 2

$g(3) = 2$ since $f(2) = 3$, then composing the functions, $f(g(3)) = f(2) = 3$.

Choice F multiples $f(2)$ and $g(3)$. Choice G multiplies $g(2)$ and $g(3)$.

41. C./ S/ 2

The probability of answering any one question correctly is $\frac{1}{4}$. Each question is answered independently so each probability is multiplied to get $\frac{1}{4} \times \frac{1}{4} \times \frac{1}{4} \times \frac{1}{4} \times \frac{1}{4} = \frac{1}{1024}$. Choice A adds the denominator of each probability for each question.

42. J./ F/1

Reflecting (4, 8) across the y-axis changes the sign of the x-coordinate so the point transforms to (–4, 8). Translating (–4, 8) up 3 units changes the y-coordinate to (–4, 8 + 3) = (–4, 11). Choice F reflects the point across the x-axis and up 3 units. Choice G reflects the point across the x-axis then to the right 3 units. Choice J reflects the point across the y-axis then down 3 units.

43. A./ IES/ 2

One rotation of the wheel encompasses the circumference of the wheel so, $C = 2\pi(6) = 12\pi$. Rotating 20 then $12\pi \times 20 = 753.98$ inches or 62.83 feet which

is approximately 63 feet. Choice B incorrectly uses 6π as the circumference of the wheel. Choice C uses the area of the circle to determine its circumference.

44. J./ G/ 2

Simplify the left side of the equation before set the corresponding component on the left and right side of the equation equal.

$$2\langle 5,3 \rangle - \langle v_1, v_2 \rangle = \langle 7,-2 \rangle$$

$$\langle 10,6 \rangle - \langle v_1, v_2 \rangle = \langle 7,-2 \rangle$$

$$\langle 10 - v_1, 6 - v_2 \rangle = \langle 7,-2 \rangle$$

Now, $10 - v_1 = 7$ and $6 - v_2 = -2$. So, $v_1 = 3$ and $v_2 = 8$. The sum of the component is 11.

Choice F and G only consider the components of V. Choice I sets $10 - v_1 = -2$ and $6 - v_2 = 7$ then finds the difference between v_1 and v_2.

45. B./ A/ 2

The pool collects $2.75a$ dollars in adult entrance fees and $1.75c$ dollars for children entrance fees. So, $2.75a + 1.75c = 271.75$. The number of people that were swimming was 130 so, $a + c = 130$.

46. J./ A/ 2

Use the difference of cubes $(a+b)(a^2 - ab + b^2)$ to factor $8x^3 - 125$ where $a = 2x$ and $b = 5$. Then, $8x^3 - 125 = (2x - 5)((2x)^2 + 2x \cdot 5 + 5^2) = (2x - 5)(4x^2 + 10x + 25)$. So, choice I, $4x^2 + 10x + 25$ is the correct choice. Choices F and H use $(a-b)(a^2 + ab + b^2)$ to factor the given expression.

47. B./ IES/ 3

Let x be the number of quarts of the 5% sugar solution to be added. So, $0.05x$ is the number of quarts of sugar in the 5% solution. The 8% sugar solution contains $0.08 \times 2 = 0.16$ quarts of sugar. Mixing the solutions to make a solution that is 7% sugar will have $0.07(x + 2)$ quarts of sugar. Now,

$$0.05x + 0.16 = 0.07(x+2)$$

$$5x + 16 = 7(x+2)$$

$$5x + 16 = 7x + 14$$

$$-2x = -2$$

$$x = 1$$

1quart of the 5% solution needs to be added.

48. F./ G/ 1

Substitute the center of the circle (5 ,3) into the answer choices to see which equation is a solution. Substituting the center into $y = 2x - 7$ you get,

$3 = 2(5) - 7$

$3 = 10 - 7$

$3 = 3$

So, choice F is the correct choice. The other answer choices do not yield an equality when substituting the center.

49. D./ G/ 2

The hypotenuse of the triangle is the length of a side of the square. Using the Pythagorean theorem,

$hyp^2 = 9^2 + 12^2$

$hyp^2 = 81 + 144$

$hyp^2 = 225$

$hyp = 15$

You may instead note the triangle is a multiple of a 3-4-5 triangle so $3 \times 3 = 9, 4 \times 3 = 12$, and $5 \times 3 = 15$. The perimeter of the deck is $9 + 12 + 15 + 15 + 15 = 66$ feet. Choice A is the area of the deck and choice E adds all 4 sides of the square when determining the perimeter of the deck.

50. F./ A/ 2

Using the properties of logarithms, $\log_x 16 = 4$ then $x^4 = 16$ so, $x = 2$, and $\log_2 32 = y$ then $2^y = 32$ so, $y = 5$. Then, $5^2 = 25$. Choice G calculates the expression as 2^5. Choice H is the product of 2 and 5.

51. D./ A/ 2

Substitute $n = 5$ into the absolute value inequality and solve for m.

$|m + 1| < 5$

$-5 < m + 1 < 5$

$-6 < m < 4$

Choice C is considering that $|m| > 0$. Choice E is a false statement since there is no value for m that is greater than 4 and less than –6.

52. G./ S/ 2

Let n be the 5th score. The formula for the average is $\dfrac{85 + 85 + 75 + 92 + n}{5} = 84$. Solving for n you have,

$\dfrac{85 + 85 + 75 + 92 + n}{5} = 84$

$\dfrac{337 + n}{5} = 84$

$337 + n = 440$

$n = 83$

Choice H is the median of the given scores.

53. B./ N /2

Using the one-to-one equality, the exponents are equal.

$x^2 - x = 6$

$x^2 - x - 6 = 0$

$(x + 2)(x - 3) = 0$

$x = -2 \text{ or } x = 3$

Choice A sets $x^2 + x - 6 = 0$ to find the roots of –3 or 2.

54. G./ G/ 3

The geometric mean for 3 numbers is the cube root of their product. Let x be the 3rd number then,

$\sqrt[3]{4 \cdot 16 \cdot x} = 12$

$64x = 12^3$

$64x = 1728$

$x = 27$

Choice I is the average of 4 and 16. Choice J takes the square root of the product of the 3 numbers.

55. C./S/1

Twenty of the thirty people prefer bananas or apples so, $\dfrac{20}{30} = 0.67$.

56. J./ N/ 2

Choose a number between 0 and 1 and substitute it into the choices to see which has the smallest value. Let $x = \dfrac{1}{2}$ then, $x^2 = \left(\dfrac{1}{2}\right)^2 = \dfrac{1}{4} > 0$, $\sqrt{x} = \sqrt{\dfrac{1}{2}} > 0$, $\dfrac{x}{2} = \dfrac{\frac{1}{2}}{2} = \dfrac{1}{4} > 0$, $x - x = \dfrac{1}{2} - \dfrac{1}{2} = 0$, and $x = \dfrac{1}{2} > 0$. So, choice J is the smallest value.

57. A./ A /2

Let x be the width and y be the length of the rectangle. The perimeter, $P = 2x + 2y$. Substituting the given perimeter and solving for y you have,

$$2x + 2y = 16$$
$$2y = 16 - 2x$$
$$y = 8 - x$$

The area, A, is $A = xy$. Substituting the y value for the perimeter, you have the quadratic equation, $A = 8x - x^2$. The maximum value for the graph of a quadratic in the form $y = ax^2 + bx + c$ can be found by using, $x = -\dfrac{b}{2a}$.

For $b = 8$ and $a = -1$ you have, $x = -\dfrac{8}{2(-1)} = 4$.

So, the dimensions have a length and width of 4 feet. Choice E satisfies the condition for the perimeter of the rectangle but not the maximum area.

58. F./ G/ 1

The sum of the measure of the interior angles in a polygon is $(n-2) \times 180°$ where n is the number of sides. A dodecagon is a 10-sided polygon so, the sum measure of the angles is $(10-2) \times 180° = 8 \times 180° = 1440°$. Since one of the angles measures 55 degrees, the sum of the other 9 angles is, $1440 - 55 = 1385°$. Choice G is the sum for a 12-gon. Choice H is for an octagon.

59. B./ A/ 2

Substitute $y = 6250$ and solve for x.

$$6250 = 8200 - 940\ln x$$
$$-1950 = -940\ln x$$
$$2.074 = \ln x$$
$$x = e^{2.074} \approx 8$$

So, it will take about 8 years.

60. H./ A/ 2

$$\frac{7.5 \times 10^8}{2.5 \times 10^{-5}} = \frac{7.5}{2.5} \times \frac{10^8}{10^{-5}} = 3 \times 10^{8-(-5)} = 3 \times 10^{13}.$$

Choice A subtract 5 from 8 to get an exponent of 3 for the power of 10. Choices D and E incorrectly subtract 2.5 from 7.5 to get 5 in the scientific notation form.

Answers to Math Practice Test 5

ANSWER KEY

#	Key	Your Answer	#	Key	Your Answer	#	Key	Your Answer	#	Key	Your Answer	#	Key	Your Answer	#	Key	Your Answer
1	B		11	B		21	B		31	C		41	C		51	C	
2	F		12	K		22	G		32	J		42	F		52	H	
3	B		13	B		23	C		33	E		43	C		53	A	
4	H		14	I		24	J		34	G		44	F		54	H	
5	E		15	D		25	B		35	C		45	E		55	C	
6	G		16	H		26	G		36	F		46	H		56	G	
7	C		17	D		27	E		37	D		47	D		57	E	
8	J		18	H		28	G		38	G		48	G		58	H	
9	A		19	A		29	C		39	A		49	B		59	B	
10	H		20	F		30	H		40	H		50	J		60	F	

ANSWERS – TEST 5

Each problem number is followed with: **Correct answer/ Topic(s)/ Level of difficulty (1-3)**.

Legends: **N** = Numerical, **A** = Algebra, **F** = Functions, **G** = Geometry, **S** = Statistics and Probability, **IES** = Integrating Essential Skills, **M** = Modeling, **1** = Easy, **2** = Medium, **3** = Difficult

1. **B./ N/ 1**

   Substituting the given values, you get, $3(2)^2 - (2 + 4(-5)^2)$
   $3 \times 4 - (2 + 4 \times 25) = 12 - (102) = -90$.

   Choice A $(-5)^2$ as -25. Choice C does not properly distribute the negative sign to $4y^2$ when simplifying, and choice D substitutes x for y and y for x when evaluating the expression.

2. **F./ IES/ 1**

   Simplifying the ratio $\dfrac{3 \text{ questions}}{4 \text{ minutes}}$ you can answer $\dfrac{\frac{3}{4} \text{ questions}}{1 \text{ minute}}$ which is $\dfrac{3}{4}$ questions per minute. In 84 minutes, you can answer $84 \times \dfrac{3}{4} = 63$ questions.

3. **B./ N/ 1**

   K. Converting the values to standard numbers, $\dfrac{7}{4} = 1.75$, $\sqrt{3} = 1.73$, and $171\% = 1.71$. So, from least to greatest the order is 171%, $\sqrt{3}$, $\dfrac{7}{4}$, 1.79. Choice E lists the values from greatest to least.

4. **H./ G/ 2**

   The hypotenuse is,

   $hyp^2 = 10^2 + 24^2$
   $hyp^2 = 100 + 573$
   $hyp = \sqrt{676} = 26$

   So, the perimeter is $26 + 24 + 10 = 60$.

   Choice F is the correct length of the hypotenuse, but not the perimeter. Choice J miscalculates the 20.

5. **E./ N/ 2**

   $(3 + 2i)(1 - 4i) + 2i(5i) = 3 - 10i - 8i^2 + 10i^2 = 3 - 10i + 8 - 10 = 1 - 10i$. Choice A converts $-8i^2$ to -8 when simplifying. Choices B and C converts $10i^2$ to 10 when simplifying.

6. **G./ N/ 3**

   Substituting the given values, you get,

   $$\dfrac{\frac{2}{3} + 2}{\frac{3}{2}} = \dfrac{\frac{8}{3}}{\frac{3}{2}} = \dfrac{8}{3} \times \dfrac{2}{3} = \dfrac{16}{9}$$

   Choice F multiplies $\dfrac{8}{3}$ by $\dfrac{3}{2}$ when simplifying. Choice H substitutes x for y and y for x when evaluating the expression.

7. **C./ S/ 1**

   Order the set to find the mean, {2, 5, 6, 9, 13}. So, the median is 6. The mean is $\dfrac{2 + 5 + 6 + 9 + 13}{5} = 7$.

   The sum of the mean and median is $6 + 7 = 13$. Choices A and B only take the mean and median into consideration. Choice D is the product of the mean and median and choice E is their difference.

8. **J./ A/ 1**

   In the form $y = a(x - h)^2 + k$, (h, k) is the vertex. So, $y = a(x - 3)^2 - 5$. Next. Substitute (6, 4) to find the value for a.

   $4 = a(6 - 3)^2 - 5$
   $4 = 9a - 5$
   $9 = 9a$
   $a = 1$

   So, the equation of the parabola is $y = (x - 3)^2 - 5$. Choice G has the correct vertex, but does not contain (6, 4). Choice H contains (6, 4) but is not the correct vertex.

9. **A./ IES/ 2**

   Brittney spends $\left(\dfrac{240}{21}\right) \times 2.25 = \$25.71$ for fuel each week, so, she spends a total of $\$25.71 + \$45 = \$70.71$ for fuel and lunch each week. She spends less than her budget allows by $\$4.29$.

10. H./ F/ 2

Using the formula to find a term, S_n, in a geometric sequence where $S_n = a_1 \cdot r^{n-1}$. $a_1 = 3$ and $r \frac{-6}{3} - 2$, so $S_n = 3 \cdot (-2)^{n-1}$. When $n = 1$, the 10th term is $S_{10} = 3 \cdot (-2)^{10-1} = 3 \cdot (-2)^9 = -1536$. Choice F is he 11th term. Choice I treats the sequence as arithmetic as does choice J where the common difference is –9 and 9 respectively.

11. B./ G/ 1

A rotation of a two-dimensional object produces a 3-dimensional figure that has at least one circular base. When a square is rotated about one of its sides, the two sides that are perpendicular to the rotated side produce circular bases for the top and the bottom of a right circular cylinder.

12. K./ G/ 2

A circle in the form $(x-h)^2 + (y-k)^2 = r^2$ has its center at (h, k) and a radius of r units. The figure shows the center to be at $(-3, 4)$ and the radius can be found by counting horizontally or vertically the number of units from the center to a point on the circle. So, $r = 4$. Substituting you get,

$(x--3)^2 + (y-4)^2 = 4^2$

$(x+3)^2 + (y-4)^2 = 16$

Choices F and G can be eliminated since the radius is not squared in either equation. Choice I incorrectly substitutes the center into the equation as $(3, -4)$.

13. B./ A/ 1

The GCF is the greatest factor that is common to both expressions. Looking at each of the common factors of the 2 expressions, the GCF of 8 and 24 is 8, the GCF of x^2 and x is x, and the GCF of z^3 and z is z. Choice A and D can be eliminated since y is not a factor of $8xz$.

14. I/ A/ 2

Factoring you have, $2x^2 + 9x - 18 = (2x - 3)(x + 6)$. The sum of the products of the inner-most terms and outer most terms in the 2 binomials must be the middle term in the expression, $+9x$.

15. D./ A/ 1

In slope-intercept form $3x - 5y = 4$ is $y = \frac{3}{5}x - \frac{4}{5}$ so, the slope is $m = \frac{3}{5}$. A perpendicular line's slope is the

negative reciprocal so, $m = -\frac{5}{3}$. Choice A is the slope of the given line. Choice C only takes the reciprocal of the slope of the given line. Choice E is the y-intercept of the given line.

16. H./ G/ 1

The form $\frac{(x-h)^2}{a^2} + \frac{(y-k)^2}{b^2} = 1$ is an ellipse with the center at (h, k) if $a \neq b$. If $a = b$, the ellipse is a circle. The equation is a hyperbola if the 2 terms on the left side of the equation are being subtracted.

17. D.,/ G,/ 2

The area of the square is $10^2 = 100$ square units. The radius of the circle is one-half the length of the side of the square so, $r = 10$. The area of the circle is $\pi(5)^2 = 25\pi$ square units. The difference between the area of the square and circle leaves the desired area so, $100 - 25\pi$ square units is the area outside of the circle and inside of the square.

18. H./ IED/ 2

The table of values is linear, since the change in any 2 distances divided by any 2 corresponding times is 48 so, choices F, G, and J can be eliminated. Since you are asked to write the equation for d in terms of t, choice I can also be eliminated.

19. A./ IED/ 2

Since you spend 35% studying for the test, you spend 65% doing other things. Of that percent of time, you spend 40% awake (since you sleep 60% of it). So, you spend 65% of 40% or $0.65 \times 0.40 = 0.26 = 26\%$ of your time doing other things.

20. F.,/ N/ 2

Choose a number less than –1 and substitute it into each answer choice. Let $x = -2$ then,

$\frac{x}{2} = -\frac{2}{2} = -1$

$2x = 2(-2) = -4$

$x^3 = (-2)^3 = -8$

$-x^2 = -(-2)^2 = -4$

$x = -2$

So, –1 is the greatest value.

21. B./ N/ 3

Simplifying you have, $\dfrac{2}{\sqrt{-8}} = \dfrac{2}{\sqrt{-1\cdot 8}} = \dfrac{2}{\sqrt{-1}\sqrt{8}} =$

$\dfrac{2}{i\sqrt{8}} \cdot \dfrac{i\sqrt{8}}{i\sqrt{8}} = \dfrac{2i\sqrt{8}}{8i^2} = \dfrac{i\sqrt{8}}{-4} = \dfrac{2i\sqrt{2}}{-4} = -\dfrac{\sqrt{2}}{2}i.$ Choice A neglects that $i^2 = -1$.

22. G./ A/ 2

One of the vertical sides of the rectangle has a length of 4 units since its endpoints are $(-7, 2)$ and $(-7, -2)$. The other vertical side has one of its endpoints at $(5, -2)$ so the other endpoint is at $(5, 2)$.

23. C./ A/ 2

$\dfrac{x^3 y^4 z}{xyz^2} \cdot \dfrac{1}{xz^{-2}} = \dfrac{x^3 y^4 z}{x^2 y} = xy^3 z$.

24. J./ G/ 2

Using the trigonometric identity $1 + \tan^2\theta = 0\sec^2\theta$, you get,

$1 + \tan^2\theta = \sec^2\theta$

$\tan^2\theta = \sec^2\theta - 1$

$\sqrt{\tan^2\theta} = \sqrt{\sec^2\theta - 1}$

$\tan\theta = \sqrt{\sec^2\theta - 1}$

Choice G takes the square root of $\sec^2\theta$ and 1 separately in the 3rd line of the solution above. Choice H neglects to take the square root of the 2nd line in the solution above.

25. B./ IES/ 2

The food stand collects $1.75x$ dollars in hotdogs sales and $3.50y$ in hamburger sales so, the total sales of \$612.50 is the sum of hotdog and hamburger sales or $1.75x + 3.50y = 612.50$. Since there are 250 hotdogs and hamburgers sold, $x + y = 250$.

26. G./ G/ 3

Two sides and the included angle are given for the triangle so, the law of cosines can be used to find the length of the side opposite the given angle. Let a be the side opposite 32 degrees then,

$a^2 = 80^2 + 92^2 - 2\cdot 80\cdot 92\cos 32°$

$a^2 = 14,864 - 14,720\cos 32°$

$a^2 = 2380.73$

$a = 48.79$

Choice F uses the Pythagorean theorem to find a. Choice H uses the sine instead of cosine when using the law of cosines to find a.

27. E./ F/ 2

$f(g(-2)) = f(3\cdot -2 + 4) = f(-2) = (-2)^2 + 2 = 4 + 2 = 6.$ Choice A takes the product of $f(-2)$ and $g(-2)$ and evaluates $f(-2)$ as -2. Choice D finds $g(f(-2))$.

28. G./ IES/ 2

Let t be the number of minutes it takes to complete the entire project. 120 minutes is $\dfrac{2}{3}$ of t so, $120 = \dfrac{2}{3}t$

$120 \times \dfrac{3}{2} = t$

$t = 180$ minutes

So, Selma needs $180 - 120 = 60$ minutes to complete the project. Choice F is the time it takes to complete the entire project. Choice J is the average of the time to complete the entire project and the time she needs to complete the project.

29. C./ F/ 1

In the form $y = af(x - h) + k$, a is vertical stretch if $a > 1$, h is a translation to the left is $h < 0$, and k is a vertical translation upwards if $k > 0$. Since the graph is stretched by a factor of 2, $a = 2$. Translating f to the left means $h = -2$, and translating upwards 4, $k = 4$. Choice A can be eliminated because $h = 3$ means f is translated to the right 3 units. Choices B and D can be eliminated because negative value for a means the graph of f is reflected across the x-axis.

30. H./ F/ 2

The slope for line l is, $m = \dfrac{3-5}{-6-2} = \dfrac{-2}{-8} = \dfrac{1}{4}$. The slope for line k is the negative reciprocal of l then, $m = -4$. Choice G only takes the negative for the slope of l and choice I only takes the reciprocal of the slope of l. Remember, perpendicular lines have slopes that are negative reciprocals of each other.

31. C./ F/ 2

Using the definition of logarithms, $\log_5 M = 2$ means $5^2 = M$ then, $M = 25$. $\log_a 64 = 3$ means $a^3 = 64$ then, $a = 4$. So, $M - a = 25 - 4 = 21$. Choice A evaluates M as the product of 5 and 2, and a as the quotient of 64 and 3. Choice B evaluates M as the sum of 5 and 7, and a as the difference of 64 and 3.

32. J./ N/ 1

Converting the dimensions of the base to yards, 15 feet = 5 yards, and 13 feet = $\dfrac{13}{3}$ yards. The area of the rectangular base is $5 \times \dfrac{13}{3} = \dfrac{65}{3}$ or 21.67 square yards. Choice F multiplies the dimensions by 3 to convert feet to yards. Choice H finds the perimeter of the base.

33. E./ A/ 2

The distance from A to B is the difference in the x-coordinates, $28 - 3 = 25$. Three-fifths of the distance is $\dfrac{3}{5} \times 25 = 15$. So, the coordinates of C are $(3 + 15, 4) = (18, 4)$. Choice A uses the distance from A to b as the x-coordinate of C. Choice B are the coordinates of C from B to A.

34. G./ F/ 1

The solution set are the points of intersection for the graphs of the 2 functions. Choice F is the y-intercepts for the 2 graphs. Choice H reverses the coordinates for the points of intersection. Choice I states the x-intercepts of the 2 graphs.

35. C./ S/ 1

For each of the 3 shirts you have a combination of choosing 2 pairs of pants and 1 pair of shoes, so you can make 2 outfits by choosing 1 of the shirts. This can be done 3 times with the shirts for a total of $3 \times 2 = 6$.

36. F./ N/ 3

Solve the 1st equation for a and the 2nd for b before substituting into $\dfrac{b}{a}$.

$\dfrac{a}{b} = 30$, then $a = 30b$ and $5a + b = 15$, then $b = 15 - 5a$. So, $\dfrac{b}{a} = \dfrac{30b}{15 - 5a} = \dfrac{6b}{3 - a}$

Choice G evaluates $\dfrac{a}{b}$. Choice H incorrectly simplifies $\dfrac{6b}{3-a}$ to $\dfrac{\not{6}b}{\not{3}-a} = \dfrac{2b}{1-a}$.

37. D./ N/ 2

Simplifying each choice,

A. $\sqrt{-9} = \sqrt{-1 \cdot 9} = \sqrt{-1} \cdot \sqrt{9} = 3i$

B. $i\sqrt{9} = 3i$

C. $i\sqrt{9} \cdot i\sqrt{3} = i^2 3\sqrt{3} = -3\sqrt{3}$

D. $(3 - i)(3 + i) = 9 - i^2 = 9 - (-1) = 10$

E. $(3 + i)(3 + i) = 9 + 6i + i^2 = 9 + 6i - 1 = 8 + 6i$

Choices A, B, and E are imaginary. Choice C is irrational. Only choice D is rational.

38. G./ A/ 2

Completing the square you have,

$x^2 - 18x$

$= x^2 - 18x + \left(\dfrac{-18}{2}\right)^2 - \left(\dfrac{-18}{2}\right)^2$

$= \left(x^2 - 18x + 81\right) - 81$

$= \left(x - 9\right)^2 - 81$

The other choices incorrectly complete the square.

39. A./ G/ 2

The ratio of the adjacent side, adj, to the hypotenuse for the triangle is 5 to 13. Since the length of the hypotenuse is 39, $\dfrac{5}{13} = \dfrac{adj}{39}$ so, $adj = \dfrac{5}{13} \times 39 = 15$. Let a be the length of the side opposite angle A so, using the Pythagorean Theorem to find side a you get,

$a^2 + 15^2 = 39^2$

$a^2 + 225 = 1521$

$a^2 = 1296$

$a = \sqrt{1296} = 36$

40. H./ IES/ 1

The dollar amount the laptop has been discounted is $550 – $485 = $65. As a percent, the discount is $\dfrac{65}{550} = 0.118$ or about 12%. Choice G divides 65 by 485. Choice A divides 485 by 550.

41. C./ G/ 2

Angle A $= \dfrac{1}{2} \cdot \overset{\frown}{BEC} = \dfrac{1}{2} \cdot 210° = 105°$. The sum of angles B and C is $75°$, angles B and C have measures of $37.5°$ each. Choice B is the measure of angle A. Choice D is one-half of the difference of the measure of arc BAC which has a measure of $150°$.

42. F./ F/ 1

The height of the object as it hits the ground is 0. Substituting $h = 0$ and solving for t,

$$0 = -16t^2 + 190$$
$$-190 = -16t^2$$
$$\dfrac{-190}{-16} = t^2$$
$$t = 3.45$$

So, it takes about 3.45 seconds for the object to hit the ground. Answer H is the value of $\dfrac{-190}{-16}$.

43. C./ G/ 2

$\left|\sin\theta\right| \leq 1$ is equivalent to $-1 \leq \sin\theta \leq 1$ which occurs for any value of θ in the first and second quadrant. So, choices A and B can be eliminated. Choices D and E can also be eliminated since they contain angles in the third and fourth quadrant respectively.

44. F./ F/ 2

Using the rule of logarithms, $5 = \log\dfrac{M}{3} \Leftrightarrow 10^5 = \dfrac{M}{3}$ so, $M = 3 \cdot 10^5$.

45. E./ N/ 2

For a matrix in the form $\begin{bmatrix} a & b \\ c & d \end{bmatrix}$, the value of the determinant is $ad - bc$. So,

$$6 \cdot 4 - k \cdot k = 3k$$
$$24 - k^2 = 3k$$
$$k^2 + 3k - 24 = 0$$
$$(k+8)(k-3) = 0$$
$$k = -8 \text{ or } k = 3$$

Only –8 is a correct choice to choose, so the correct choice is E. Choices A and B factor $k^2 + 3k - 24$ as $(k - 8)$ and $(k + 3)$ to get values of 8 and –3 respectively. Choices C and D factor $k^2 + 3k - 24$ as $(k - 4)$ and $(k + 6)$ to get values of 4 and –6 respectively.

46. H./ F/ 1

Reflecting a function across the x-axis changes the signs of y values for the function so, the graph of $y = x^2$ is transformed to $y = -x^2$. Finally, shifting the function right 3 units to the right transforms the function to $y = -(x - 3)^2$. Choices G and J can be eliminated since the neither is reflected across the x- axis. Choice F is a horizontal translation left 3 units, and choice J is a vertical shift down 3 units.

47. D./ G/ 1

The period for $y = a\cos(bx)$ is $\dfrac{2\pi}{|b|}$ where $b = \dfrac{\pi}{2}$ so, the period is $\dfrac{2\pi}{\left|\dfrac{\pi}{2}\right|} = 2\pi \times \dfrac{2}{\pi} = 4$. Choice A uses $\dfrac{1}{2}$ [for b when determining the period. Choice B is the fundamental period for cosine. Choice C is the value for b that is used to find the period.

48. G./ N/ 2

Let x be her homework average, then $0.5 \times 86 + 0.3 \times 88 + 0.2x = 85$. Solving for x,

$$0.5 \times 86 + 0.3 \times 88 + 0.2x = 85$$
$$43 + 26.4 + 0.2x = 85$$
$$69.4 + 0.2x = 85$$
$$0.2x = 15.6$$
$$x = 78$$

Choice H equally weighs the test, quiz, and homework average.

49. B./ I/ 1

If you simplify $\dfrac{12}{\sqrt{3}} \times \dfrac{\sqrt{3}}{\sqrt{3}} = \dfrac{12\sqrt{3}}{3} = 4\sqrt{3}$. $\sqrt{3}$ is an irrational number (since it is not a perfect square) and the produce of a rational number and irrational number is an irrational number.

50. J./ F/ 2

The dashed line of $y = \dfrac{1}{2}x - 1$ is shaded above and the solid line of $y = -x - 2$ is shaded below, so the solution is $y \leq -x - 2$ and $y > \dfrac{1}{2}x - 1$.

51. C./ A/ 2

Before finding any zeros, the function must be simplified.

$\dfrac{x^2 - 81}{x^2 - 9x} = \dfrac{(x+9)(x-9)}{x(x-9)} = \dfrac{x+9}{x}$. Setting the numer-

ator equal to 0 to find the zeros, $x + 9 = 0$ then, $x = -9$. Choice A factors the numerator without simplifying the expression to find the zeros. Choice B takes all the factors in the numerator and denominator without simplifying to find the zeros.

52. H./ G/ 1

For $y = f(x)$ is even if $f(-x) = f(x)$, and odd if $f(-x) = -f(x)$. Cosine is an even function so, $\cos(-\theta) = \cos(\theta)$. Choice F is the answer for $\sin(-\theta)$. Choice G assumes cosine is an odd function.

53. A./ S/ 2

There are 26 letters to choose from for the first 3 values and 10 number to choose from for the last four values. Since each letter and number can be used repeatedly the total number of combinations is $26 \times 26 \times 26 \times 10 \times 10 \times 10 \times 10 = 175,760,000$. Choice B assumes the letters and numbers cannot be repeated.

54. H./ A/ 2

Since $x = 6$ is a root, $y = 0$. Substituting you get,

$0 = 6^2 - 6b - 24$

$0 = -6b + 12$

$-12 = -6b$

$b = 2$

Choice I and K only take factors of –24 for their answers.

55. C./ F/ 1

The range for a function is the domain of its inverse. The graph of $y = \sqrt{x}$ that has a range of $y \geq 0$, is shifted horizontally right 5 units and vertically up 3 units to get the transformed graph $y = \sqrt{x+5} + 3$. So, its range is $y \geq 3$. The domain of the inverse is $x \geq 3$. Choice A is the domain of $y = \sqrt{x+5} + 3$.

56. G./ N/ 1

Since $\triangle ABC \sim \triangle DEF$, $\dfrac{a}{d} = \dfrac{c}{f}$. Substituting you have,

$\dfrac{18}{3} = \dfrac{42}{f}$

$6 = \dfrac{42}{f}$

$6f = 42$

$f = 7$

Choice D incorrectly sets the ratio up as $\dfrac{3}{18} = \dfrac{42}{f}$ to find f. Choice E uses the ratio $\dfrac{3}{42} = \dfrac{f}{18}$ to find f.

57. E./ G/ 2

The sum of $\angle CBD$ and $\angle ABD$ is $230°$ (because $360° - 130°$). Then,

$x + (x + 10) = 230°$

$2x = 220°$

$x = 110°$

Then $\angle ABD = 120°$. Choice A is the measure of $\angle ABC$. Choice B is the sum of $\angle CBD$ and $\angle ABD$.

58. H./ N/ 2

Simplify the left side of the equation to compare the exponents.

$\left(3x^4 y\right)^2 = 9x^m y^n$

$3^2 x^8 y^2 = 9x^m y^n$

$9x^8 y^2 = 9x^m y^n$

So, $m = 8$ and $n = 2$ by the one-to-one property then, $8 + 2 = 10$. Choice I is the product of m and n. Choice J is the difference of m and n.

59. B./ N/ 1

$\dfrac{7.2 \times 10^{12}}{2.4 \times 10^{-5}} = \dfrac{7.2}{2.4} \times \dfrac{10^{12}}{10^{-5}} = 3 \times 10^{12-(-5)} = 3 \times 10^{17}$.

Choice A takes the difference of 12 and 5 for the bases of 10. Choice C is the product of the exponents for the bases of 10. Choices D and E can be eliminated since 7.2 and 2.4 are being subtracted to get 4.8.

60. F./ G/ 2

Using the tangent function, $\tan 37° = \dfrac{10}{11+x}$.

Solving for x,

$$\tan 37° = \frac{10}{11+x}$$

$$\tan 37° (11+x) = 10$$

$$11 + x = \frac{10}{\tan 37°}$$

$$x = \frac{10}{\tan 37°} - 11$$

$$x = 2.27$$

So, the length of the side opposite C is $11 + 2.27 = 13.27$. Choice G is only the value for x. Choice I uses cosine of 37 degrees to find x and choice J is the length of the side opposite C using the incorrect answer from choice I.

Answers to Math Practice Test 6

ANSWER KEY						

#	Key	Your Answer	#	Key	Your Answer	#	Key	Your Answer	#	Key	Your Answer	#	Key	Your Answer	#	Key	Your Answer
1	B		11	D		21	D		31	B		41	A		51	B	
2	K		12	J		22	J		32	H		42	H		52	G	
3	D		13	A		23	B		33	A		43	E		53	C	
4	H		14	F		24	H		34	H		44	K		54	F	
5	C		15	B		25	A		35	D		45	D		55	D	
6	G		16	H		26	G		36	G		46	G		56	H	
7	A		17	B		27	B		37	C		47	B		57	C	
8	H		18	H		28	F		38	H		48	H		58	J	
9	D		19	B		29	C		39	B		49	A		59	B	
10	G		20	G		30	F		40	F		50	H		60	J	

ANSWERS – TEST 6

Each problem number is followed with: **Correct answer/ Topic(s)/ Level of difficulty (1-3)**.

Legends: **N** = Numerical, **A** = Algebra, **F** = Functions, **G** = Geometry, **S** = Statistics and Probability, **IES** = Integrating Essential Skills, **M** = Modeling, **1** = Easy, **2** = Medium, **3** = Difficult

---

1. B./ N/ 1

   Substituting the values for x and y and simplifying you get, $3(5) - ((-2)^2 + 2 \times 5 \times (-2)) + 4(5 - (-2)) = 15 - (4 - 20) + 4(7) = 15 + 16 + 28 = 59$. Choice B evaluates $(x - y)$ as $(5 - 2)$. Choice C evaluates $(y^2 + 2xy)$ as $(-4 - 20)$. Choice D switches x and y when evaluating the expression.

2. K./ N/ 2

   Cross multiply to find mn.

   $$\frac{4}{mn} = \frac{24}{1}$$
   $$24mn = 4$$
   $$mn = \frac{4}{24} = \frac{1}{6}$$

   Choice F takes the product of 4 and 24 to find mn. Choice H cross multiplies incorrectly when finding mn as does choice J.

3. D./ G/ 1

   The exterior angle of 120 degrees is equal to the sum of its 2 remote interior angles A and C so, $\angle A + \angle C = 120°$. $\angle CBD = 120°$ since $\angle CBD$ and $\angle ABE$ are vertical angles. Then $\angle A + \angle C + \angle CDB = 240°$. Choice A finds only part of the whole. Choice B finds $\angle ABC$. Choice C finds the interior angles, and choice E finds the sum of the exterior angles.

4. H./ G/ 2

   The easier method is to solve the equation for x and substitute its value into the expression. $4x + 7 = 43$, then $x = 9$. Substituting you have, $2(9) - 5 = 13$. Choice F solves $2x - 5 = 43$ for x. Choice C substitutes $x = 13$ into $2x - 5$.

5. C./ A/ 1

   Factoring $2x^2 + -x - 15$ into a product of 2 binomials you have, $2x^2 - x - 15 = (2x + 5)(x - 3)$. So, the only correct factor to choose from is choice C. The sum of

the products of the inside terms and the outside terms must be $-x$ when determining the correct combination of factors. The product of the factors for choices D and E is $2x^2 + 7x - 15$.

6. G./ S/ 1

   Order the data to get the median. 23.1, 23.1, 23.7, 23.7, 23.8 so, the median is 23.7. The mean is, $23.1 + 23.8 + 23.7 + 23.8 + 23.1$
   $$\frac{23.1 + 23.8 + 23.7 + 23.8 + 23.1}{5} = 23.5.$$ So, the sum of the median and mode is $23.7 + 23.5 = 47.2$. Choice H uses a median of 23.1 when finding the sum, and choice F uses a mode of 23.8 when finding the sum.

7. A./ F/ 2

   $g(2) = 2^2 + 1 = 5$ so, a function for f must be chosen so that $f(5) = 25$. If $f(x) = 4x + 5$ then, $f(5) = 4(5) + 5 = 25$. Choices B and C would be correct if 4 and 1 were not combined with $5x$. Choice E is $f(x) \times g(2)$.

8. H. A 1

   You can find the equation of the line using the given information, but we suggest, counting from the x-intercept to the y-intercept using the slope. Since slope is rise over run, move 4 units to the left and 3 units upwards 2 times from $(8, 0)$ to $(0, 6)$ so, the y-intercept is 6. Choice G moves $(8, 0)$ four units to the left and 3 units 2 times to $(0, -6)$.

9. D./ N/ 2

   One-half of 108 is 54, so the first number is 108. Let x be the other number then, $\frac{1}{4} \cdot \frac{1}{2} \cdot x = 12$
   $$\frac{1}{8} \cdot x = 12$$
   $$x = 96$$

   The sum of the 2 numbers is, $108 + 96 = 204$. Choice B takes the sum of one-half of 54 and one-half of 12. Choice C is the sum of one-half of 54 and 96.

10. G./ A/ 2

The GCF in the numerator and denominator is $2xy$. Simplifying you get,

$$\frac{6xy^2 - 12x^5 y}{2xy^3} = \frac{2\cancel{xy}\,(3y - 6x^4)}{2\cancel{xy}\,(y^2)} = \frac{3y - 6x^4}{y^2}$$

Choice F can be eliminated since $6xy^2$ and $2xy^3$ are reduced by 2 but $12x^5y$ is reduced by 3. Choice H can be eliminated since $6xy^2$ and $2xy^3$ have a common factor of y^2 but $12x^5y$ does not when the expression is simplified.

11. D./ G/ 1

$\overset{\frown}{ADE} = 70°$ since $\overset{\frown}{ACE} + \overset{\frown}{ADE} = 360°$. $\angle ACE$ is one-half the measure of its intercepted arc of $\overset{\frown}{ADE}$ so, $\angle ACE = \dfrac{1}{2} \times 70 = 35°$. Choice B incorrectly determines that $\angle ACE$ is twice the measure of its intercepted arc. Choice C incorrectly determines $\angle ACE$ equals the measure of its intercepted arc (this is true if $\angle ACE$ were a central angle for circle O).

12. J./ G/ 2

The perimeter, P, of an equilateral triangle is, $P = 3s$. Solving the perimeter in terms of P you have $s = \dfrac{P}{3}$.

The area, A, of an equilateral triangle is, $A = \dfrac{\sqrt{3}}{2}s^2$. Substituting for s you get,

$A = \dfrac{\sqrt{3}}{2}\left(\dfrac{P}{3}\right)^2 = \dfrac{\sqrt{3}}{2}\left(\dfrac{P^2}{9}\right) = \dfrac{\sqrt{3}}{18}P^2$. Choices F and G can be eliminated since the area is written in terms of s. Choice J can also be eliminated since the equation is incorrectly written for the perimeter.

13. A./ N/ 2

A student can score in only 1 of the 3 categories, a 90 or above, between an 80 and 89, or an 80 or below. So, the 3 categories combine determines the whole. The portion of the class that makes a 90 or above and between an 80 and 89 is $\dfrac{1}{5} + \dfrac{2}{7} = \dfrac{17}{35}$. So, the portion that makes an 80 or below is $1 - \dfrac{17}{35} = \dfrac{18}{35}$. Choice E is portion of the class that makes a 90 or above and between an 80 and 89. Choice E incorrectly adds the portion of the class that makes a 90 or above and between an 80 and 89. Choice C uses choice E to determine the portion of the class that makes an 80 or below of $1 - \dfrac{3}{4} = \dfrac{1}{4}$.

14. F./ A/ 2

Since $x = -3$ and 4 are the x-intercepts then, $x + 3$ and $x - 4$ are factors. The product of the factors is $x^2 - x - 12$. The parabola opens downward if the leading coefficient is negative. Multiplying the expression by -1 gives you $-x^2 + x + 12$. Choices G and H gives the correct x-intercepts but opens upwards. Choices I and J open downwards but do not contain the correct intercepts.

15. B./ IES/ 2

The fixed charge of $55 plus the variable charge of $40x where x is the number of hours worked equals $425. So,

$$55 + 40x = 425$$
$$40x = 370$$
$$x = 9.25$$

So, the plumber works 9.25 hours to complete a service call. Choice A divides 425 by 55. Choice B switches the fixed cost and variable cost and solves $40 + 55x = 425$ for x. Choice E neglects the fixed charge and only divides 425 by 40.

16. H./ N/ 2

Put the values in their imaginary form using $\sqrt{-1} = i$.

$$\sqrt{-36} - \sqrt{-8}$$
$$= \sqrt{-1 \cdot 36} - \sqrt{-1 \cdot 8}$$
$$= \sqrt{-1}\sqrt{36} - \sqrt{-1}\sqrt{8}$$
$$= i \cdot 6 - i2\sqrt{2}$$
$$= 6i - 2i\sqrt{2}$$

Choice F incorrectly simplifies $\sqrt{8}$ as $4\sqrt{2}$. Choice I and J incorrectly combine $6i$ and $2i\sqrt{2}$ but they are not like terms so, they cannot be combined.

17. B./ G/ 1

To find the period, count the horizontal distance from one point on the graph to the next point where the domain repeats itself. This can easily be done by counting from the maximum point of (0 4) to the next maximum point to the right of $(0, \pi)$. Choice A is the fundamental period for the graph of cosine or sine. Choice D and E can be eliminated since the function is even (has symmetry about the y-axis).

18. H./ F/ 2

Set f equal to -7 and solve for x.
$$-7 = x^2 - 6x + 2$$
$$0 = x^2 - 6x + 9$$
$$0 = (x - 3)^2$$
$$x = 3$$

Choice I appears to factor $x^2 - 6x + 9$ to $(x + 3)^2$ to get $x = -3$ as the zero. Choice J appears to combine $x^2 - 6x + 2$ and -7 to get $x^2 - 6x - 5$ then incorrectly factor it to $(x - 1)(x - 5)$ to get $x = 5$ as one of the zeros.

19. B./ A/ 2

Using the factoring form $a^3 + b^3 = (a+b)(a^2 - ab + b^2)$ where $a = 2$ and $b = 8$ for choice B you get $x^3 + 8 = (x+2)(x^2 - 2x + 4)$ which has $x + 2$ as one of its factors. Choice A uses the factoring form $a^3 - b^3 = (a-b)(a^2 + ab + b^2)$ so $x^3 - 8 = (x-2)(x^2 + 2x + 4)$. Choices C and D can be eliminated since they do not factor. Choice E factors to $3(x - 2)$.

20. G./ F/ 1

Since the functions are inverses of each other and $f(2) = 5$, $g(5) = 2$. Now, $f(g(5)) = f(2) = 5$. The function value $f(3) = 6$ is an arbitrary value that is a distractor in the problem

21. D./ F/ 2

Set the determinant (top left · bottom right - top right · bottom left) equal to 14 and solve for a.

$$\begin{bmatrix} 4 & 5 \\ 6 & -a \end{bmatrix} = 14$$
$$4 \cdot -a - 6 \cdot 5 = 14$$
$$-4a - 30 = 14$$
$$-4a = -44$$
$$a = 11$$

So, $a = 11$, not -11 as choice D suggests. Choice E incorrectly cross multiplies the determinant as $4 - a - (6 - 5)$ to get $a = -19$.

22. J./ S/ 2

The probability of one of you being chosen 1st is $\frac{2}{6}$. The probability that the other person is chosen 2nd is $\frac{1}{5}$ since one of the 6 people has been chosen. The events of choosing a person at random are independent so the probability is $\frac{2}{6} \times \frac{1}{5} = \frac{2}{30} = \frac{1}{15}$. Choice F and H

only take the probabilities of one person being chosen 1st and 2nd. Choice G assumes the probability of one of you chosen first is $\frac{1}{6}$. Choice J adds incorrect individual probabilities.

23. B./ IES/ 2

Let x be the number then,
$$152 = 4x - 8$$
$$160 = 4x$$
$$x = 40$$

Choice A uses $8x - 4$ when solving for x. Choice C uses $8 - 4x$ when solving for x.

24. H./ F/ 1

$y = \cos x$ is an even function. The rest of the answer choices are odd functions.

25. A./ F/ 1 or 2

The perpendicular line's slope is the negative reciprocal of $-\frac{1}{5}$ so, the slope is $m = 5$. Using the point of intersection as a point on the line and the point-slope form of a line, $y - y_1 = m(x - x_1)$ where (x_1, y_1) is a point on the line, you get $y + 1 = 5(x - 4)$. Choices C and D can be eliminated since only the reciprocal of the slope is taken. Choice E can also be eliminated since only the negative of the slope was taken.

26. G./ G/ 2

Using the trigonometric identities $\csc x = \frac{1}{\sin x}$ and $\sec x = \frac{1}{\cos x}$ you can simplify the expression as follows;

$$\frac{\sin^2 x \csc^2 x}{\cos^2 x} = \frac{(\sin x)^2 \cdot \frac{1}{(\sin x)^2}}{\cos^2 x} = \frac{1}{(\cos x)^2} = (\sec x)^2$$
$$= \sec^2 x.$$

27. B./ IES/ 2

Converting gallons per hour to ounces per minute, you get $\frac{30 \, gal}{1 \, hr} \times \frac{1 \, hr}{60 \, min} \times \frac{128 oz}{1 \, gal} = \frac{64 oz}{1 \, min}$ so, the lawn sprinkler waters the yard at 10 more ounces each minute.

28. F./ F/ 2

Before finding any x-intercepts, the function must be simplified.

$y = \dfrac{x^2 - 9}{x + 3} = \dfrac{(x-3)\cancel{(x+3)}}{\cancel{x+3}} = x - 3$. Setting the y equal

to 0 to get the x-intercept, $0 = x + 3$ then, $x = -3$. Set $x = 0$ for the original function to find the y-intercept

then, $y = \dfrac{0^2 - 9}{0 + 3} = -3$. So, the sum of the intercepts

is $-3 - 3 = -6$. Choice J finds the x-intercepts of -3 and 3 by neglecting to simplify the function first to get $-3 + 3 - 3 = -3$. Choice J uses an x-intercept of 3 to get a sum for the intercepts of $3 - 3 = 0$.

29. C./ F/ 1

Only B needs to be transformed to answer the question. Reflecting B across the origin changes the sign of the coordinates to $(5, -4)$. Then, shifting 6 units to the right changes the x-coordinate only to $(5 + 6, -4) = (11, -4)$. Choice A reflects B correctly but then shifts it up vertically 6 units. Choice B also reflects point B correctly but then shifts it down vertically 6 units. Choice D shifts B to the left 6 units after reflecting it across the origin.

30. F./ A/ 1

The dashed line has a y-intercept of 2 so its equation is $y = x + 2$. Also, since the shaded region is below its graph, the inequality is $y < x + 2$. The solid line then, is $y = -x + 3$. Since the shaded region is above the graph, the inequality is $y \geq -x + 3$.

31. B./ F/ 2

The distance, a_n, Kylie runs each day can be modeled by an arithmetic sequence,

$a_n = a_1 + d(n - 1)$ where $a1$ is the distance she runs on the first day, d is the additional distance she runs each day, and n is the day. Now,

$a_{30} = 3 + \dfrac{3}{7}(30 - 1) = 15.4$. So, she will have run 15.4

miles on the 30th day. Choice E incorrectly uses

$3 + \dfrac{3}{7}(30)$ to determine the number of miles run on

day 30.

32. H./ N/ 1

$\dfrac{x}{y} = -3$ then, $\dfrac{y}{x} = -\dfrac{1}{3}$. Substituting you get, $4\left(-\dfrac{1}{3}\right)$

$^2 = 4(\dfrac{1}{9}) = \dfrac{4}{9}$. Choice only substitutes -3 in for $\dfrac{y}{x}$

before simplifying and choice G substitutes 3 in for $\dfrac{y}{x}$ before simplifying.

33. A./ A/ 2

Factoring $x^3 - 27$ using the form $a^3 - b^3 = (a - b)(a^2 + ab + b^2)$ where $a = x$ and $b = 3$ you have $x^3 - 27 = (x - 3)(x^2 - 3x + 9) = 0$. Setting $x - 3 = 0$ then, $x = 3$ is a real number. Setting $(x^2 - 3x + 9) = 0$ produces 2 conjugate complex roots.

34. H./ N/ 2

Using the distance formula to find the distance between A and B,

$5^2 = (m - 4)^2 + (3 - -1)^2$

$25 = (m - 4)^2 + 16$

$9 = (m - 4)^2$

$3 = m - 4$

$m = 7$

35. D./ N/ 2

The length of the major axis can be ± 0.001 inches of 8 inches so, the axis can be as small as 7.999 or as large as 8.001 inches. Solving choice D you have,

$|k - 8| \leq 0.001$

$-0.001 \leq k - 8 \leq 0.001$

$-0.001 + 8 \leq k \leq 0.001 + 8$

$7.999 \leq k \leq 8.001$

The inequality for choice A describes the difference in the length of the axis and the error produced by the machine is less than or equal to 8. The inequality for choice E describes the desired length must be less than or equal to the error produced by the machine.

36. G./ G/ 2

For the right triangle with vertex angle θ, $\tan \theta = \dfrac{x}{y}$,

and for the right triangle with the vertex angle

α, $\tan \alpha = \dfrac{x}{a}$. The ratio and $\tan \theta$ to $\tan \alpha$ is,

$\dfrac{\tan \alpha}{\tan \theta} = \dfrac{\dfrac{x}{y}}{\dfrac{x}{a}} = \dfrac{x}{y} \cdot \dfrac{a}{x} = \dfrac{a}{y}$

Choices F and J are the same answers so they can be eliminated.

37. C./ S/ 3

The sum of the first 7 numbers in the set is $24 \times 7 = 168$. Adding another number, n, to the set changes the mean to 27 so,

$$\frac{168 + x}{8} = 27$$

$$168 + x = 216$$

$$x = 48$$

Choices D is just the difference in the new and original mean. Choices A and E are the original and new means so they could probably be eliminated.

38. H./ A/ 1

Find the slope of the line with the given intercepts of $(-7, 0)$ and $(0, 12)$.

$m = \frac{12 - 0}{0 - -7} = \frac{12}{7}$. So, the parallel line also has a slope

of $\frac{12}{7}$. Choice F is for the line that is perpendicular.

Choice J takes the difference in the x and y-intercepts to determine the slope of the given line.

39. B./ A/ 1

The radical form of an exponential expression $x^{\frac{m}{n}}$ is

$\sqrt[n]{x^m}$. So, $2x^{\frac{3}{5}} = 2\sqrt[5]{x^3}$. Choice A reverse the radical and the power of x. Choices D and E can be eliminated since both put the 2 inside of the radical.

40. F./ F/ 2

Substituting $A = 24,000$ and using logarithms to find the time, t,

$$24,000 = 1200(1 + 0.08)^t$$

$$20 = (1 + 0.08)^t$$

$$\ln 20 = \ln 1.08^t$$

$$\ln 20 = t \ln 1.08$$

$$t = \frac{\ln 20}{\ln 1.08}$$

$$t = 38.93$$

So, it takes about 39 years for the investment to have a value of $24,000. Choice G divides 24,000 by 1200 to get 20 years. Choice H divides 20 by 1.08 to get 19 years.

41. A./ F/ 2

Switch the x and y values and solve for y to find the inverse.

$$y = \sqrt[3]{x + 2}$$

$$x = \sqrt[3]{y + 2}$$

$$x^3 = \left(\sqrt[3]{y + 2}\right)^3$$

$$x^3 = y + 2$$

$$y = x^3 - 2$$

Choices D and E can be eliminated since they are solved for x in terms of y. Choice B incorrectly subtracts 2 on both of the equation after the 2nd step in the solution above before cubing both sides of the equation.

42. H./ G/ 1

Adding any multiple of 360 degrees to a given angle determines a coterminal angle since its terminal side coincides with the given angle. So, adding 360 n times to 32 degrees produces the set of coterminal angles to 32 degrees. So, $32° + 360°n$. Note that if $n < 0$, the rotation is counterclockwise.

43. E./ N/ 1

The column values for the 1st matrix in the solution are the coefficients for x and y in each equation. The 2nd matrix is the variable or solution matrix, and the 3rd matrix column values are the right-hand side of each equation.

44. K./ G/ 3

Since two sides and the included angle are given, the law of cosines can be used to find the side opposite the given angle.

$$a^2 = 6^2 + 8^2 - 2 \cdot 6 \cdot 8 \cos 62°$$

$$a^2 = 36 + 64 - 96 \cos 62°$$

$$a^2 = 100 - 96 \cos 62°$$

$$a^2 = 54.93$$

$$a = 7.4$$

Choice G used $\sin 62°$ instead of $\cos 62°$ in the above solution. Choice F solves for a².

45. D./ A/ 2

The coordinates for P are $(x, \sqrt{x - 4})$ and the origin $(0, 0)$. Using the distance formula, you have,

$$d = \sqrt{(x-0)^2 + \left(\sqrt{x-4}-0\right)^2}$$
$$d = \sqrt{x^2 + x - 4}$$

Choice B goes too far and takes the square root of x^2 and $(x-4)$ in solution above.

46. G./ G/ 2

Since the square and triangle are adjacent, the lengths of the sides of the triangle are also 8 units. Combining the area of the square and triangle, the area of the polygon is,

$$8^2 + \frac{\sqrt{3}}{4}(8)^2 = 64 + 16\sqrt{3}.$$ Choice F use 4 as the length of the side of the equilateral triangle. Choice H incorrectly uses the base and height of the equilateral triangles as 8 and 8 to determine an area of 32, then combining it with the area of the square.

47. B./ F/ 1

In the form $y = ax^2 + bx + c$ the graph of a parabola opens downward if $a < 0$ and upwards of $a > 0$. The y-intercept can be found on the graph, so $c = 3$. Choices A, D, and E can be eliminated since $a > 0$. Choice C and be eliminated since $c = 3 > 0$.

48. H./ IES/ 2

Let x be the number of 2 x 4 and y be the number of 2 x 6 needed. Then,

$$x + y = 54$$
$$4x + 7y = 288$$

Substituting the 1st equation into the 2nd you have,

$$x + y = 54 \text{ then } y = 54 - x.$$
$$4x + 7(54 - x) = 288$$
$$4x + 378 - 7x = 288$$
$$-3x = -90$$
$$x = 30$$

So, $y = 54 - 30 = 24$. Then there are 30 – 2 x 4 boards and 24 – 2 x 6 boards needed. Choices I and J can be eliminated since the total number of boards is not 54.

49. A./ G/ 1

$\angle B = \angle E$ so, $\angle B = 47°$. Now, $\angle C = 180° - \angle A - \angle B$ so, $\angle C = 180° - 32° - 47° = 101°$.

Choice C incorrectly assumes $\angle A = \angle C$ and choice D incorrectly assumes $\angle A = \angle E$.

50. H./ G/ 2

Complete the square for x to put the equation of the circle in standard form $(x - h)^2 + (y - k)^2 = r^2$.

$$x^2 + 8x + \left(\frac{8}{2}\right)^2 + (y - 6)^2 = 36 + \left(\frac{8}{2}\right)^2$$
$$x^2 + 8x + 16 + (y - 6)^2 = 36 + 16$$
$$(x + 4)^2 + (y - 6)^2 = 52$$

So $r = \sqrt{52} = \sqrt{4 \times 13} = 2\sqrt{13}$. Choice I factors 4 out of the square root as 4 in the solution.

51. B./ N/ 2

Using the rule of logs for $\log_M 16 = \frac{3}{2}$,

$$M^{\frac{2}{3}} = 64$$
$$M = 64^{\frac{2}{3}} = \sqrt[3]{64^2} = 4^2 = 16$$

For the exponential function $e^{\ln N} = 7$,

$$\ln(e^{\ln N}) = \ln 7$$
$$\ln N = \ln 7$$
$$N = 7.$$

So, $M + N = 16 + 7 = 23$.

52. G./ G/ 2

Use the circumference to find the radius of the circle.

$$100 = 2\pi r$$
$$r = \frac{100}{2\pi} = \frac{50}{\pi}$$

The area, A, of a circle is $A = \pi r^2$ then, $A = \pi \left(\frac{50}{\pi}\right)^2 = \frac{2500}{\pi}$. Choice C incorrectly uses 50π as the radius of the circle when determining the area. Choice E multiplies 50 by 2 instead of squaring 50 in the solution.

53. C./ F/ 1

The coordinates of the points for $f(2) = 5$ and $f(7) = -9$ are (2, 5) and (7, –9) respectively. Find the slope using the change in the y-coordinates divided by the change in the x-coordinates $\left(\frac{y_2 - y_1}{x_2 - x_1}\right)$ for the 2 points you get:

$$m = \frac{-9 - 5}{7 - 2} = -\frac{14}{5}.$$ Choice A calculates the slope as the change in the x-coordinates divided by the change

in the y-coordinates. Choice D takes the difference in the 1st x value and 2nd y value divided by the 1st y value and 2nd x value for the 2 points.

54. F./ N/ 2

Only choices F and I produce positive values so, choices G, H, and J can be eliminated. Choose $n = -2$ then, $(-2)^2 = 4$ and $\sqrt{-(-2)} = 1.414$ so, n^2 has the greatest value. Also, squaring a number less than -1 produces a positive value that is always greater than the square root of its negative value.

55. D./ IES/ 3

Let h be the number of hours it takes to complete the project working together. Hudson can complete $\frac{1}{6}$ of the project in one hour, and Kaden can complete $\frac{1}{4}$ of the same project in one hour. Combining the fraction of the project each completes in h hours you have,

$$\frac{1}{6}h + \frac{1}{4}h = 1$$
$$\frac{5}{12}h = 1$$
$$h = \frac{12}{5}$$

So, it takes $\frac{12}{5}$ hours to complete the project working together. Choice A takes the average each person takes to complete the project.

56. H./ G/ 2

For coordinate trigonometry, $sin\theta = \frac{y}{r}$ and $cos\theta = \frac{x}{r}$ where $r^2 = x^2 + y^2$ for the point (x, y) that passes through the terminal side of θ. Since $sin\theta = \frac{12}{13}, y = 12$ and $r = 13$ then,

$$13^2 = x^2 + 12^2$$
$$169 = x^2 + 144$$
$$25 = x^2$$
$$x = \pm 5$$

Since θ is in the 2nd quadrant, $x = -5$ and $cos\theta = -\frac{5}{13}$.

Choice F neglects that θ is in the 2nd quadrant when finding the value for x.

57. C./ A/ 2

MN and MP are perpendicular segments since $\angle NMP$ is a right angle, so the slope of MP is the negative reciprocal of the slope of MN. The slope of MN is
$$m = \frac{8-4}{-5-3} = \frac{4}{-8} = -\frac{1}{2}$$ so, the slope of MP is 2.
Choice A only uses the negative of the slope of MN. Choice D only uses the reciprocal for the slope of MN.

58. J./ S/ 2

The probability of rolling a 4 with the die is $\frac{1}{6}$ and the probability of getting a tails with the coin flip is $\frac{1}{2}$. Since one event has no bearing on the other, the events are independent so the product of each is taken to find the combined probability. Now, $\frac{1}{6} \times \frac{1}{2} = \frac{1}{12}$.
Choice F and G only consider the individual probabilities of rolling a 4 and getting a tails. Choice J combines the individual probabilities.

59. B./ N/ 2

Let x be the 1st integer, then $x + 1$ is the 2nd and $x + 2$ is the 3rd. The sum of twice the 2nd and three times the 1st is $2(x + 1) + 3x$. Setting the sum equal to 82 and solving for x you get,

$$2(x + 1) + 3x = 82$$
$$2x + 2 + 3x = 82$$
$$5x = 80$$
$$x = 16$$

So, the 3rd integer is $16 + 2 = 18$. Choice C is the 1st integer. Choice D is twice the 1st integer and choice E is twice the 2nd integer.

60. J./ N/ 1

Only choice I is a true statement. Choices F and G state that $m > n$. Choice H states that m is also greater than 3. Choice J states that m and n are less than 1.

Answers to Math Practice Test 7

\#	Key	Your Answer	\#	Key	Your Answer	\#	Key	Your Answer	\#	Key	Your Answer	\#	Key	Your Answer	\#	Key	Your Answer
1	B		11	B		21	B		31	B		41	C		51	B	
2	F		12	K		22	H		32	F		42	G		52	J	
3	C		13	D		23	D		33	C		43	D		53	B	
4	K		14	G		24	J		34	J		44	H		54	G	
5	E		15	C		25	E		35	C		45	D		55	B	
6	G		16	H		26	J		36	K		46	G		56	F	
7	C		17	B		27	B		37	A		47	B		57	E	
8	J		18	J		28	H		38	G		48	H		58	H	
9	C		19	C		29	B		39	C		49	D		59	B	
10	G		20	D		30	H		40	J		50	F		60	J	

ANSWER KEY

ANSWERS – TEST 7

Each problem number is followed with: **Correct answer/ Topic(s)/ Level of difficulty (1-3)**.

Legends: **N** = Numerical, **A** = Algebra, **F** = Functions, **G** = Geometry, **S** = Statistics and Probability, **IES** = Integrating Essential Skills, **M** = Modeling, **1** = Easy, **2** = Medium, **3** = Difficult

---

1. B./ A/ 2

   Dividing $3x - 9y^2 = 81$ by -3 gives you $-x + 3y^2 = -27$ so, $3y^2 - x$ or $-x + 3y^2$ equals -27. Choice A divides the equation by 3 only. Choice C only divides the left side of the equation by -3 and, choices D and E divide the equation by 9 and -9 respectively.

2. F./ F/ 1

   To evaluate the composition, find the value for $g(2)$ and substitute it as the x value for f. Now, $f(g(2)) = f(7) = 7^2 - 5(7) = 14$. Choice G finds the value for $f(2) - g(2)$. Choice J find the value for $f(2) \times g(2)$.

3. C./ G/ 2

   The ratio of the adjacent side to the opposite side of 30 degrees for the right triangle is $\sqrt{3}$ to 1 so, $\dfrac{a}{16} = \dfrac{1}{\sqrt{3}}$ then, $a = \dfrac{16}{3}\sqrt{3}$. Choice A incorrectly finds the hypotenuse as twice the length of the side opposite 60 degrees. Choice B views the triangle as an isosceles right triangle. Side D uses the ratio incorrectly as $\dfrac{a}{16} = \dfrac{\sqrt{3}}{1}$. Choice E takes one-half of the adjacent side.

4. K./ S/ 1

   Putting the scores in order, 73, 87, 91, 93, the median is the average of 87 and 91. So, the median is 89. The mean is $\dfrac{73 + 93 + 87 + 91}{4} = 86$. The difference in the median and mean is 3.

5. E./ F/ 1

   The rate of change for a linear function is the slope for its graph. Putting the equation in slope-intercept form, $y = -\dfrac{3}{5}x + \dfrac{6}{5}$ so, the slope is $m = -\dfrac{3}{5}$. Choice B is the constant for the line in standard form. Choice D is the y-intercept of the line.

6. G./ F/ 1

   Using FOIL to multiply the 2 binomials you have,

$(3x + 1)(x - 4) = 3x \cdot x + 3x \cdot -4 + 1 \cdot x + 1 \cdot -4 = 3x^2 - 12x + x - 4 = 3x^2 - 11x - 4$.

7. C./ N/ 2

   $n = \dfrac{1}{2} \times 40 = 20$. So $\dfrac{2}{5} \times 20 = 8$. Choice A incorrectly takes three-fifths of 20. Choice B misinterprets one-half of 40 is n as 40 is one-half of n to get $n = 80$. Choice E takes one-half of 40 as the answer.

8. J./ F/ 1

   Choice I, $y = \sin x$ is an odd function. All other answer choices are even functions since they are all symmetric about the y-axis.

9. C./ F/ 2

   The rate of change is the same between any 2 given points so, the equation is linear. Choices D and E can be eliminated. The rate of change or the slope using the 1st two points is, $m = \dfrac{10 - 4}{5 - 3} = 3$. So, Choices A and B can be eliminated. Using the point-slope form for a line with the point (3, 4) you get, $y - 4 = 3(x - 3)$ or $y = 3x - 5$.

10. G./ G/ 2

    Completing the square to put the equation in standard form $(x - h)^2 + (y - k)^2 = r^2$ where, (h, k) is the center you have,

    $x^2 - 10x + (-5)^2 + y^2 + 6x + (3)^2 + 9 = 0 + (-5)^2 + (3)^2$

    $\left(x^2 - 10x + 25\right) + \left(y^2 + 6x + 9\right) = 25 + 9 - 9$

    $(x - 5)^2 + (y + 3)^2 = 25$

    So, the center is $(5, -3)$

11. B./ N/ 2

    Using the one to one property for exponents,

    $3(3^3)^x = 3^2$

    $3(3^{3x}) = 3^2$

    $3^{3x} + 1 = 3^2$

    $3x + 1 = 2$

    $3x = 1$

$$x = \frac{1}{3}$$

The other answer choices simplify the problem incorrectly or use the wrong exponent property.

12. K./ G/ 1

Since $\triangle ABC \sim \triangle DEF, \frac{a}{d} = \frac{b}{e} = \frac{c}{f}$. Substituting you get,

$\frac{4}{8} = \frac{9}{e} = \frac{2}{f}$ so, $e = 18$ and $f = 4$. The perimeter of triangle DEF is $8 + 18 + 4 = 30$. Choice F is the perimeter of triangle ABC. Choice I is the sum of sides d, b, and c. Choice G finds the area of triangle DEF using d as the base and e as the height.

13. D./ N/ 2

If $2n - 1$ is the 1st consecutive integer, the 2nd is $2n + 1$, and the 3rd is $2n + 3$. Now,

$$(2n-1)+(2n+1)+(2n+3)=159$$
$$6n+3=159$$
$$6n=156$$
$$n=26$$

So, the smallest odd integer is $2(26) - 1 = 51$. You can also choose x as the first integer, $x + 2$ as the next, and $x + 4$ as the largest. Choices C and E can be eliminated since they are both even integers. Choices B and A are the 2nd and 3rd consecutive integers respectively.

14. G./ N/ 2

The common difference, d, of the sequence is $7 - 11 = 3 - 7 = -1 - (-3) = -4$. Using $a_n = a1 + d(n - 1)$ you get $a_n = 11 - 4(n - 1) = 11 - 4n + 4 = 15 - 4n$. Choices I and J can be eliminated since they appear to be geometric sequences. Choice H uses $a_n = a1 + d(n)$ as the nth term.

15. C./ F/ 1

a is positive since the graph of the parabola opens upwards. c is negative since it is the y-intercept for the graph of the parabola. More information is needed in order to determine the sign of b, so choices D and E can be eliminated.

16. H./ A/ 1

A line parallel to the x-axis must have a slope of 0. Choice F has no slope. Choices G and I have a slope of 1 and choice J has a slope of $\frac{1}{5}$.

17. B./ F/ 2

The domain and range for the given function are $[-4, \infty)$ and $[0, \infty)$ respectively. Interchanging its domain and range gives you the domain and range for the inverse so, $[0, \infty)$ and $[-4, \infty)$ are the domain and range of the inverse respectively. You can not close in infinity with a square bracket so, choices A and E can be eliminated.

18. J./ S/ 2

Let g be the number of green marbles. The probability of choosing a green marble is, $\frac{g}{g+11+5} = \frac{1}{5}$.
Solving for g,

$$\frac{g}{g+16} = \frac{1}{5}$$
$$5g = g+16$$
$$4g = 16$$
$$g = 4$$

So, there must be 4 green marbles in the bag. Choice F only adds the red and blue marbles. Choice G is the total number of marbles needed.

19. C./ F/ 2

Using the sum of 2 perfect cubes to factor $8x^3 + 125$ where $a = 2x$ and $b = 5$ you get, $8x^3 +125 = (2x + 5)$ $((2x)^2 - 2x \cdot 5x + 5^2 = (2x+5)(4x^2 -10x+25)$. So, choice C is correct factor. The other answer choices can be eliminated since all answers use $a = x$ when factoring.

20. D./ N/ 2

Substituting vector u and solving for the components of v,

$$\langle 5,4 \rangle - \langle v_1, v_2 \rangle = \langle 4,11 \rangle$$
$$\langle 5-v_1, 4-v_2 \rangle = \langle 4,11 \rangle$$
$$5-v_1 = 4 \text{ and } 4-v_2 = 11$$
$$v_1 = 1 \text{ and } v_2 = -7$$

So $v = \langle 1,-7 \rangle$.

21. B./ IES/ 2

Let h be hours, $400h$ is the distance, in miles, the 1st plane travels, and $475(h - 1)$ is the distance the 2nd plane travels. The sum of the 2 distances is 215 then,

$$400h + 475(h-1) = 2150$$
$$400h + 475h - 475 = 2150$$
$$875h = 2625$$
$$h = 3$$

So, it will take 3 hours for the planes to be 2150 apart.

22. H./ A/ 2

Square both sides of the equation to solve for x.

$$x^2 = \left(\sqrt{8-2x}\right)^2$$
$$x^2 = 8 - 2x$$
$$x^2 + 2x - 8 = 0$$
$$(x+4)(x-2) = 0$$
$$x + 4 = 0 \ \square or \ x - 2 = 0$$
$$x = -4 \ \square or \ \square = 2$$

Generally, a square root equation only involves a principal root which means the square root of a value cannot be negative. Substituting x = −4 into the equation gives you $-4 = \sqrt{16}$. So, choices F and G can be eliminated. Substituting $x = 0$ into the equation yields an inequality so choice I can also be eliminated.

23. D./ N/ 2

Choice A is the complex number $2i + 1$. Choice B simplifies to the irrational number $2\sqrt{2}$. Choice C also simplifies to an irrational number $6\sqrt{2} + 1$ and, choice E is also irrational.

24. J./ G/ 1

The measure of an exterior angle is one-half the difference of the measures of the 2 arcs it intercepts on a circle. Since $\overline{CE}$ is tangent to circle O at B,

$$\angle ACE = \frac{1}{2}\left(\overset{\frown}{ADB} - \overset{\frown}{AB}\right)$$
$$\angle ACE = \frac{1}{2}(245 - 115)$$
$$\angle ACE = \frac{1}{2} \cdot 130°$$
$$\angle ACE = 65°$$

If the vertex for $\angle ACE$ is at the center of the circle choice F is correct. Choice H would be true if C were on the circle. Choice J would be true if $\overline{AC}$ were tangent to the circle.

25. E./ A/ 2

Parallel lines have the same slope so, $m_l = m_p$. Then,

$$\frac{8-4}{5-3} = \frac{5-(-3)}{k-(-5)}$$
$$2 = \frac{8}{k+5}$$
$$2k + 10 = 8$$
$$2k = -2$$
$$k = -1$$

Choice A is the slope of line l. Choice B sets the slopes perpendicular to each other.

26. J./ N/ 3

You can solve the 1st equation for a and substitute the value into the 2nd equation.

$$\frac{a}{b+3} = 2 \text{ then, } a = 2b+6 \text{ and,}$$
$$\frac{a}{2+\dfrac{6}{b}} = \frac{2b+6}{2+\dfrac{6}{b}} = \frac{2b+6}{\dfrac{2b+6}{b}} = \left(2b+6\right) \times \frac{b}{2b+6} = b.$$

27. B./ F/ 1

The maximum for A is 5. The maximum for B is 7. The maximum for C is 3. The maximum for D is 4, and the maximum for E is 1.

28. H./ A/ 1

If $t = 1350$ then, $\left(\dfrac{1}{2}\right)^{\frac{1350}{1350}} = \dfrac{1}{2}$, so it takes 1350 years for the initial amount of 26 gms of the isotope to be reduced by one-half.

29. B./ N/ 1

Substituting the subtraction operator into the blank you get an equality.

$$5 - 2(8 - 15 + 1) = 17$$
$$5 - 2(-6) = 17$$
$$5 + 12 = 17$$
$$17 = 17$$

30. H./ F/ 1

The y value has a minimum of -3 and a maximum of 2. Since the graph is continuous (contains all real numbers for -3 to 2), the range is $[-3, 2]$. Choice G is the domain. Choices F, I, and J use a domain and range coordinate in each interval.

31. B./ F/ 2

Substituting $x = 4$ you get, $g(4) = f(4 - 2) + 1 = f(2) + 1 = -3 + 1 = -2$. You can also shift $(2, -3)$ on the graph of f 2 units right and 1 unit up to obtain the point on g of $(2 + 2, -3 + 1) = (4, -2)$. There are not values of x where $g(x) = -3$ for choice A. $g(-2.50$ and $g(5) = 0$ for choice C, and $g(-4)$ and $g(5.5) = 0$ for choice D.

32. F./A/ 2

You can factor $x^4 - 5x^2 - 36$ like you would a quadratic where the x^4 factors to x^2 and x^2 to get,

$x^4 - 5x^2 - 36 = 0$
$(x^2 - 9)(x^2 + 4) = 0$
$(x + 3)(x - 3)(x^2 + 4) = 0$
$x + 3 = 0$ or $x - 3 = 0$ or $x^2 + 4 = 0$
$x = -3, 3,$ or $x = \pm 2i$

Choice G neglects to use $x^2 + 4$ when finding all the solutions. Choice H factors the expression on the left side of the equation to $(x^2 + 9)(x^2 - 4)$ and choice I factors the expression the same way as choice H but neglects to use $x^2 + 9$ when incorrectly finding all the solutions.

33. C./ N/ 2

Solve the first equation for y using the one to one property for exponents.

$3^y(3^2) = 81$
$3^{y+2} = 3^4$
$y + 2 = 4$
$y = 2$

Substitute $y = 2$ into the 2nd equation to find x.

$5^{x-2} = 125$
$5^{x-2} = 5^3$
$x - 2 = 3$
$x = 5$

Choice A mistakenly takes the exponent for $81 = 3^4$ as the answer for x. Choice B mistakenly take the difference of x = 5 and y = 4 from choice A. Choice D takes the difference in x = 5 and y = 2.

34. J./ G/ 2

The circumference or the length that the car has travelled in 1 revolution is $C = 32\pi$ inches. In one minute, the car has travelled $32\pi \times 100 = 3200\pi$ inches. In ten minutes, the car travels $3200\pi \times 10 = 32,000\pi$ or 100,531 inches or 8378 feet. Choice F is the correct answer in inches. Choice H uses $r = 32$ inches when determining the distance the car has travelled. Choice J finds the area instead of the circumference of the tire when determining the distance the car has travelled.

35. C./ A/ 1

Reflecting the graph about the x-axis transforms the equation to $y = -\sqrt[3]{x}$. A horizontal translation to the right 3 units transforms $y = -\sqrt[3]{x}$ to $y = -\sqrt[3]{x-3}$. Choices B and D shift down 3 and up 3, respectively. Choice A shifts left 3 instead of right 3. Choice E is a vertical stretch of 3.

36. K./ G/ 3

In the form $(x-h)^2 + (y-k)^2 = (r)^2$ where $r = 8$ and the intersection of the lines is the point (4, 4) is the center of the circle (h, k), you have $(x-4)^2 + (y-4)^2 = 64$. Choice F incorrectly substitutes the center as $(-4, -4)$ and uses the diameter for r^2. Choice G incorrectly substitutes the center as $(-4, -4)$. Choice H neglects to square the radius when writing the equation of the circle, and choice I squares the diameter of the circle to get 256 instead of squaring the radius.

37. A./ F/ 2

You can use the rule of 72, $\frac{72}{r}$ where r is the interest rate, to approximate the time an investment will double in value. The given equation is the continuous compounded amount. $A = Pe^{rt}$ where r the interest rate. Be careful to state the interest rate as a standard number, not in its decimal form when using the rule of 72. So, $r = 0.08 = 8\%$ and the investment will double in approximately $\frac{72}{8} = 9$. years.

38. G./ IES/ 2

The area of the circle is $A = \pi(4.5)^2 = 20.25\pi$, and the circumference is $C = 2\pi(4.5) = 9\pi$. As a rational number, the ratio of the area to the circumference is $\frac{20.25\pi}{9\pi} = \frac{20.25}{9} = \frac{9}{4}$ or 9 to 4. Choice F is the ratio of the circumference to the area. Choice H use the radius when finding the area but the diameter when finding the circumference when determining the ratio. Choice J uses the diameter for the radius when determining the area and circumference.

39. C./ S/ 1

To determine the sum of the scores, each score is multiplied by the frequency of customers to get, $1 \times 25 = 25, 2 \times 100 = 200, 3 \times 52 = 156, 4 \times 17 = 68, 5 \times 115 = 575$. The mean is the sum of the scores divided by 219 customers,

$$\frac{25+203+156+468+575}{219}=\frac{1024}{219}=4.7.\,\text{So, the mean}$$

score is 4.7. Choice A is the median. Choice B is the mode.

40. J./ G/ 2

Find the difference of the adjacent side of the 30-degree angle for the larger right triangle and the adjacent side of the 60-degree angle of the smaller triangle. Let x be the larger adjacent side and y be the smaller adjacent side.

$$\tan 30 = \frac{15}{x} \qquad \tan 60 = \frac{15}{y}$$

$$x = \frac{15}{\tan 30} \quad\text{and}\quad y = \frac{15}{\tan 60}$$

$$x = 25.98 \qquad y = 8.66$$

So, $a = x - y = 25.98 - 8.66 = 17.32$. Choice F is the x value and choice G is the y value. Choice H is the sum of x and y. Choice J uses the sine ratio when finding x and y.

41. C./ N/ 2

Choose any value between 0 and 1 and substitute into the answer choices. Let $n = 0.5$,

A. $0.5^2 = 0.25$

B. $\sqrt{0.5} = 0.71$

C. $\dfrac{1}{0.5} = 2$

D. 0.5

E. $0.5 - 1 = 0.5$

So, choice C will have the greatest value.

42. G./ F/ 1

In function notation, $y = f(x)$. Solve the equation for y to put it in function notation.

$3x + 2y - 4(x - y) = 12$

$3x + 2y - 4x + 4y = 12$

$-x + 6y = 12$

$6y = x + 12$

$y = \dfrac{x}{6} + 2$ So, $f(x) = \dfrac{x}{6} + 2$. Choice F neglects to divide 12 by 6 when solving the equation for y. Choices H, I, and J are not in function notation so can be eliminated.

43. D./ A/ 1

A perfect square trinomial is in the form $(x - a)^2 = x^2 - 2ax + a^2$. Since $-2ax = -16x$, $a = 8$ then $a^2 = 8^2 = 64$. So, $c = 64$. Choice A divided 16 by to get 8. Choice B divides -16 by 2 to get -8. Choice C squares -8 to get -64 not 64. Choice C halves $(-8)^2$ to get 32.

44. H./ A/ 2

Substitute $x = 4$ and $y = 3$ into the system to find a and b.

$$4a + 3b = 5$$
$$+(4a - 3b = 11)$$
$$\overline{8a = 16}$$
$$a = 2$$

Substituting $a = 2$ into the 1st equation you get, $4(2) + 3b = 5$ then, $b = -1$. Choice F uses the given solution for the values of a and b. Choice G uses the solutions for the 2 equations written in terms of a and b. Choice I reverses the correct values for a and b.

45. D./ A/ 2

The slope for line l is, $m = \dfrac{9-1}{1-3} = -2$. Since line k is perpendicular to l, its slope is $m = \dfrac{1}{2}$. Writing the equation for k in point-slope form using the point $(3, 5)$ you get, $y - 5 = \dfrac{1}{2}(x - 3)$. Substituting the coordinates of $(11, 9)$ into the equation you get,

$$9 - 5 = \frac{1}{2}(11 - 3)$$
$$4 = 4$$

which is a true statement. Choice A uses a slope of $-\dfrac{1}{2}$ for k so the equality holds when the point $(7, 3)$ is substituted into the equation $y - 5 = -\dfrac{1}{2}(x - 3)$. Choice C uses a slope of 2 for k so, the equality holds when the point $(1, 1)$ is substituted in the equation $y - 5 = 2(x - 3)$.

46. G./ N/ 1

$$\frac{8.4 \times 10^{12}}{2.8 \times 10^{-3}} = \frac{8.4}{2.8} \times \frac{10^{12}}{10^{-3}} = 3 \times 10^{12-(-3)} = 3 \times 10^{15}.$$

Choice F subtracts 3 from 12 for the exponents with a base of 10. Choice H divides the exponents. Choice I subtracts 2.8 from 8.4.

47. B./ G/ 2

Using trigonometric identities to simplify you have,

$$\frac{\sin x \cdot \cot x}{\sec x} = \frac{\sin x \cdot \dfrac{\cos x}{\sin x}}{\dfrac{1}{\cos x}} = \frac{\cos x}{\dfrac{1}{\cos x}} = \cos x \cdot \cos x = \cos^2 x.$$

48. H./ A/ 2

Set the denominator equal to zero and solve for x to get the vertical asymptote.

$$2x + 6 = 0$$
$$2x = -6$$
$$x = -3$$

Let x approach infinity to find the horizontal asymptote so, you only need to take the terms with the highest powers of x in the numerator and denominator when simplifying to get the horizontal asymptotes.

$y = \dfrac{4x}{2x} = 2$. So, $y = 2$ is the horizontal asymptote. The sum of the asymptotes is $-3 + 2 = -1$. Choice F is the sum of the root and the vertical asymptote. Choice G is the sum of the root and the horizontal asymptote. Choice J is the sum of the y-intercept and the root.

49. D./ S/ 2

Andrew scores in order from least to greatest are, {50, 61, 68, 69, 70, 74, 74, 75, 75, 82, 86, 86, 86, 86, 88, 90, 91, 95, 95}. The median is the middle score. Since there a total of 19 scores, the 10th score of an 82 is the median score. Choice B is the mean score and choice E is the mode.

50. F./ A/ 2

The polynomial has one negative root, a root that is zero, and 2 positive roots. Since the graph bounces off the x-axis at the smallest positive root, the factor that produces it will an even degree factor. The negative root is produced by $(x + 3)$, the root of zero is produced by the factor x, the smallest positive root is produced by $(x - 2)^2$, and the largest positive root is produced by the factor $(x - 5)$. The factor $(x - 2)$ for choice G should be squared since the graph bounces off the x-axis at x = 2. The factors of $(x + 2)$ and $(x + 5)$ produce roots of x = −2 and −5 but are not part of the graph for choice H. The graph has a root of x = 0 so, there needs factor of x added to the equation for choice I.

51. B./ IES/ 2

Let w be the width of the rectangle, then the length, l, is 2.5w. Substituting into the perimeter formula you have $2(2.5w) + 2w = 182$ so, $w = 26$. Then, $l = 65$ and the area is $26 \times 65 = 1690$. Choice C divides the perimeter by 2 to get a length and width of 91 to determine the area. Choice A uses a width and length of 26 to determine the area and choice D uses a width and length of 65 to determine the area.

52. J./ F/ 2

The composition $f(g(x))$ tells you to substitute $g(x) = x^2 - x$ into the x value for some function f to get $3x^2 - 3x - 1$. Substituting $x^2 - x$ into $3x - 1$ you get, $3(x^2 - x) - 1 = 3x^2 - 3x - 1$. Choice G produces a composition of $x^2 - x - 2$ when substituting $x - 1$ into f. Choice J produces a composition of $2x^2 - 2x - 1$ when substituting $x - 1$ into f. Choice J incorrectly takes the difference in $f(g(x))$ and $g(x)$.

53. B./ F/ 1

The y-coordinate for g minus the y-coordinate for f must be 9 for the corresponding points on f and g that have the same x-coordinate. Now, $g(-1) - f(-1) = 4 - (-5) = 4 + 5 = 9$. For choice A you have, $g(2) - f(2) = 0$. For choice C you get, $g(0) - f(0) = 6$. For choice D, $g(3) - f(3) = -3$, and for choice E you get $g(4) - f(4) = -6$.

54. G./ N/ 2

The common ratio, r, among terms is 3 since $\dfrac{3}{1} = 3$. To find the number of terms in the sequence use, $a_n = a_1 (r)^{n-1}$ where $a_1 = 1$ and $a_n = 6561$. Then,

$$6561 = (3)^{n-1}$$
$$3^8 = 3^{n-1}$$
$$8 = n - 1$$
$$n = 9$$

So, we know there are 9 terms in the sequence. The sum of a geometric sequence, Sn, is $S_n = a_1 \dfrac{(1 - r^n)}{1 - r}$ then,

$$S_9 = \frac{(1 - 3^9)}{1 - 3} = \frac{-19,682}{-2} = 9841$$

Choice F uses $n = 10$ when finding the sum. Choice I uses $n = 8$ when finding the sum and, choice J is the only the sum of the first and last term in the sequence.

55. B./ IES/ 2

Let h be the hours each person rakes leaves. Todd rakes $\frac{1}{4}$ of the leaves in the yard each hour, and Patty rakes $\frac{1}{7}$ of the leaves in the yard each hour. In h hours, Todd rakes $\frac{h}{4}$ of the leaves in h hours, and Patty rakes $\frac{h}{7}$. Together they rake $\frac{h}{4} + \frac{h}{7}$ of the leaves in the yard. To complete the entire job together $\frac{h}{4} + \frac{h}{7} = 1$. Solving for h,

$$\frac{h}{4} + \frac{h}{7} = 1$$

$$\frac{7}{28}h + \frac{4}{28}h = 1$$

$$\frac{11}{28}h = 1$$

$$h = \frac{28}{11}$$

So, it takes $\frac{28}{11} = 2.5$ hours. Choice F is the average of 4 hours and 7 hours. Choice H is a guesstimate. You know it should take less time for them working together than it will take Todd working alone. Choice J only takes Todd's time to rake the leaves since it is the shorter time.

56. F./ G/ 2

Convert $\frac{25}{6}\pi$ to degrees. $\frac{25}{6}\pi \times \frac{180°}{\pi} = 750°$. Coterminal angles share the same terminal side. Subtract as many full rotations from $750°$ to determine a coterminal angle. Subtracting $360°$ twice from $750°$ you get, $750° - 2 \cdot 360° = 30°$. So, $30°$ is coterminal to $750°$. Choice G would be coterminal to $690°$. Choice H would be coterminal to $780°$. $30°$ that was calculated for choice F was mistakenly placed in the 2nd quadrant as a reference angle for $150°$.

57. E./ N/ 2

Let n be the number. Then,
$12 + n^2 = 8n$
$n^2 - 8n + 12 = 0$
$(n - 6)(n - 2) = 0$
$n = 6$ or $n = 2$
Choice E is the only correct answer choice. Choices A and B incorrectly uses factors of $(n + 6)(n + 2)$ and choices C and D incorrectly uses factors of $(n - 4)$ $(n - 3)$.

58. H./ IES/ 3

Let x be the number of quarts that contain the 5% insecticide mixture, then the % mixture contains $0.05x$ quarts of insecticide. The 9% mixture contains $0.09 \times 3 = 0.27$ quarts of insecticide. The 8% mixture contains $0.08(x + 3)$ quarts of insecticide. Combining the 5% and (5 mixtures to produce the 8% mixture you get,

$$0.05x + 0.27 = 0.08(x + 3)$$
$$5x + 27 = 8(x + 3)$$
$$5x + 27 = 8x + 24$$
$$-3x = -3$$
$$x = 1$$

So, 1 quart is needed to produce a mixture that is 8% insecticide.

59. B./ G/ 3

You can use the law of sines to find the measure of the angle opposite one of the given sides, the measure of another side and its opposite angle, or SSA, for the triangle. The formula for the law of sines is,
$$\frac{\sin A}{a} = \frac{\sin C}{c}.$$
Substituting you get,

$$\frac{\sin A}{15} = \frac{\sin 125°}{21}$$

$$\sin A = 15 \times \frac{\sin 125°}{21}$$

$$\sin A = 0.5851$$

$$A = 35.8°$$

Choice A uses $\cos A$ and $\cos C$ for the law of sines. Choice C uses $21 \times \frac{\sin 125°}{15}$ in the 2nd step of the correct solution above, and choice D uses $\cos A = 21 \times \frac{\cos 125°}{15}$.

60. J./ A/ 1

Dividing each term by the GCF (greatest common denominator) of $3x$ you have,
$$\frac{\frac{42x}{3x} - \frac{3x^2}{3x}}{\frac{6x}{3x}} = \frac{14 - x}{2} = \frac{14}{2} - \frac{x}{2} = 7 - \frac{x}{2}.$$ Choice F can be eliminated since $42x$ is only divided by x not $3x$. Choice H is divided by a common factor of 3 but

should be divided by the GCF $3x$ to completely simplify the expression. Choice J is divided by a common factor of x but should be divided by the GCF $3x$ to completely simplify the expression.

This page is intentionally left blank

Answers to Math Practice Test 8

ANSWER KEY

#	Key	Your Answer	#	Key	Your Answer	#	Key	Your Answer	#	Key	Your Answer	#	Key	Your Answer	#	Key	Your Answer
1	C		11	D		21	D		31	B		41	A		51	B	
2	K		12	G		22	F		32	H		42	H		52	G	
3	E		13	C		23	D		33	A		43	B		53	C	
4	F		14	F		24	J		34	J		44	H		54	J	
5	B		15	C		25	C		35	B		45	D		55	C	
6	H		16	G		26	G		36	H		46	G		56	K	
7	B		17	C		27	C		37	E		47	C		57	C	
8	K		18	G		28	G		38	J		48	J		58	G	
9	E		19	D		29	B		39	D		49	B		59	D	
10	H		20	H		30	J		40	J		50	F		60	J	

ANSWERS – TEST 8

Each problem number is followed with: **Correct answer/ Topic(s)/ Level of difficulty (1-3)**.

Legends: **N** = Numerical, **A** = Algebra, **F** = Functions, **G** = Geometry, **S** = Statistics and Probability, **IES** = Integrating Essential Skills, **M** = Modeling, **1** = Easy, **2** = Medium, **3** = Difficult

1. C./ A/ 1

   Divide both sides of the equation by –4 to get,

   $$\frac{4a-16b^3}{-4}=\frac{48}{-4}$$
   $$-a+4b^3=-12$$
   $$4b^3-a=-12$$

   So, $4b^3 - a$ equals –12. Choice A divides 48 by 4. Choice B only multiplies the equation by –1 to get –48. Choice E is the is the divisor used to reduce the equation.

2. K./ F/ 1

   Since f and f^{-1} are inverses of each other, $f^{-1}(2) = a$ and $f(a) = 2$. $f(1) = 2$ then, $f^{-1}(2) = 1$. Now, $f(f^{-1}(2)) = f(1) = 2$. Choice F evaluates $f(2)$ only. Choice G finds $f^{-1}(2)$. Choice H interprets $f^{-1}(2)$ as the reciprocal of 2 and choice I interpret $f^{-1}(2)$ as the negative of 2.

3. E./ N/ 1

   If $x > 0$, it must be positive. If $y < 0$, it must be negative. A positive number times a negative number is negative number. For choice A, you are combining a negative and a negative number which yields a negative number. For choice C, $\frac{y}{x}$ yields a proper fraction since $x > y$.

4. F./ G/ 1

   $AC = BD$ only if the parallelogram is a rectangle. For a parallelogram opposite sides are congruent so choice A is true, opposite angles are congruent so choice C is true, and consecutive angles are supplementary so choice D is also correct.

5. B./ A/ 2

   Factoring $16x^4 - 81$ as a difference of 2 perfect squares, $16x^4 - 81 = (4x^2 - 9)(4x^2 + 9) = (2x - 3)(2x + 3)(4x^2 + 9)$. Choice A is the factorization of a perfect square trinomial. For choice C, $4x^2 - 9$ is incorrectly factored to $(2x - 3)^2$ and $4x^2 + 9$ is prime (does not factor). Choice D factors $16x^4 - 81$ as $16x^2 - 81$.

6. H./ IES/ 2

   Let n be the number, then $n(n + 7) = 60$. Solving for n,

   $$n(n+7)=60$$
   $$n^2+7n=60$$
   $$n^2+7n-60=0$$
   $$(n+12)(n-5)=0$$
   $$n+12=0 \text{ or } n-5=0$$
   $$n=-12 \text{ or } n=5$$

   So, $n = -12$ is the correct answer choice. Choices F and G incorrectly factor $n^2 + 7n - 60$ to $(n - 12)$ and $(n + 5)$ to get $n = 12$ and –5 respectively.

7. B./ IES/ 2

   Let h be the number of hours worked then, the total cost for the repair is $45n + 75$. Setting the total cost to the budget you get,

   $$45n + 75 = 480$$
   $$45n = 405$$
   $$n = 9$$

   So, the plumber will have 9 hours to repair the problem. Choice C divides 480 by the sum of 45 and 75. Choice D divides 480 by 75. Choice E divides 480 by 45.

8. K./ F/ 2

   Write the equation of the line in slope-intercept, $y = mx + b$ where b is the y-intercept. The slope, $m = \frac{8-0}{3-5} = -4$. First, use the point-slope form of a line, $y - y_1 = m(x - x_1)$ where $(x_1, y_1) = (5, 0)$, to get, $y - 0 = -4(x - 5)$. So, the slope intercept form is $y = -2x + 20$ and the y-intercept is 20. Choice F is the x-intercept. Choice G is the x-coordinate for the y-intercept. Choice I finds y-intercept of the perpendicular line. Choice H is the slope of the line.

9. E./ G/ 2

   The radius of the circle is 4 so, in the form $(x - h)^2 + (y - k)^2 = r^2$ choices A, B, and C can be eliminated since $(x-h)^2 +(y-k)^2 =16$. The vertex of the parabola is (0, –5) and the center of the circle for choice E is (0, –5) so the parabola intersects the center of the circle $x^2 +(y+5)^2 =16$ on the y-axis.

10. H./ S/ 1

$\frac{3}{7}$ of the students surveyed failed the test. Of 42 students in the class, $\frac{3}{7}\times 42 =18$ failed the test, according to the survey. Choice H is the number of students that passed the test. Choice I is the sum of 3 and 7. Choice J is the difference in 42 and 3.

11. D./ N/ 1

Substituting the values for x and y you get,
$3\cdot 2(2-4(-5))-(-5)^2 =6(2+20)-25 =6(22)-25$
$=132-25=107$. Choice C evaluates $(x-4y)$ as 24. Choice B evaluates $(x-4y)$ as –18. Choice C substitutes $x=-5$ and $y=2$ into the expression before simplifying.

12. G./ F/ 1

The graph of a parabola opens down when a is a negative value. The y-intercept for the graph of a parabola is the value of c. So, $a<0$ and $c=-4<0$. The value for b could be positive, negative, or zero depending on the values for a and c so more information is needed to determine the sign of b.

13. C./ N/ 2

Let n be the number you are asked to find. 25% of 156 is $0.25\times 156 =39$. Now,
$2n-3=39$
$2n=42$
$n=21$

Choice A takes 3 less then twice 39 to get 75. Choice B takes twice the number is 3 less than 39 to get 18. Choice E takes 25% of 3 less then 156 to get 38.

14. F./ N/ 2

The difference in the 5th and 1st terms in the sequence is $-7-9=-16$ so, since there are $5-1=4$, $d=-4$. The nth term in an arithmetic sequence, a_n is $a_n =a_1 +d(n-1)$ where a_1 is the first term. Now, $a_n =9-4(n-1)$ and $a_{10} =9-4(10-1)=9-36=-27$. Choice I uses –7 as the 1st term when writing a_n. Choice J uses 4 as the common difference when writing a_n. Choice I uses 16 as the common difference when writing a_n.

15. C./ F/ 1

Substitute $t=20$ into the equation and solve for C.
$20=2\sqrt{C-15}$
$10=\sqrt{C-15}$
$10^2 =(\sqrt{C-15})^2$
$100=C-15$
$C=115$

So, the temperature is 115 degrees Celsius after 20 seconds. Choice A neglects writing 2 in the equation and only uses $20=\sqrt{C-15}$ when solving for C. Choice B subtracts 2 from 20 in the equation when solving for C. Choice D squares 20 and $\sqrt{C-15}$ but not 2 when solving for C.

16. G./ A/ 2

Use the FOIL technique to check the answer,
$3x\times x+3x\times 3-4\times x-4\times 3=3x^2 +9x-4x-12 =3x^2 -5x-12$. The signs for the 2 binomials are reversed for choice F. The product of +4 and +3 gives +12 not – for choice H. The middle term after foiling choice I is 16x not –5x, and –16x for choice J.

17. C./ G/ 2

The sides must satisfy the Pythagorean Theorem, $leg^2 +leg^2 =hypotenuse^2$ where the hypotenuse is the longest side. Substituting legs of 10 and 24, and hypotenuse of 26 you have,
$10^2 +24^2 =26^2$
$100+576=676$
$676=676$

So, the equality holds thus, choice C are the sides of a right triangle. The sides for each of the other answer choices do not form a triangle since the sum of any 2 sides must be greater than the 3rd side.

18. G./ N/ 2

Zack spends 30% of his day at school or $0.30\times 24=7.2$ hours at school. He spends 20% of $0.70\times 24=16.8$ hours doing homework so, he spends $0.20\times 16.8=3.36$ hours doing homework. Subtracting the sum of 7.2 and 3.36 hours he spends in school and doing homework from 24 hours in a day, you get $24-(7.2+3.36)=13.44$ hours Zack has left in his day. Choice F only considers spending 20 % of the other 70% he spends on his day. Choice H only considers the time he spends the other 70% of the day. Choice I is the difference in time spent the other 70% of the day and 13.44 hours.

19. D./ A/ 2

Writing the equation of the parabola in the form $y = a(x - h)^2 + k$ where (h, k) is the vertex and a is a constant you get, $y = a(x - 4)^2 + 3$. Substitute $(6, -1)$ into the equation to find the value for a.

$-1 = a(6 - 4)^2 + 3$
$-1 = 4a + 3$
$-4 = 4a$
$a = -1$

So, $y = -(x - 4)^2 + 3$. The vertex for choice A is (6. –1), choice B is (–6, –1), and choice C is (6, 1) not (4, 3). The vertex for choice E is (4, –3) not (4, 3).

20. H./ G/ 1

An angle formed by 2 chords in a circle measures one-half the sum of the 2 arcs it intercepts on the circle. $\angle AGB$ is formed by chords AC and BE so,

$\angle AGB = \frac{1}{2}\left(\widehat{EFC} + \widehat{ADB}\right)$

$74 = \frac{1}{2}\left(\widehat{EFC} + 120\right)$

$148 = \widehat{EFC} + 120$

$\widehat{EFC} = 28°$

Choice F only takes one-half of 74 degrees. Choice G calculates one-half the sum of 120 and 74 degrees to find $\widehat{EFC}$.

21. D./ G/ 1

The graph of g is a horizontal shift to the right 7 units of the graph of f. A horizontal shift does not change the period for a graph, so the graph of g is also 14 units. Also, since the period is +14 units, the other answer choices can be eliminated.

22. F./ F/ 1

Substitute $t = 20$ and solve for A.

$A = 2500(1 + 0.06)^{20}$
$A = 2500(1.06)^{20}$
$A = 8017.84$

Choice G takes 2500 × 10.6 × 10. Choice H takes 2500 + 06 × 10 × 2500. Choice I only takes 2500 × 10. Choice I can be eliminated since the initial amount

is earning a positive interest the amount after 20 years is greater than the initial investment.

23. D./ N/ 2

Substituting x and y into the expression you get,

$\frac{3+2}{\frac{1}{4}} = \frac{5}{\frac{1}{4}} = 5 \times 4 = 20$. Choice A substitutes $x = 4$ and

$y = 3$ into the expression. Choice B substitutes correctly but simplifies $\frac{5}{\frac{1}{4}}$ as $\frac{5}{4}$, and choice C simplifies $\frac{5}{\frac{1}{4}}$ as $\frac{4}{5}$.

24. J./ F/ 1

The graph of f is constant over an interval (the x-values) where the y-values for any point on the graph are the same over the interval. The points on the graph from $0 \le x \le 4$ have y-coordinate of 3 so, the graph is constant from [0, 4]. The graph is increasing for the interval in choice F. The graph is constant and decreasing for the interval in choice G. The graph in decreasing for the interval in choice J.

25. C./ F/ 1

Choices C and E are positive in value so, choices A, B, D can be eliminated since they have negative values. $f(2) > f(6)$ so $f(2)$ has the greatest value.

26. G./ A/ 2

Expanding using the binomial expansion you get,

$_5C_0(2x)^5 + {_5C_1}(2x)^4(-4) + {_5C_2}(2x)^3(-4)^2 +$
$_5C_3(2x)^2(-4)^3 + {_5C_1}(2x)(-4)^4 + {_5C_5}(-4)^5$
$= 32x^5 + 5 \cdot 16x^4(-4) + 10 \cdot 8x^3 \cdot 16 + 10 \cdot 4x^2(-64) +$
$5 \cdot 2x \cdot 256 - 1024$
$= 32x^5 - 3206x^4 + 1280x^3 - 2560x^2 + 2560x - 1024$

The 3rd degree term is $1280x^3$ which has a coefficient of 1280. Choice F incorrectly calculate (-4^2) as -16 when determining the 3rd degree term. Choice H calculates $(2x)^3$ as $4x^3$ when finding the 3rd degree term. Choice K is the coefficient of the 2nd degree term.

27. C./ G/ 1

The volume of a right circular cone is $\frac{1}{3}\pi r^2 h$ where πr^2 is the area of the base and h is the height. Substituting you have, $\frac{1}{3}(6\pi)4h = 8\pi h$. Choice A uses $\pi r^2 h$ as the volume formula. Choice E uses $\frac{1}{2}\pi r^2 h$ as the volume formula.

28. G./ F/ 1

$x = f(y)$ is the inverse of $y = f(x)$ and its graph is a side-ways parabola. Switching the x and y values for $f(x)$ for the vertex and y-intercept give you the vertex and x-intercept for $f(y)$. So, (3, 2) and (5, 0) are the vertex and y-intercept give you the vertex and x-intercept for $f(y)$. The vertex and y-intercept are switched for choice F. The y-intercept of (0, 5) is the y-intercept for f(x) not f(y) for choice. There is not enough information to determine the x-intercepts for choices I and J so they can be eliminated.

29. B./ F/ 2

Write the equation of the line in slope-intercept form $y = mx + b$, then substitute the given points to find which one is a solution. The slope of the line is, $m = \dfrac{10 - 0}{0 - (-4)} = \dfrac{5}{2}$ and the y-intercept is $b = 10$ so, the equation of the line is $y = \dfrac{5}{2}x + 10$. Substituting the point (–15, –10) you get $-8 = \dfrac{5}{2}(-10) + 10$

$$-8 = -25 + 10$$
$$-15 = -15$$

So, the equality holds, and (–15, –10) is on the line. Choice A uses the line in the form $y = \dfrac{5}{2}(x + 4)$. Choice C uses the slope of the perpendicular line to get the equation $y = -\dfrac{2}{5}x + 10$.

30. J./ IES/ 2

The linear distance the bicycle travels for one revolution of the tire is equivalent to the circumference, C, of the tire. So, $C = 2\pi(15) = 30\pi$ inches. At 2 revolutions per second, the distance travelled is $\times 2 = 60\pi$ inches. After 10 seconds, the bicycle travels $60\pi \times 10 = 600\pi = 1885$ inches or 157 feet. Choice F is the correct answer but in inches. Choice G is one-half of the correct number of inches. Choice H is one-half of the correct number of feet traveled. Choice K uses the area of the tire instead of the circumference.

31. B./ S/ 1

Since each question has 5 answer choices, the probability of getting any one question correct is $\dfrac{1}{5}$. Each question is answered independently so, the probability of getting all 4 questions correct (which would be a perfect score) is the product of each question's probability or $\dfrac{1}{5} \times \dfrac{1}{5} \times \dfrac{1}{5} \times \dfrac{1}{5} = \dfrac{1}{625}$.

32. H./ G/ 1

The period is the interval along the x-axis where the graph reproduces itself. It is easiest to find the period by counting horizontally from maximum point to maximum point, or minimum point tot minimum point on the graph. The interval from the maximum point of (0, 7) to or minimum point tot minimum point on the graph. The interval from the maximum point of (0, 7) to $(4\pi, 7)$ is 4π. Choice F is the fundamental period for a sinusoidal graph. Choice I is the maximum value of the graph. Choice J is the difference in the maximum and minimum y-values of the graph.

33. A./ N/ 2

Write the numerator as an imaginary number before rationalizing the expression.

$\dfrac{\sqrt{-9}}{1 - 4i^2} = \dfrac{\sqrt{-1} \cdot \sqrt{9}}{1 - 4(-1)} = \dfrac{3i}{1 + 4} = \dfrac{3i}{5}$. Choice B simplifies the denominator to $1 - 4 = -3$. Choice C mistakenly simplifies the denominator as $1 - \sqrt{4i^2} = 1 - 2 = -1$. Choice D simplifies $\sqrt{-9}$ to -3, and choice E simplifies the numerator $\sqrt{-9}$ to $-3i$.

34. J./ N/ 1

Convert the 3 values to standard form before finding their products. $\dfrac{2}{5} = 0.40$, $45\% = 0.45$ then, $0.40 \times 0.45 \times 235 = 42.3$. Choice F changes $\dfrac{2}{5}$ to 0.20 when taking the products of the 3 numbers. Choice K finds the value of $\dfrac{235 \times \dfrac{5}{2}}{45}$.

35. B./ N/ 2

Let $v = \langle v_1, v_2 \rangle$ then, combining the components of u and v you have.

$$\langle -3, 7 \rangle - \langle v_1, v_2 \rangle = \langle 12, -16 \rangle$$
$$-3 - v_1 = 12 \text{ and } 7 - v_2 = -16$$
$$v_1 = -15 \text{ and } v_2 = 23$$

So, $v \langle -15, 23 \rangle$. Choice A incorrectly takes the sum of u and $\langle 12, -16 \rangle$. Choice C reverses the coordinates for u before subtracting them from $\langle 12, -16 \rangle$. Choice D also reverses the coordinates for u before incorrectly subtracting them from $\langle 12, -16 \rangle$.

36. H./ G/ 1

The distance between A and B is the difference in their y-coordinates, $27 - 6 = 21$. Two-thirds of the distance is $\frac{2}{3} \times 21 = 14$. Adding 14 to the y-coordinate of A to find the point so, $(5, 6 + 14) = (5, 20)$. Choice F incorrectly adds 6 and 14 to get 21. Choice G is the point that is two-thirds of the way from B to A. Choices I and J reverses the coordinates for answer choices H and F respectively.

37. E./ G/ 2

Regardless of their periods, sine and cosine have a minimum and maximum value of -1 and 1 respectively so, the minimum and maximum values for $\sin(2A)$ and $\cos(B)$ are -1 and 1. Substituting 1 for $\sin(2A)$ and -1 for $\cos B$ gives you the maximum value of the expression.

$$7\sin(2A) - 3\cos(B) + 1 = 7 \times 1 - 3(-1) + 1 = 7 + 3 + 1 = 11.$$

Choice A uses 1 for $\sin(2A)$ and $\cos B$. Choice B evaluates $7\sin(2A)$ as $7 \times 2\sin(A)$ where $\sin(2A) = 1$ and $\cos B = 1$. Choice C evaluates $7\sin(2A)$ as $7 \times 2\sin(A)$ where $\sin(2A) = 1$ and $\cos B = -1$.

38. J./ N/ 2

The area of the rectangle is $8 \times 5 = 40$. The perimeter is $2 \times 5 + 2 \times 8 = 10 + 16 = 26$. The ratio of the area to the perimeter is 40 to 26 which can be reduced by a factor of 2 to 20 to 13. Choice F is the ratio of the perimeter to the area. Choice G calculates the perimeter as $5 + 8 = 13$. Choice H is the is the reverse of choice G but would be the ratio of the perimeter to the area.

39. D./ A/ 2

The dashed line has a y-intercept of 1 and shaded below so, the inequality $y < \frac{1}{2}x + 1$ is used in the system. The solid line has a y-intercept of -2, and is shaded above so, $y \geq x - 2$ is also used in the inequality. Choices A and B can be eliminated since each inequality in the system is strictly less than. Choices C and E can be eliminated since one of the graphs is a dashed line so, one of the inequalities in the system must be strictly less than or greater than.

40. J./ F/ 1

In the form $y = af(x - h) = k$, h is a horizontal translation right if $h > 0$, and a horizontal translation left if $h < 0$. Since $y = \ln(x + 4)$ can be written as $y = \ln(x - (-4))$, $h = -4 < 0$ so, the graph of $y = \ln(x + 4)$ translates the graph of $y = \ln x$ left 4 units. Choice F would produce $y = \ln(x) + 4$. Choice G would produce $y = \ln(x) - 4$. Choice H would produce $y = \ln(x - 4)$, and choice K would produce $y = 4\ln(x)$.

41. A./ A/ 2

The coordinates of the point that is the zero for the graph are $(3, 0)$. Substituting the point into the equation you have,

$$0 = 2(3)^2 + 3b - 6$$
$$0 = 18 + 3b - 6$$
$$0 = 12 + 3b$$
$$-12 = 3b$$
$$b = -4$$

Choice B incorrectly solves for b using $12 = 3b$. Choice I substitutes x incorrectly to get

$0 = 3 + bx - 6$ when solving for b. Choice E mistakenly uses 0 for b when told 3 is a zero for the graph.

42. H./ S/ 2

Since 100 people prefer apples and 20 of them prefer both apples and oranges then, $100 - 20 = 80$ people in the survey prefer only apples. The probability that a person chosen at random prefers only apples out of the 130 people in the survey is $\frac{80}{130} = 0.62$. Choice F is the probability of a person only preferring oranges. Choice J is the probability of a person preferring both apples and oranges. Choice I is the probability of a person preferring apples. Choice J is the probability of a person preferring oranges.

43. B./ G/ 2

Using the trigonometric identities, you get,

$$\frac{\cos x \tan x}{\sin^2 x} = \frac{\cos x \cdot \frac{\sin x}{\cos x}}{\sin^2 x} = \frac{\sin x}{\frac{\sin^2 x}{\sin x}} = \csc x. \text{ Choice A}$$

incorrectly identifies the reciprocal of sine as secant. Choice C rewrites $\tan x$ as $\frac{\cos x}{\sin x}$ when simplifying the expression to get $\cot^2 x$. Choice E incorrectly identifies the reciprocal of sine as cosine.

214

44. H./ N/ 3

Solve each equation for m and n.

$x^n = \left(x^4 \cdot x^{-1}\right)^3$

$x^n = \left(x^{4\,1}\right)^3$

$x^n = \left(x^3\right)^3$ and

$x^n = x^{3\cdot3}$

$x^n = x^9$

$n = 9$

$y^m = \left(\dfrac{y^5}{y^2}\right)^{-1}$

$y^m = \left(y^{5-2}\right)^{-1}$

$y^m = \left(y^3\right)^{-1}$

$y^m = y^{3\cdot-1}$

$y^m = y^{-3}$

$m = -3$

So, $m + n = 9 - 2 = 7$. Choice F simplifies $x^4 \cdot x^{-1}$ to x^{-4} to find m. Choice G simplifies $\left(x^4 \cdot x^{-1}\right)^3$ to x^{-4+3} when finding m. Choice I simplifies $\left(x^4 \cdot x^{-1}\right)^3$ to $\left(x^3\right)^3 = x^{27}$ when finding m.

45. D./ G/ 1

An exterior angle is the sum of its 2 remote interior angles for a triangle. Then,

$\angle BCA + \angle B = \angle BAE$

$\angle BCA + 100 = 133$

||||||||$\angle BCA = 33°$

$\angle BCD$ and $\angle BCA$ form a linear pair (their sum is 180 degrees). Then,

$\angle BCD + 33 = 180$

||||||||$\angle BCD = 147°$.

Choice A assumes that angles A and C inside of the triangle are congruent so their supplements $\angle BCD$ and $\angle BEA$ are also congruent. Choice B mistakes $\angle BCD$ with $\angle B$. Choice C is the measure of $\angle BCA$.

46. G./ N/ 2

A rational number contains no square root as part of its value. Choice F simplifies to $14 + 6\sqrt{5}$. Choice H has the same value as choice F. Choice I simplifies to $\dfrac{3-\sqrt{5}}{4}$. Choice J simplifies to $\dfrac{3\sqrt{5}}{5}$. Choice G simplifies to 4 so it is the only rational number for the answer choices.

47. C./ F/ 1

Reflecting across the x-axis transforms (–5, 7) to (–5, –7). Translating (–5, –7) horizontally right 4 units transforms it to (–5, –7 + 4) = (–5, –3). Choice A

reflects the point across the y-axis then 4 units to the right. Choice B reflects the point across the y-axis then 4 units down. Choice E reflects the point across the x-axis then up 4 units.

48. J./ F/ 1

The center of the circle is (–4, 5). Substituting the center into the equation $y = -x + 1$ you get the equality $5 = -(-4) + 1 = 5$ so, the line passes through the center of the circle. Substituting the center into the equations of the other answer choices does not result in an equality.

49. B./ G/ 1

A dodecagon has 12 sides and 12 angles. The sum of the degrees of the angles in any polygon is $(n - 2) \times 180$. So, the sum of the angles in the dodecagon is $(12- 2) \times 180 = 1800$. You are told the dodecagon is a regular polygon so the angle measures are equal then, each angle measures $\dfrac{1800}{12} = 150$. The interior and exterior angles for a polygon form a linear pair so, 180 –150 = 30. Thus, the exterior angle is 30 degrees. Alternatively, the sum of the exterior angles of every regular polygon total 360, so 360/12 = 30 will work just as well.

Choice A is the measure of the interior angle. Choice C mistakenly calculates the interior angle as $(8 - 2) \times 180$ and divides the result by 12 to get 120 degrees. Choice C uses the incorrect interior angle of 120 degrees calculated in choice C and finds the exterior angle by subtracting 120 degrees from 180 degrees.

50. F./ F/ 1

By the definition of a logarithm, $log_2 32 = M$ then, $2^M = 32$ so, $M = 5$. Next, $ln\,e = 1$ so,

$3ln\ e = N$

$3 \times 1 = N$

$N = 3$

Thus, $M + N = 5 + 3 = 8$. Choice G incorrectly evaluates $log_2 32 = M$ as $2 \times 16 = 32$ so $M = 16$ when taking the sum of M and N. Choice H evaluates $ln\,e$ as 1 but neglects to multiply by 3 so $N = 1$ when taking the sum of M and N. Choice H incorrectly evaluates $3ln\,e$ as zero to get $N = 0$ when finding the sum. Choice I is the difference of M and N.

51. B. /IES/ 2

Let a be the number of adults and c be the number of children at the event then , $a+c=165$ is the sum of adults and children at the event, and $10a+7c=1455$ is the total cost of tickets at the event. Substituting the 1st equation into the 2nd and solving for a,

$a+c=165$ then, $c=165-a$. Now,

$$10a+7(165-a)=1455$$
$$10a+1155-7a=1455$$
$$3a=300$$
$$a=100$$

So, there are 100 adults at the event. Choice A is the number of children at the event.

52. G./ F/ 1

In component form (when the tails of the vectors are at the origin), vectors can be added by combining the coordinates of their head points. Then, $(3+2, 4+-3)=(5,-1)$.

You can also combine the 2 vectors using head to tail addition. Let v be the vector whose head is $(2, -3)$ be the vector whose head is $(3, 4)$. Translate the tail of v to the head of u. The resultant vector, u + v has its tail at the origin and head at the head of the translated vector v as shown below.

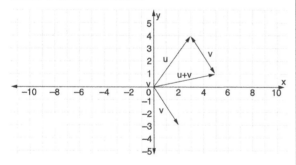

Choice F is the difference in the vectors (3, 4) and (2, –3). Choice H incorrectly takes the sum of the vectors as (3, 4) and (–3, 2). Choices I and J only consider the vectors (3, 4) and (2, –3) respectively.

53. C./ N/ 1

6400 glasses of juice is equivalent to $\dfrac{6400}{16}=400$ gallons. The machine can bottle 50 gallons of juice every 2 hours or 25 gallons each hour. To bottle 400 gallons, it takes $\dfrac{400}{25}=16$ hours. Choice A divides 400 gallons by 50 gallons. Choice B only divides 6400 glasses by 16 glasses. Choice D divides 2 by the quotient of 6400 and 50.

54. J./ F/ 2

Solving the inequality, you get,

$$|x-16|<4$$
$$-4<x-16<4$$
$$-4+16<x<4+16$$
$$12<x<20$$

Choice F only solves half of the inequality $x - 16 < 4$. Choice G only solves half of the inequality $-4 < x - 16$. Choice H incorrectly sets up the combined inequality as $4 < x-16 < -4$. Choice K neglects to add 16 to the left side of the combined inequality when solving for x.

55. C./ A/ 2

Choices A, D, and E only have 1 possible zero since they are one-to-one functions, so they can be eliminated. Choice B has a zero at $x = -2$ but not 3 so, the correct answer is C by elimination.

56. K./ G/ 1

Using coordinate trigonometry, $\cos\theta = \dfrac{x}{r}$ and $\sin\theta = \dfrac{y}{r}$ where $r = \sqrt{x^2+y^2}$. Since θ is in the 3rd quadrant and $\cos\theta = -\dfrac{1}{2}$, $x = -1$ and $r = 2$. Now,

$$2=\sqrt{(-1)^2+y^2}$$
$$2^2=\left(\sqrt{(-1)^2+y^2}\right)^2$$
$$4=1+y^2$$
$$3=y^2$$
$$y=\pm\sqrt{3}$$

Again, since θ is in the 3rd quadrant, $y=-\sqrt{3}$. So, $\sin\theta = -\dfrac{\sqrt{3}}{2}$.

57. C./ G/ 3

Since SAS (side included angle and side) are given, the law of cosines can be used to find the remaining side. Let a be the side opposite angle A, $b = 11$ and $c = 15$ for $a^2 = b^2 + c^2 - 2bc\cos A$,

$$a^2=11^2+12^2-2(11)(15)\cos115°$$
$$a^2=121+144-330\cos115°$$
$$a^2=404.464$$
$$a=20.1$$

So, the perimeter is $11 + 15 + 20.1 = 46.1$. Choice A assumes a is the hypotenuse for a right triangle. Choice B also assumes ABC is a right triangle and finds the area using sides 11 and 15. Choice D incorrectly uses the law of cosines by using $sin115°$ formula instead of $cos115°$.

58. G./ N/ 2

The geometric mean is the nth root of the product of n values. Since you are given the geometric mean for 3 numbers, $n = 3$. Now,

$$6 = \sqrt[3]{3 \times 9 \times x}$$
$$6 = \sqrt[3]{27x}$$
$$6^3 = \sqrt[3]{27x}^3$$
$$216 = 27x$$
$$x = 8.$$

Choice F calculates the 3rd number using the arithmetic mean. Choice H divides 6 by the sum of 3 and 9. Choice I takes divides the product of 3, 6, and 9 by 3.

59. D./ F/ 2

Using the rules of logarithms, you get,

$\log_2 x + 3\log_2 y - \log_2 z^4 = \log_2 x + \log_2 y^3 - \log_2 z^4 = \log_2\left(xy^3\right) - \log_2 z^4 = \log_2\left(\dfrac{xy^3}{z^4}\right)$. Choices A an B can be eliminated since neither is written as a single logarithm. Choices C and E incorrectly use the addition and subtraction rules for logarithms.

60. J./ F/ 2

The sequence is recursive since any term is the sum of its 2 previous terms. The first 5 terms are given so, the 6th term is $11 + 18 = 29$, 7th term is $18 + 29 = 47$, 8th term is $29 + 47 = 76$, 9th term is $47 + 76 = 123$, and 10th term is $76 + 1231 = 199$. Choice F is the 9th term in the sequence. Choice G incorrectly identifies the sequence as arithmetic with a common difference of 3 determine the 10th term. Choice H incorrectly identifies the sequence as geometric with a common ratio of 3 multiply it to each successive term to the 10th term to get 4374.

NOTES

Made in the USA
Monee, IL
18 November 2020